Radial Basis Function Networks 1

Studies in Fuzziness and Soft Computing

Editor-in-chief

Prof. Janusz Kacprzyk
Systems Research Institute
Polish Academy of Sciences
ul. Newelska 6
01-447 Warsaw, Poland
E-mail: kacprzyk@ibspan.waw.pl
http://www.springer.de/cgi-bin/search_book.pl?series=2941

Robert J. Howlett
Lakhmi C. Jain

Editors

Radial Basis Function Networks 1

Recent Developments
in Theory and Applications

With 85 Figures
and 14 Tables

Physica-Verlag

A Springer-Verlag Company

Dr. Robert J. Howlett
University of Brighton
School of Engineering
Intelligent Signal Processing Laboratories (ISP)
Moulsecoomb, Brighton BN2 4GJ
United Kingdom
r.j.howlett@brighton.ac.uk

Professor Lakhmi C. Jain
Knowledge-Based Intelligent
Engineering Systems Centre
University of South Australia
Adelaide, Mawson Lakes
South Australia 5095
Lakhmi.Jain@unisa.edu.au

ISSN 1434-9922
ISBN 978-3-7908-2482-7
e-ISBN 978-3-7908-1827-7

Cataloging-in-Publication Data applied for
Die Deutsche Bibliothek – CIP-Einheitsaufnahme
Radial basis function networks 1 / Robert J. Howlett; Lakhmi C. Jain, ed. – Heidelberg; New York: Physica-Verl., 2001
Recent Developments in Theory and Applications; with 14 tables. – 2001
  (Studies in fuzziness and soft computing; Vol. 66)

Physica-Verlag Heidelberg New York
a member of BertelsmannSpringer Science+Business Media GmbH

© Physica-Verlag Heidelberg 2010
Printed in Germany

Hardcover Design: Erich Kirchner, Heidelberg

88/2202-5 4 3 2 1 0 – Printed on acid-free paper

This book is dedicated to all our students

Preface

The Radial Basis Function (RBF) network has gained in popularity in recent years. This is due to its desirable properties in classification and functional approximation applications, accompanied by training that is more rapid than that of many other neural-network techniques. RBF network research has focused on enhanced training algorithms and variations on the basic architecture to improve the performance of the network. In addition, the RBF network is proving to be a valuable tool in a diverse range of applications areas, for example, robotics, biomedical engineering, and the financial sector.

The two-title series *Theory and Applications of Radial Basis Function Networks* provides a comprehensive survey of recent RBF network research. This volume, **Recent Developments in Theory and Applications**, covers advances in training algorithms, variations on the architecture and function of the basis neurons, and hybrid paradigms. The sister volume to this one, **New Advances in Design**, contains a wide range of applications in the laboratory and case-studies describing current use. The combination of the two volumes will prove extremely useful to practitioners in the field, engineers, researchers, students and technically accomplished managers.

There has been debate over whether the RBF network is truly a "neural" network, and thus whether it is correct to use the term "RBF neural network." Whether the operation of the RBF network is more or less biologically plausible than that of the Multi-Layer Perceptron using back-propagation training can be debated. However, this is something of a sterile discussion. Of greater importance is that the RBF network represents a useful tool with increasingly widespread application. For this reason we have not prevailed on authors to be consistent about the use of the term "RBF network" or "RBF neural network."

This book contains 11 chapters, each contributed by an accomplished researcher in the field. Chapter 1, by Ciocoiu, begins by describing standard and proposed RBF networks in the context of system theory. Several extensions to conventional architectures are then introduced to make better use of temporal information.

A problem faced by designers of RBF networks is the need to determine the number of RBF nodes, and the centres and widths of the Gaussians. Chapter 2, by Kubat, proposes a recently developed method to facilitate this by using decision trees to divide the input space into relatively homogeneous hyperrectangular regions. An RBF node is then associated with each region.

In Chapter 3, Borghese explains a technique in which grids of Gaussians are stacked, at decreasing scale, one over the other, forming a Hierarchical Radial Basis Function (HRBF) network. The network carries out Multi-Scale Analysis, different to Wavelet decomposition, and has the potential for real-time operation. The use of the network in a 3-D scanner application is described.

Chapter 4, by András, introduces the minimal spectral RBF network, which has some parallels with Support Vector Machines. The construction of spectral neural networks with orthogonal basis functions that are minimal orthogonal representations of the true minimal data model is described. The approach is illustrated using some practical applications.

In Chapter 5, Li and Leiss propose the use of the least trimmed squares approach to achieve an RBF network that has very high noise immunity. The resulting network balances the requirements for robustness and efficiency in the presence of outliers and Gaussian noise. The approach is validated by the presentation of experimental results.

Chapter 6, by Borş and Pitas, describes training algorithms for RBF networks that use robust statistics in a two-stage algorithm. The Median

RBF training algorithm and the Alpha-Trimmed Mean RBF are introduced. Applications in data classification and object modelling are provided.

Kernel methods are increasingly popular because they offer a rigorous approach to training learning machines and the superior performance achieved can be theoretically justified. The next two chapters are on kernel methods. Chapter 7, by Campbell, introduces methods that use RBF kernels for classification, regression and novelty detection. Algorithmic approaches to training these systems are explained and some recent applications are described.

Chapter 8, by Fyfe, MacDonald, Lai, Rosipal, and Charles, continues the kernel theme to first cover the use of radial kernels for Kernel Principal Components Analysis (KPCA). Kernel methods are then applied to a number of other paradigms, and illustrated using real and artificial data.

In Chapter 9, Hamker proposes a growing RBF network that determines the number of nodes needed for a particular application during training and also automatically varies the learning rate dynamically. The results of several simulations are presented to show that the network has the major characteristics needed to cope with the classical stability-plasticity dilemma.

The field of Operations Research has produced several new RBF learning rules and design algorithms. In Chapter 10, Roy presents new techniques which have arisen from this source that can lead to the development of truly autonomous learning methods. The chapter also introduces a new theory for brain-like learning. In addition algorithms that use linear programming models to generate RBF networks for function approximation and classification are described.

The final chapter in the book describes a hybrid technique formed from the fusion of two intelligent paradigms. In Chapter 11, by Lacerda, de Carvalho, and Ludermir, the selection of RBF parameters using evolutionary algorithms is discussed. An overall view of the methods used for the genetic optimisation of artificial neural networks and the inherent problems is presented. Finally the authors propose a model and describe experimental results using this model.

We would like to express our sincere thanks to Berend-Jan van der Zwaag for his efficient help in preparing the manuscript. We are grateful to the authors for their high-quality contributions and to the publishers for their editorial assistance.

R.J. Howlett, University of Brighton, U.K.
L.C. Jain, University of South Australia

Biographical Notes

Dr Robert J. Howlett has a PhD from the University of Brighton, an MPhil from the University of Sussex, and a BSc(Hons) from Portsmouth Polytechnic. He is a member of the British Computer Society and a Chartered Engineer. Dr Howlett is the Director of the University of Brighton TCS Centre, which currently has over 15 technology and knowledge transfer programmes in partnership with UK companies. He is also Head of the Intelligent Signal Processing Laboratories at the University.

Dr Howlett has a number of years experience of applying neural-networks and other intelligent techniques to industrial problems. He is leader of a research team in this area, has published widely on the subject, and has presented invited talks, keynote addresses, etc. He is currently Editor-in-Chief of the International Journal of Knowledge-Based Intelligent Engineering Systems. He is a past and current member of the International Scientific Committees of a number of conferences, and was the General Chair of the Fourth International Conference in Knowledge-Based Intelligent Engineering Systems and Allied Technologies (KES 2000) at the University of Brighton, UK, and is Executive Chair of KES 2001. He is the UK head of two Anglo-French projects funded by the European Union Interreg Programme, and a multi-national Framework V project. He is an Expert Evaluator for European Framework 5 projects.

L.C. Jain is a Director/Founder of the Knowledge-Based Intelligent Engineering Systems (KES) Centre, located in the University of South Australia. He is a fellow of the Institution of Engineers Australia. He has initiated a postgraduate stream by research in the Knowledge-based Intelligent Engineering Systems area. He has presented a number of Keynote addresses in International Conferences on Knowledge-Based Systems, Neural Networks, Fuzzy Systems and Hybrid Systems.

He is the Founding Editor-in-Chief of the International Journal of Knowledge-Based Intelligent Engineering Systems and served as an Associate Editor of the IEEE Transactions on Industrial Electronics. Dr Jain was the Technical chair of the ETD2000 International Conference in 1995, and Publications Chair of the Australian and New Zealand Conference on Intelligent Information Systems in 1996. He also initiated the First International Conference on Knowledge-based Intelligent Electronic Systems in 1997. This is now an annual event. He served as the Vice President of the Electronics Association of South Australia in 1997. He is the Editor-in-Chief of the International Book Series on Computational Intelligence, CRC Press U.S.A. His interests focus on the applications of novel techniques such as knowledge-based systems, artificial neural networks, fuzzy systems and genetic algorithms and the application of these techniques

Contents

Chapter 4.
RBF neural networks with orthogonal basis functions
P. András

Chapter 5.
On noise-immune RBF networks
S.-T. Li and E.L. Leiss

Chapter 6.
Robust RBF networks
A.G. Borş and I. Pitas

Chapter 7.
An introduction to kernel methods
C. Campbell

Chapter 8.
Unsupervised learning using radial kernels
C. Fyfe, D. MacDonald, P.L. Lai, R. Rosipal, and D. Charles

Chapter 9.
RBF learning in a non-stationary environment: the stability–plasticity dilemma
F.H. Hamker

Chapter 10.

**A new learning theory and polynomial-time autonomous learning
algorithms for generating RBF networks**
A. Roy

Chapter 11.
Evolutionary optimization of RBF networks
E. Lacerda, A. de Carvalho, and T. Ludermir

Chapter 1

Dynamic RBF Networks

I.B. Ciocoiu

This chapter covers dynamic RBF networks, which are systems that take explicitly into account temporal information. Inspired by the remarkable performances of multilayer perceptrons with FIR/IIR synapses, we introduce RBF networks with dynamic synapses. Basically, the scalar values of the output weights in the standard architecture are replaced by linear discrete-time FIR/IIR filters. We extend the existing results to novel filter types such as gamma and Laguerre.

While focusing on the discrete-time version of such systems, we also introduce the RBF approach in the context of analog networks. Specifically, gradient-type systems with RBF-type Lyapunov functions are presented, and the influence of the associated parameters on the dynamics is investigated. The main goal is related to the possibility of computing with attractors, namely to storing both stable equilibrium points and limit cycles and making controlled transitions between them. Conclusions revealed by theoretic analysis are verified through computer simulations related to benchmark applications.

1   Introduction

"When you have a hammer in your hands everything looks like a nail" says an old English proverb, but when applying neural networks to real life difficult tasks it seems not to be exaggerated. Although not fully meeting the expectations of the early 1980s, the neural approach has proved to be one of the more attractive solutions to solve complex problems related to speech processing, pattern recognition, or nonlinear control, to cite just a few. Nowadays, neural techniques have become popular in biomedicine, finance, and automotive industry, while

computer simulation environments integrate increasingly more of the novel architectures and learning algorithms.

The present contribution is related to Radial Basis Functions networks (RBFs), which have been traditionally used as a multidimensional interpolation technique, implementing general mappings $f : R^m \rightarrow R$ according to [7]:

$$f(\mathbf{X}) = w_0 + \sum_{i=1}^{M} w_i \phi\left(\left\|\mathbf{X} - \mathbf{C}_i\right\|\right) \tag{1}$$

where ϕ is a nonlinear function selected from a set of typical ones, $\|\cdot\|$ denotes the Euclidean norm, w_i are the tap weights and $C_i \in R^m$ are called RBF centers. It is easy to see from the formula above that such networks belong to the broader family of feedforward architectures: it defines a special form of a 2-layer perceptron, which is *linear in the parameters* by fixing all the centers and nonlinearities in the hidden layer [2]. The output layer simply performs a linear combination of the (nonlinearly) transformed inputs and thus the tap weights w_i can be obtained by using standard tools from linear adaptive filter theory such as the LMS algorithm or its momentum version. This generally leads to a dramatic reduction of the computing time with the supplementary benefit of avoiding the problem of local minima, usually encountered when simulating standard multilayer perceptrons (MLPs).

Since RBF networks also possess universal approximation capabilities (critically dependent of the choice of the centers) they have been traditionally used in the same applications as MLPs. Anyway, when dealing with complex temporal processing tasks such as speech processing, their performances are generally inferior to those of recurrent networks, basically due to limited memory length. The usual approach relies on using time-delayed data windows in order to cope with the inherent *static* character of the input-output mapping. Larger memory means increasing the data window length (that is, the dimensionality of the input space), which in turn would require a substantial growth of the number of the centers to yield satisfactory approximation results.

We introduce several extensions to the standard architecture in order to better use temporal information, focused on the following directions:

a) replacement of the scalar values of the output weights in the standard architecture by linear discrete time FIR/IIR filters. Learning algorithms for the proposed networks are presented, and their performances tested on nonlinear system identification and chaotic time series prediction applications.

b) proper use of the space localization properties of RBF networks (with gaussian-type activation functions) in the context of analog recurrent networks. Associative memory design is considered as an implementation of the *"computing with attractors"* paradigm, along with a soft decoding procedure for data transmission applications.

In order to have a broader view on the theoretical aspects related to the subject, we begin by presenting a brief characterization of standard and proposed RBF networks in the light of system theory. It offers a unified view on existing solutions and makes clearer the novel aspects to be covered.

2   A System Theoretic Perspective

RBF networks have been an active research area in the last decade, both from theoretical and applicative points of view. Original contributions have addressed all three elements characterizing general neural networks, namely the individual neuron model, the architecture, and the learning algorithm. In the sequel we present a brief characterization of useful properties and capabilities offered by RBF nets based on established terminology and classification criteria provided by system theory:

(a) *Input-output mapping*: as pointed out before, RBFs have similar universal approximation capabilities as MLP networks. Moreover, for a particular choice of the centers, they hold the so-called *best approximation property* [19] in the sense that there exists at least one set of output weights such that the network output has minimum distance from a given function to be approximated. The local activation function $\phi(\mathbf{X})$ generates a qualitatively different nonlinear character of the resulting mapping, exhibiting well-localized spatial responses for data points close to the centers.

(b) *Memory*: in standard form, RBF networks provide *static* input-output mappings. In order to make it useful for temporal processing applications, the basic architecture should be modified to allow explicit representation of time information. Switching from purely algebraic to dynamic (time-varying) behavior is possible if *memory* is included into the network design. This leads to a more suitable description in terms of state equations and may be accomplished in two forms: introducing dynamic synapses by replacing scalar values of the output weights by discrete-time FIR/IIR filters, or by building global feedback paths. In Figure 1, we present standard and proposed dynamic RBF architectures to be used for time-varying input data.

(c) *Linear versus nonlinear*: Interesting enough, both previous design ideas can be related to a powerful decomposition theorem stating the uniqueness of the structure presented in Figure 2, where $L_1(\cdot)$ and $L_2(\cdot)$ designate the transfer functions of two linear time-invariant systems, and $N(\cdot)$ represents a memoryless strictly nonlinear operator [6]. As a corollary of this theorem, it follows that the two block diagrams from the right side of Figure 1 correspond to *completely disjoint* systems. Moreover, input-output measurements alone may reveal useful information about the internal structure of an unknown nonlinear dynamic system.

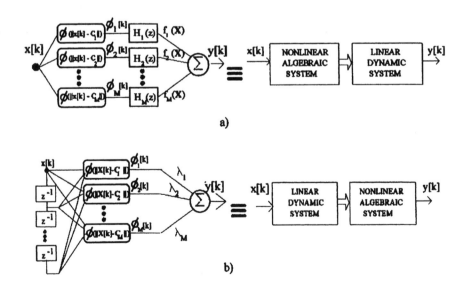

Figure 1. RBF architectures for temporal processing applications:
a) proposed solution; b) standard.

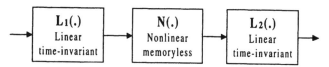

Figure 2. Generic structure for the decomposition theorem.

(d) *Analog versus discrete*: RBF networks generally operate in discrete-time. As will be shown in Section 4, it is possible to speculate their intrinsic space localization properties in order to extend the functionality towards continuous-time networks. The link between the two is represented by the formulation of a special Lyapunov function in terms of RBF expansion, whose parameters are tailored to the application at hand.

(e) *Adaptivity*: adapting RBF parameters to optimally cope with the (possibly continuing) changes of the environment has been an area of intensive research in the last years. Two distinct directions have been mainly considered:

- fixed architectures with improved learning strategies: owing to the convergence speed limitations of standard LMS-type algorithms, a set of superior solutions have been proposed for training both output weights and centers position. They originate from different theoretical grounds, such as functional approximation, estimation theory, and nonlinear optimization. Examples include first order (gradient descent or OLS [8]) and second order (Extended Kalman Filter [33]) fully-supervised algorithms, and global optimization tools such as Genetic Algorithms.

- time-varying architectures: constructive methodologies follow both learn-and-grow (RAN [26]) and pruning strategies. A flexible solution combining the two approaches is MRAN [33], while trimming the network complexity according to generalization error is considered in PCP [18].

3   Discrete-Time Dynamic RBF Networks

Introducing time delays into the structure of a static neural network provides a straightforward possibility of turning it into a dynamic one. This form of memory is not only biologically motivated, but also more computationally attractive, since learning algorithms bear a close resemblance with the back-propagation family. Existing solutions include Wan's MLPs with FIR synapses [32] and time-delay neural networks (TDNN [13]) and have been used in speech processing, nonlinear system identification and prediction applications. The mathematical background is offered by the celebrated Takens' embedding theorem introducing the notion of reconstruction space, and the capability of standard MLP networks to act as universal approximators in this space [28].

Inspired by the remarkable performances of existing solutions, we propose a novel RBF architecture obtained by replacing the scalar values of the output weights by linear discrete time FIR/IIR filters, as in Figure 1a. Since RBF learning algorithms have clear advantages in terms of convergence speed and optimality of solution over MLPs, it is expected that such networks would deal with temporal processing problems without excessive computational burden. When compared to the classical structure used for time processing applications, it is easy to see that the new one performs a *"z^{-1}-ϕ" exchange* that enables the input to the hidden layer to become *unidimensional*. This will moderate the effect of the well-known *curse of dimensionality* and simplify the hardware implementation.

3.1   The Learning Algorithms

Adaptive IIR filters suffer from two important drawbacks, namely potential instability problems and the presence of local minima in the error function [29]. Even when the stability conditions are easily met, such as in the case of lattice or biquads, the computational complexity is higher than for FIR adaptive filters. This is why we decided to use a recently introduced IIR structure called *the gamma filter* [31], which both imposes trivial stability conditions and is computationally effective. It may be considered as a generalization of the classical transversal filter, the standard delay operator z^{-1} being replaced by the so-called *gamma operator*:

$$G(z) = \frac{\mu}{z - (1 - \mu)} \qquad (2)$$

where μ is a real parameter that controls the memory depth of the filter. As pointed out in [30], gamma filters are superior to standard FIR filters in terms of number of parameters required to model a given dynamics.

The filter is stable if $0 < \mu < 2$. For $\mu = 1$, $G(z)$ reduces to the usual delay operator, so the learning algorithm to be presented below is easily applicable for the simpler case of FIR synapses.

The system output at time k is given by

$$y[k] = \sum_{i=1}^{M} f_i[k] \tag{3}$$

and the instantaneous error at time k is

$$E[k] = \tfrac{1}{2}\{e[k]\}^2 = \tfrac{1}{2}\left\{d[k] - \sum_{i=1}^{M} f_i[k]\right\}^2 \tag{4}$$

where $d[k]$ is the target output at time k and M is the number of centers to be used.

The transfer function $H_i(z)$ may be written

$$H_i(z) = \sum_{d=0}^{D} w_{id} \left[G_i(z)\right]^d, \qquad i = 1,\dots,M \tag{5}$$

where every $G_i(z)$ function has its own μ_i parameter and D is the maximum delay (for simplicity, D is the same for all filters). Equivalently, we may write

$$\phi_{id}[k] = (1 - \mu_i)\phi_{id}[k-1] + \mu_i\phi_{i(d-1)}[k-1], \quad d=1,\dots,D;\ i=1,\dots,M \tag{6}$$

where $\phi_{i0}[k] = \phi_i[k]$, $\phi_{iD}[k] = f_i[k]$ and $\phi_{id}[k]$ represent (gamma) delayed versions of the incoming signals $\phi_i[k]$.

Following the derivation of the learning algorithm presented in [30], the weights w_{id} and coefficients μ_i modify according to a gradient descent rule as

$$\Delta w_{id}[k] = \eta e[k]\phi_{id}[k], \quad d = 0,\dots,D;\ i = 1,\dots,M \tag{7}$$

$$\Delta\mu_i = \eta \sum_{d=0}^{D} e[k]w_{id}[k]\alpha_{id}[k], \quad d = 0,\dots,D;\ i = 1,\dots,M \tag{8}$$

where $\alpha_{id}[k] = (\partial_{id}[k]/\partial\mu)$ verifies the recursive equation ($\alpha_{i0}[k]=0$):

$$\alpha_{id}[k] = (1-\mu)\alpha_{id}[k-1] + \mu\alpha_{i(d-1)}[k-1] + \phi_{i(d-1)}[k-1] - \phi_{id}[k-1],$$
$$d = 1,...,D; \ i = 1,...,M \tag{9}$$

It is important to note that the memory depth of the system can be adjusted on-line, making it more suitable for capturing the dynamics of the analyzed time series. In this respect, the learning algorithm can be related to temporal back-propagation with adaptive time delays [13].

Gamma filters provide a flexible compromise between memory depth and resolution (defined as the number of taps per sample). Since the filter is linear, the signals on each tap may be regarded as the convolution between the impulse response of the leaky integrator defined by the gamma operator in equation (2) and the signal on the previous tap. As a consequence, the tap signals have increasingly smaller amplitude as the order of the memory filter increases. There is a superior alternative to gamma operator, based on approximation theory involving Laguerre polynomials. From a system theoretic point of view, Laguerre filters are formed by a front-end low-pass filter followed by a cascade of all-pass filters having the transfer functions [27]:

$$H_{LP}(z) = \frac{\sqrt{1-(1-\mu)^2}}{1-(1-\mu)z^{-1}}; \ H_{AP}(z) = \frac{z^{-1}-(1-\mu)}{1-(1-\mu)z^{-1}} \tag{10}$$

It can be proved that, in this case, the tap signals become orthogonal and, as a consequence, the training procedure is much faster.

3.2 Simulation Results

We have tested the efficiency of the proposed approach on two distinct applications:
   (a) identification of dynamic nonlinear systems
   (b) chaotic time series prediction

In both cases we used Gaussian-type activation functions of the form $\phi(x) = \exp(-x^2/\sigma^2)$. Centers have been selected using Kohonen's self-organizing maps [16], since they are known to offer a proper image of the distribution density of the data, and because the algorithm is computationally efficient. We used the *k-nearest neighbors* algorithm [13] to obtain the values of the spread parameter σ, although universal approximation is still possible by taking constant width [25]. The stopping criterion of the learning phase was based on monitoring the evolution of the Mean-Square Error (MSE) on a cross-validation set (10% of the whole database).

3.2.1 System Identification

First of the examples to be considered was also analyzed in [24], and is included merely as a confirmation of the fact that the two systems presented in Figure 1 yield completely different performances:

$$y[k+1] = 0.1f(u[k-1]) + f(u[k-2]) + 0.5f(u[k-3])$$
$$f(u) = 4u^2 + 4u \tag{11}$$

The input signal was a random sequence of 500 points with amplitude uniformly distributed in the interval [−1, 1]. Simulation results for varying number of centers and filter order are presented in Figure 3. Final values of Mean-Square Error (MSE) are indicated in Table1 (these were obtained by averaging over 10 separate runs for each experiment).

Approximation results of the RBF network with dynamic synapses are clearly superior to the standard architecture for this particular example. Since the nonlinearity is mild, a small number of centers are sufficient in order to obtain accurate models.

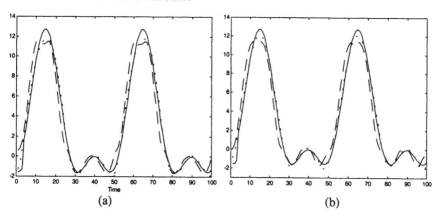

(a)   (b)

Figure 3. Simulation results (solid line – target data, dotted line – gamma synapses, dashed line – standard RBF architecture); (a) 5 centers, filter order 3; (b) 7 centers, filter order 3.

Table 1. MSE values for system identification application ($\times 10^{-3}$).

Centers	Training set				Cross-validation set			
	Gamma		Standard		Gamma		Standard	
	Order 2	Order 3	Order 2	Order 3	Order 2	Order 3	Order 2	Order 3
5	0.16	0.113	2.35	1.35	1.32	0.94	20.8	11.8
7	0.055	0.091	2.25	0.66	0.4	0.76	19.8	5.72

We consider a second system identification example, defined by a more complicated mapping of the form

$$y[k+1] = y[k]\cos y[k] + y[k]e^{-\dfrac{y^2[k]}{8}} + \dfrac{u^3[k]}{1 + u^2[k] + 0.5\cos y[k]} \qquad (12)$$

The training database contained 500 input-output pairs and the input signal was $u[k] = \sin(\frac{2\pi k}{10}) + \sin(\frac{2\pi k}{25})$. Simulation results using 7 centers and gamma synapses of order 3 are presented in Figure 4b.

We also tested a general architecture as in Figure 2, by including gamma filters at the input layer of an RBF network (the structure is sometimes called *focused*) with gamma synapses, and the results are presented in Figure 4a.

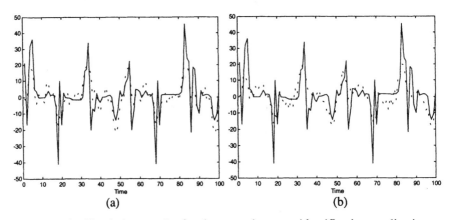

Figure 4. Simulation results for the second system identification application (7 centers, gamma filter order 3); (a) focused RBF network and gamma synapses; (b) unidimensional input RBF network with gamma synapses.

3.2.2 Chaotic Time Series Prediction

A training sequence of 500 points was obtained by integrating the well-known Lorenz equations by Runge-Kutta method with step size 0.1. The resulting signal has been used as input to the RBF networks and one-step ahead prediction has been performed. The results of the simulations are presented in Figure 5 for FIR and gamma synapses of order 5 and 20 centers. It is easy to see that the neural networks are able to closely approximate the original time series. MSE values are given in Table 2 (average over 10 separate runs for each experiment).

The results show that the errors decrease when the number of centers and/or the order of the filters increase, but a number of 20 centers and synapses of order 10 are sufficient in order to obtain satisfactory performances.

Table2. MSE values for time series prediction application on the training set ($\times 10^{-3}$).

No. centers	FIR synapses of order:			Gamma synapses of order:			RBF standard	
	5	10	15	5	10	15	5	10
5	2.286	1.917	1.991	2.286	1.917	1.991	17.33	19.54
10	0.848	0.66	0.442	0.774	0.663	0.442	11.8	21.02
15	0.591	0.47	0.368	0.591	0.442	0.368	10.69	21.02
20	0.585	0.42	0.331	0.591	0.402	0.365	9.95	20.28
25	0.555	0.4	0.295	0.545	0.368	0.331	9.95	20.28
30	0.516	0.25	0.258	0.442	0.331	0.33	9.95	21.02

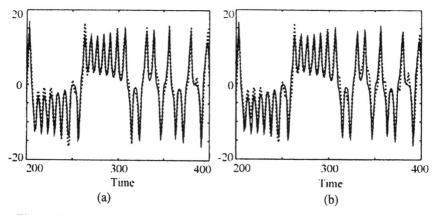

Figure 5. Simulation results for 20 centers and filter order 5 (solid line – target data, dotted line – approximating sequence); (a) FIR synapses 3; (b) gamma synapses

In order to validate the model, we may chose between two alternatives:

(a) computing correlation functions between the prediction error (residual sequence) and several linear and non-linear combinations of past inputs and outputs and verify if all of them fall within the 95% confidence interval [4], [5], since if the model structure is adequate the residuals should be uncorrelated with any combination of this kind. Another widely-used statistical method is represented by the so-called chi-squared tests [5];

(b) split the data into a training sequence and a testing one and performing *iterative prediction*, which means that the *predicted* value at time k is used as an input to predict the value at moment $(k+1)$. We have used both approaches, although the first one is more suitable in this case, since the number of data points is not very large.

Simulation results for iterative prediction are presented in Figure 6. The network is clearly able to closely predict several values into the future, and the performances improve when the order of the synaptic filters is larger. We have also tested the case of common μ for all synaptic filters, but the results were poorer than in previous cases, and the learning parameter had to be set to smaller values in order to obtain stable convergence.

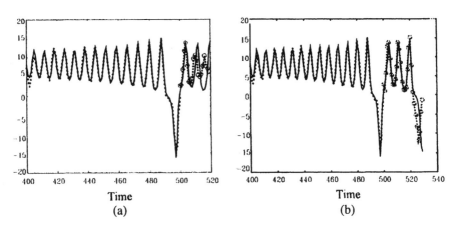

Figure 6. Iterative prediction with FIR synapses of order 10 (the dotted line with circles defines starting the iteration): (a) 20 centers; (b) 25 centers.

4   Continuous-Time RBF Networks

RBF networks have been traditionally used in discrete-time version, and all practical applications have been related to this point of view. Nevertheless, there exists a possibility of establishing a link towards analog, continuous-time networks, by speculating the very essence of such networks: space localization. The basic idea to be presented in the following is very simple: design gradient-type analog networks by constructing an RBF-like Lyapunov function as in equation (1). The main benefit of the approach is the possibility of placing stable equilibrium points in *predefined positions* in state-space, where the Lyapunov function has local minima. This is a highly desirable property in many important applications, such as pattern recognition or associative memory design. We include two examples, related to soft decoding of linear block codes used in data transmission, and to optical character recognition. The later application includes a significant enhancement to the main approach, by providing a mechanism allowing *controlled transitions* among different stable equilibria stored in the system. Moreover, a novel hierarchical associative memory is proposed, by considering a pair of gradient-type systems operating on a master-slave basis.

All systems define higher-order analog neural networks. While this leads to greater complexity compared to classical recurrent architectures such as the Hopfield net, spurious responses are practically eliminated and the basins of attraction around stable equilibria are tailored simpler.

4.1   Storing Stable Equilibria and Limit Cycles

Results presented in the following are mainly related to associative memory design. Basically, a set of patterns is to be stored using a training database and a proper learning procedure. In the testing phase, the system should output correct results even if noisy, incomplete or distorted data is applied as input.

We consider a special gradient-type analog recurrent network of the form:

$$\frac{dx_i}{dt} = -\frac{\partial V(\mathbf{X})}{\partial x_i}, \quad i = 1, ..., N \tag{13}$$

where $\mathbf{X}=\{x_i\}$ defines the state-vector, N is the order of the system, and $V(\mathbf{X})$ is the associated Lyapunov function. A well-known result states that all isolated minima of $V(\mathbf{X})$ are asymptotically stable states of system (13) [14]. Function $V(\mathbf{X})$ will be chosen in a particular way, in order to satisfy the following requirements [20]:
- any desired memory pattern should be stored as a point in a multidimensional state space where the Lyapunov function $V(\mathbf{X})$ has a minimum
- no spurious memories (stable states which do not correspond to the desired ones) should exist
- the number of desired equilibria should be arbitrarily large
- the addition/elimination of an equilibrium should be performed without redesigning the system.

In order to have the desired memory patterns placed specifically at the equilibrium points of the dynamic system we use an idea previously presented in [12] to solve a pattern recognition task. We construct the Lyapunov function as a sum of individual functions exhibiting good *space localization* properties, having deep minima at the desired locations and been practically constant in rest:

$$V(\mathbf{X}) = \sum_{m=1}^{M} w_m g_m(\mathbf{X}) \tag{14}$$

where M is the number of memories to be stored, w_m are scalar weights, and functions $g_m(\mathbf{X})$ are:

$$g_m(\mathbf{X}) = 1 - e^{-\frac{d_p^{\,p}(\mathbf{X},\mathbf{X}_m)}{2\sigma_m^{\,2}}} \tag{15}$$

where $d_p(\mathbf{X},\mathbf{X}_m)$ is the distance induced by the L_p measure defined on the N-dimensional vector space. It is easy to observe that equation (14) defines a standard RBF formula, where the desired equilibrium points act as the centers.

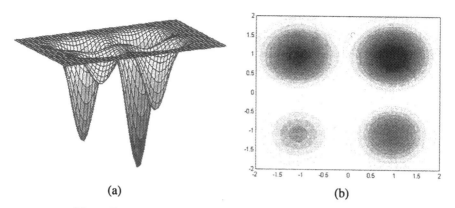

Figure 7. (a) RBF-type Lyapunov function; (b) contour plot.

In Figure 7, we present an example of the function $V(\mathbf{X})$ for a system with $N = 2$ and $M = 4$ stable equilibrium points, namely, $(-1, -1)$; $(-1, 1)$; $(1, -1)$; $(1, 1)$. We used a common value for $\sigma_m = 0.25$, and the weights vector was $\{w_m\}=\{1, 2, 3, 4\}$.

We tested the efficiency of the proposed idea on a data transmission application, namely the problem of analog (sometimes called *soft*) decision decoding of linear block codes. In order to generate such a code, the source encoder maps blocks of k binary information symbols into output codewords of n bits $(n > k)$. The mapping must be carefully chosen in order to improve the reliability of transmission. There are 2^k codewords to be selected from a set of 2^n possible combinations in a way that maximizes the Hamming distance between the chosen words (the Hamming distance between two binary numbers equals the number of positions they differ). If d is the minimum Hamming distance between any two codewords than it can be shown [35] that up to e errors can be corrected if $d \geq 2e+1$. A block code is usually denoted (n, k) and the ratio $R_m = (k/n)$ is called the *code rate*. The received distorted noisy analog codewords will act as initial conditions for such a (neural) dynamical system which will eventually settle down to one of the stable equilibrium points which should be predefined to coincide with the correct versions of the codewords used by the source, hopefully to the closest in terms of Hamming distance.

Computer simulations have been performed using two different block codes, namely (7,4) Hamming code and (7,4) cyclic redundancy code. (they both are single error correcting codes). The decoding performances are usually analyzed in terms of the post-decoding bit-error rate (BER) versus the signal-to-noise ratio per information bit E_b/N_0. The last term strongly depends on the modulation scheme and the type of channel that is used. For additive white Gaussian noise (AWGN channel), baseband unipolar transmission and for optimal demodulator (matched filter followed by a sampler) the ratio E_b/N_0 can be expressed as a function of the signal amplitude A_s and the noise variance σ^2 [35].

$$\frac{E_b}{N_0} = \frac{n}{k} \frac{A^2{}_s}{8\sigma^2} \tag{16}$$

The factor n/k indicates that E_b is the *energy per information bit* and not per channel symbol.

Many simulations have been performed by selecting one of the codewords and adding gaussian noise with zero mean and σ^2 variance to each bit then delivering this analog vector to the neural network, as an initial condition. Two different types of distances have been used, the Euclidean ($p = 2$) and Manhattan ($p = 1$) distance. Special care must be taken in the later case, since the function is *not* differentiable:

$$d_1 = \sum_{i=1}^{N} \left| x_i - x_i^s \right| \tag{17}$$

A proper approximation for the modulus function has been used:

$$f(x) = \frac{1}{\alpha} \ln(\cosh(\alpha x)) \tag{18}$$

where parameter α controls the slope of the derivative around origin.

The results are presented in Figure 8a for the (7,4) Hamming code and in Figure 8b for the (7,4) cyclic redundancy code. For comparison, the results obtained by using a standard hard decision decoder are also presented. It is obvious that the soft decision neural decoders perform better than the hard one, which illustrates in fact a well-known principle. The post-decoding bit error rate is one order of magnitude smaller for the neural decoder using the Euclidean distance at 7 dB signal-to-noise ratio for the (7,4) Hamming code and slightly better for the cyclic code.

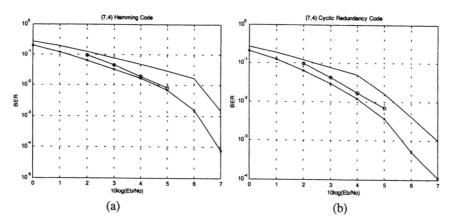

(a)   (b)

Figure 8. Simulation results (σ=0.5, x – L2 network; o – L1 network ; solid
line – using the hard-decision decoder); (a) (7,4) Hamming code; (b) (7,4)
cyclic redundancy code.

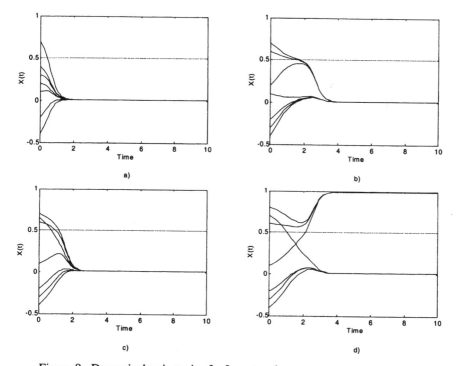

a)   b)

c)   d)

Figure 9. Dynamical trajectories for L_2 network:
(a) one component of the initial state vector exceeds the threshold value;
(b) two components of the initial state vector exceed the threshold value;
(c) three components of the initial state vector exceed the threshold value;
(d) convergence towards a wrong stable state.

In Figure 9, typical dynamical trajectories are shown. In Figure 9a, only one component of the initial state vector exceeds the threshold set at 0.5 (half distance between the two signaling levels) and the final state of the system is the correct (0 ... 0) vector. The same result would had been obtained if a hard-decision decoder have been used since after thresholding the Hamming distance between the resulting word and the correct one would have been 1 (and the (7,4) Hamming code is able to correct up to 1 error). Anyway, for the trajectories presented in Figures 9b and 9c, the resulting Hamming distance after thresholding would be 2 and 3, respectively, and the hard decoder would not be able to reconstruct the correct codeword. In Figure 9d, convergence to a wrong codeword is shown. These graphics indicate that the basin of attraction of a specific codeword may include states that, after thresholding, give binary words whose Hamming distances from it exceed 1 (which is the limit for the hard-decision decoder to operate well).

4.2 Computing with Attractors

Attractor networks, such as the one presented in the previous paragraph, define mappings from an input (usually continuous) space to a discrete output space, and have been the subject of much interest in the last decade [2], [13], [34]. Many of the existing solutions, such as the Hopfield network, suffer from the presence of spurious attractors and have limited memory capacity. Even when such drawbacks are largely eliminated, as in the remarkable case of networks using nonmonotonic activation functions [22], the design strategy cannot accommodate storing more complex dynamics like oscillatory (or even chaotic) attractors. Moreover, learning algorithms relating the network weights to a predefined set of patterns to be stored are rare [2], and generally computationally intensive.

The proposed design procedure has a number of important advantages, including:
- a clear correspondence between the set of memories to be stored and the equations governing the system dynamics
- a transparent interpretation of the effect of the parameters (centers, weights, width) on the time and state-space evolution
- guaranteed convergence based on Lyapunov stability theory
- implementation advantages in terms of limited number of interconnections. In fact, the core elements of the architecture,

namely distance computing cells and gaussian-type activation functions have already been implemented in VLSI circuits [15].

Important applications such as speech processing or written word recognition require not only the necessity of storing separate pieces of information in a robust manner, but also the means by which the memory patterns can be sequentially visited, ideally in a predefined order. Existing solutions include chaotic memory search [23] and nonmonotonic networks [22]. We propose a novel method, based on the use of the tunneling effect proposed in [3] as a global optimization method. Basically, the idea relies on the violation of Lipschitz condition at an equilibrium point of a dynamic system, which enables state trajectories to approach an attractor or escape from a repeller in finite time. In fact, we modify equation (13) by introducing an additional energy term which transforms any particular equilibrium $\mathbf{X}^*$ in a terminal repeller:

$$\frac{dx_i}{dt} = -\{1 - \Theta[V(\mathbf{X}) - V^*]\}\frac{\partial V(\mathbf{X})}{\partial x_i} + \alpha\Theta[V(\mathbf{X}) - V^*]\frac{\partial}{\partial x_i}(\mathbf{X} - \mathbf{X}^*)^{\frac{4}{3}},$$

$$i = 1, ..., N \tag{19}$$

where Θ is the Heaviside step function, V^* is the value of Lyapunov function from equation (14) at $\mathbf{X}^*$, and α is a scalar.

Remarks

(a) The dynamic system $\frac{\partial x_i}{\partial t} = \frac{\partial}{\partial x_i}\left(\mathbf{X}^{\frac{4}{3}}\right) = \frac{4}{3}\mathbf{X}^{\frac{1}{3}}$ has a repelling unstable equilibrium at $\mathbf{X} = 0$ which violates the Lipschitz condition.

(b) This elegant global optimization method has also been used as a supervised learning algorithm for standard feedforward networks, as an enhancement to the well-known backpropagation family [10].

We make the dynamics of the system *switch* between a tunneling phase and a gradient-descent phase as follows: we select one of the desired memory patterns as vector $\mathbf{X}^*$, and define the initial state of the system $\mathbf{X}_0$ by perturbing $\mathbf{X}^*$ with a small random amount. Since $\mathbf{X}^*$ corresponds to a local minimum of function $V(\mathbf{X})$ we have $V(\mathbf{X}_0) > V(\mathbf{X}^*)$ and, as a consequence, the system enters the tunneling phase: as long as $V(\mathbf{X})$ is higher than V^* the state of the system moves away from $\mathbf{X}^*$. When it reaches a point for which $V(\mathbf{X})$ is less than V^* the system enters the gradient descent phase and stabilizes to a different equilibrium point. In order to enable visiting other (lower $V(\mathbf{X})$ energy) memories, the last local minimum becomes $\mathbf{X}^*$, the new initial state is again a slightly perturbed version of it, and the process reenters the tunneling phase. Eventually, the system state rests on the lowest energy equilibrium.

Remarks

(a) Usually, the weights vector $\{w_m\}$ is hardwired to fixed values. Anyway, if these values are allowed to gradually change and if the stored memories are to be visited in a predefined order, they should be carefully readjusted at the transition between the gradient descent and the tunneling phase, to ensure that the next equilibrium to be reached has lower energy than the preceding one.

(b) In a multidimensional space $(N > 1)$ a successful search is not always guaranteed. Typically, multiple runs starting from different initial conditions must be performed in order to reach the desired memory. We have successfully tried a (mostly empirical) solution to this problem, by choosing each vector of initial conditions on the direction defined by two consecutive memories to be visited, namely

$$\mathbf{X}_n(0) = a\mathbf{X}^*_n + (1-a)\mathbf{X}^*_{n+1} \tag{20}$$

where a is a positive constant, and $\mathbf{X}^*_n$, $\mathbf{X}^*_{n+1}$ are distinct stable equilibrium points of the gradient system. This is justified by the assumption of constant direction of repelling [3]. Successful "trapping" of the dynamics into the basin of attraction of a desired equilibrium implies sufficiently strong surface gradients along that direction of repelling. In our case, this is accomplished by choosing a proper value of the (common) σ parameter.

We have tested the proposed approach on a memory storing the 0-9 digits. The data was represented as 6×6 pixels, as in Figure 10: white pixels were coded as 1s and black pixels as –1s. Each digit is stored as an equilibrium point of a dynamic system of order $N = 36$. Other parameter values are: $\sigma_m = 0.5$, $\alpha = 0.5$. The weight vector was: $\{w_m\} = \{1, 2, 3, 4, 5, 6, 7, 8, 9, 10\}$ in order to force visiting the stored memories in an ascending order (the equilibrium points of the system (1) have progressively lower energy from 0 to 9). In Figure 11a, we present typical evolution of the combined energy function of the system, that includes both function $V(\mathbf{X})$ given in equation (2) and the contribution of the repelling term, when initialized with a slightly perturbed version of the 0 digit. This proves that the system successively passes through all the stored equilibria, in a predefined (*e.g.*, ascending) order. In Figure 11b, typical evolution of one component (namely, the seventh) of the state vector during the search procedure is presented.

The proposed synthesis method is related to storing only stable equilibrium points in predefined positions in the corresponding state space of the system. More interesting phenomena arise when a dynamic system exhibits periodic behavior or even chaotic dynamics. Not only such dynamics seem prevalent in the brain, but also important technical applications are related to storing, recovering, and controlling such dynamics (*e.g.*, speech processing or chaotic based data transmission).

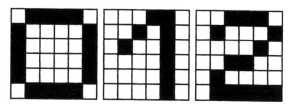

Figure 10. Examples of the stored patterns.

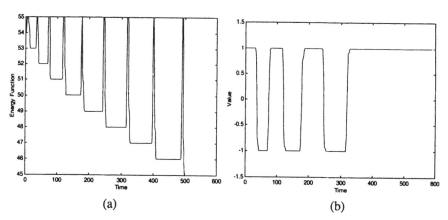

| (a) | (b) |

Figure 11. (a) Typical evolution of the combined energy function of system (15); (b) Evolution of one component of the state vector during the search period.

We may model single frequency *oscillatory patterns* (cycles) by the relation $\vec{r}e^{j\vec{\Phi}} = \vec{r}e^{j\vec{\theta}}e^{j\omega_0 t}$, where $\mathbf{r} \in \mathbf{R}^N$ defines the amplitude vector, and $\theta \in \mathbf{T}^N$ (N-torus) defines a vector of relative phases [2]. We may use the previously presented synthesis techniques in order to store such cycles by describing the system dynamics in *polar coordinates* instead of standard Cartesian ones:

$$x_{2i-1} = r_i \cos\Phi_i$$
$$x_{2i} = r_i \sin\Phi_i$$

(21)

The vector field of the dynamics (in polar coordinates) is then given as two *decoupled equations*: the evolution of the amplitude vector $\mathbf{r}$ is governed by an equation of type (13) (or (15) if "migration" among attractors is wanted), and the phase equation is simply of the form ($d\Phi_i/dt = \omega_0$). Stable fixed points of the amplitude equations will correspond to stable limit cycles of the system in Cartesian coordinates. Combined storing of both static and oscillatory patterns is possible by choosing some of the ω_i components equal to zero. The number of patterns to be stored is theoretically unlimited, although the basins of attraction around the equilibrium points (controlled by the σ parameter) should be large enough for practical applications. Moreover, a particular choice of the amplitude and phases of the stored patterns offers the possibility of memorizing any periodic sequence, based on its Fourier expansion. The proposed method is close to the Normal Form Projection Algorithm [2], which is based on the Hopf bifurcation theory, and uses a different method for the transition among attractors. While they both implement high-order neural networks, our solution is not constrained by patterns orthogonality.

4.3   A Hierarchical Associative Memory

We may use the search technique described in the previous paragraph in order to design a modular, two-level hierarchically organized associative memory as in Figure 12. AM1 designates an RBF-type memory whose dynamics is governed by equation (15), storing P_1 patterns of dimension N_1. The set of weights $\mathbf{W}^1 = \{w_i^1, i = 1, ..., P_1\}$ are programmed as stable equilibria of a second system (AM2) defined as in equation (13): each searching "itinerary" corresponds to a distinct equilibrium point of AM2. Since these equilibria control the visiting order of the memories stored in AM1, the dimension of the system implementing AM2 should be P_1.

The searching procedure starts by initializing AM2 within the basin of attraction of a specific (predefined) search schedule. After the state vector settles to the corresponding equilibrium its values are copied into the weights vector of AM1, and this system is initialized with a proper state vector close to the first of the (maximum) P_1 patterns to be visited during the current searching session. After the itinerary is completed, AM2 is reinitialized to a new value and the procedure is repeated. The design procedure should take into account the following aspects:

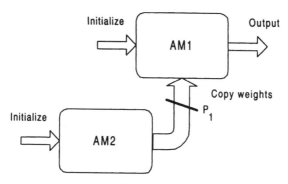

Figure 12. Block diagram of the hierarchical associative memory.

- the stable equilibria of AM2 must have *distinct* component values in order to ensure the unicity of the visiting sequence of the patterns in AM1
- the length of the search itinerary may be shorter than P_1. To implement this, simply set all the components of an equilibrium of AM2 lower than the one corresponding to the first pattern to be visited
- as pointed out in the previous paragraph, successful search is not always guaranteed in a multidimensional space (N>1). Running multiple tests starting from different initial conditions could be alleviated by using proper initialization of AM1 along the direction between the currently reached stable equilibrium and the one to be visited next. Since there is a one-to-one correspondence between the P_1 patterns and the vector $\mathbf{W}^1$, identifying *consecutive* memories in AM1 may be easily performed after ordering the components of this weight vector.

To illustrate the proposed idea consider the problem of (arbitrary length) word storing and retrieving. The patterns to be stored in AM1 should be the 26 letters of the English alphabet, coded as images with specific resolution or simply as binary vectors placed in the corners of a $[0, 1]^{26}$ hypercube. AM2 codes the dictionary, as a collection of distinct search sessions through the AM1 memories. When a specific word is to be retrieved, AM2 is first initialized and, after relaxing to the corresponding equilibrium point, it provides the search sequence among the letters in AM1. Patterns stored in AM2 may be represented as (allowed by the dictionary content) permutations of a monotonic sequence of 26 positive values such as $\mathbf{L}=\{\frac{1}{26},\frac{2}{26},....,\frac{25}{26},1\}$, plus 0 to allow for the absence of specific letters. Specifically, each word is coded as a 26-dimensional vector including (a) a subset of (properly ordered) $\mathbf{L}$ values, and (b) a number of 0s corresponding to absent letters.

Supposing the dictionary was fully stored as a collection of such $\mathbf{W}^1$ vectors in system AM2, we may consider several distinct query types including constraints on the information to be recovered, as in the following examples:
-   retrieve all three-letter words with D in the third position, and any letter but E in the second position, such as BAD. System AM2 should be repeatedly initialized within the basins of attraction of $\mathbf{W}^1$ vectors sharing several common features: have 1 as the fourth component (to force stopping the search session at letter D), 0 in the fifth position (to eliminate letter E as a possible pattern to be retrieved), and only 2 more *distinct* components among the remaining 24 positions;
-   retrieve all four-letter words that have the same 2-letter prefix, such as LOVE, LOCK, LOAD. In this case, candidate $\mathbf{W}^1$ vectors should have $\frac{1}{26}$ in the 12-th position, $\frac{2}{26}$ in the 15-th, and only 2 more distinct components in the rest;
-   retrieve words that include *repeating* letters (consecutive or not). Since the search procedure based on the tunneling effect guarantees relaxation only towards lower energy levels than the current one, the design principles used so far no longer apply. A straightforward solution is to use the same synthesis technique for *both* memory modules, namely to code $\mathbf{W}^1$ not as a single equilibrium of AM2, but as a sequence of distinct stable points, each one related to a

section of the original one formed only by distinct letters. The retrieving procedure would involve a sequential triggering of the dynamics of the two memory modules as follows:

Step1: initialize AM2
Step 2: wait for relaxing towards the first fixed point in AM2
Step 3: copy weights in AM1 and initialize AM1
Step 4: wait for sequentially visiting a group of (distinct) letters from AM1 (forming a word section)
Step 5: tunnel towards the next fixed point in AM2 (or stop if no more fixed points are found)
Step 6: copy weights in AM1 and initialize AM1
Step 7: go to *Step 4*

Attractor networks have been widely used for constructing psychological models of human cognition [34]. There are two biologically motivated elements governing such models:
- *priming*: faster reaching of a specific attractor if it has been visited recently
- *gang effect*: mutually influence between attractors, generated by their spatial distribution.

The associative memory design strategy proposed previously can easily accommodate both effects. Priming is achieved by increasing the probability of reaching a specific recently visited pattern by enlarging the basins of attraction around it. This is implemented by increasing the value of the width parameter σ_m and, if necessary, of the w_m weight. Gang effects are induced by a specific placement of the patterns to be stored, although parameter σ_m also substantially contributes to the shape of the energy landscape.

5   Conclusions

We have presented several methods of enhancing the capabilities of RBF networks to deal with temporal processing applications. There are some open problems related to the aspects covered in this chapter that are worth taken into consideration:

- *RBF networks with dynamic synapses*: while the proposed architecture exhibits distinct features when compared to the classical one, more general structures comprising memory both at the input and at the synaptic level can be constructed. Moreover, the local recursive character induced by the special gamma operator could be combined to the global feedback model analyzed in [4]. In both cases, mathematical proof of universal approximation capabilities of the resulting networks could outline the range of possible practical applications. Another interesting topic for further research is related to constructive techniques considering pruning of both centers and the order of the synaptic filters.

- *analog RBF networks*: systems presented in Section 4 define higher-order recurrent networks. In order to simplify the implementation phase it would be useful to find an approximation procedure to reduce the order. Moreover, learning algorithms for trimming the parameters of the networks (weights and widths in equation 13) according to the application at hand could improve the results. An interesting idea is the examination of a possible link between the proposed systems and neural networks with nonmonotonic activation functions.

References

[1] Back, A.D. and Tsoi, A.C. (1991), "FIR and IIR synapses, a new neural network architecture for time series modelling," *Neural Computation*, vol. 3, no. 3, pp. 375-385.

[2] Baird, B. and Eeckman, F. (1992), "A normal form projection algorithm for associative memory," in *Associative Neural Memories: Theory and Implemenation*, Oxford University Press, New York.

[3] Barhen, J., Protopopescu, V., and Reister, D. (1997), "TRUST: a deterministic algorithm for global optimization," *Science*, vol. 276, no. 5, pp.1094-1097.

[4] Billings, S.A. and Fung, C.F. (1995), "Recurrent radial basis function networks for adaptive noise cancellation," *Neural Networks,* vol. 8, no. 2, pp. 273-290.

[5] Billings, S.A. and Chen, S. (1989), "Extended model set, global data and threshold model identification of severely non-linear systems," *Int. J. Control*, vol. 50, no. 5, pp. 1897-1923.

[6] Boyd, S. and Chua, L.O. (1983), "Uniqueness of a basic nonlinear structure," IEEE Trans, Circ. & Syst., vol. 30, no. 9, pp. 648-651.

[7] Broomhead, D.S. and Lowe, D. (1988), "Multivariable functional interpolation and adaptive networks," *Complex Systems*, vol. 2, pp. 321-355.

[8] Chen, S., Cowan, C.F.N., and Grant, P.M. (1991), "Orthogonal least squares learning algorithm for radial basis function networks," *IEEE Trans. on Neural Networks*, vol. 2, no. 2, pp. 302-309.

[9] Chen, S., Billings, S.A., Cowan, C.F.N., and Grant, P.M. (1990), "Non-linear systems identification using radial basis functions," *Int. J. Systems Sci.*, vol. 21, no. 12, pp. 2513-2539.

[10] Chowdhury, P.R., Singh, Y.P., and Chansarkar, R.A. (1999), "Dynamic tunneling technique for efficient training of multilayer perceptrons," *IEEE Trans. Neural Networks*, vol. 10, no. 1, pp. 48-55.

[11] Ciocoiu, I.B. (1996), "RBF networks with FIR/IIR synapses," *Neural Processing Letters*, vol. 3, no. 1, pp. 17-22.

[12] Han, J.Y., Sayeh, M.R., and Zhang, J. (1989), "Convergence and limit points of neural networks and its application to pattern recognition," *IEEE Trans. Syst., Man, Cybern.*, vol. 15, no. 5, pp. 1217-1222.

[13] Haykin, S. (1994), *Neural Networks – a Comprehensive Foundation*, IEEE Press.

[14] Hirsch, M.W. and Smale S. (1974), *Differential Equations, Dynamical Systems, and Linear Algebra*, Academic, New York.

[15] IBM, *ZISC036*, 1996

[16] Kohonen, T. (1988), *Self-Organization and Associative memory*, Springer-Verlag, New York.

[17] Lapedes, A. and Farber, R. (1987), "Nonlinear signal processing using neural networks: prediction and system modelling," LA-VR-87-2662, Los Alamos National Laboratory.

[18] Levin, A.U.,. Leen, T.K., and Moody, J.E. (1994), "Fast pruning using principal components," in Cowan, J., Tesauro, G., and Alspector, J. (Eds.), *Advances in Neural Information Processing Systems 6*, San Mateo, CA: Morgan Kaufmann

[19] Liu, B. and Si, J. (1994), "The best approximation to C^2 functions and its error bounds using regular-center Gaussian networks," *IEEE Trans. Neural Networks*, vol. 5, no. 5, pp. 845-847.

[20] Michel, A.N. and Farrell, J.A. (1990), "Associative memories via artificial neural networks," *IEEE Control Systems Magazine*, vol. 10, pp. 6-17.

[21] Moody, J. and Darken, C.J. (1989), "Fast learning in networks of locally-tuned processing units," *Neural Computation*, vol. 1, pp. 281-294.

[22] Morita, M. (1993), "Associative memory with nonmonotone dynamics," *Neural Networks*, vol. 6, pp. 115-126.

[23] Nara, S., Davis, P., and Totsuji, H. (1993), "Memory search using complex dynamics in a recurrent neural network model," *Neural Networks*, vol. 6, pp. 963-973.

[24] Narendra, K.S. and Parthasarathy, K. (1991), "Gradient methods for the optimization of dynamical systems containing neural networks," *IEEE Trans. Neural Networks*, vol. 2, no. 2, pp. 252-262.

[25] Park, J. and Sandberg, I.W. (1991), "Universal approximation using radial basis function networks," *Neural Computation*, vol. 3, pp. 246-257.

[26] Platt, J. (1991), "A resource-allocating network for function interpolation," *Neural Computation*, vol. 3, no. 2, pp. 213-225

[27] Principe, J.C., Euliano, N.R., and Lefebvre, W.C. (2000), *Neural and Adaptive Systems – Fundamentals through Simulations*, Wiley and Sons, New York.

[28] Sandberg, I. and Xu, L. (1997), "Uniform approximation of multidimensional myopic maps," *IEEE Trans. Circ. & Syst.*, vol. 44, pp. 477-485.

[29] Shynk, J.J. (1989), "Adaptive IIR filtering," *IEEE ASSP Magazine*, pp. 4-21.

[30] de Vries, J.C. and de Oliveira, P.G. (1993), "The gamma-filter – a new class of adaptive IIR filters with restricted feedback," *IEEE Trans. on Signal Proc.*, vol. 41, no. 2, pp. 649-656.

[31] de Vries, J.C. and Principe, J.C., (1992), "The gamma model – a new neural model for temporal processing," *Neural Networks*, vol. 5, pp. 565-576.

[32] Wan, E.A. (1994), "Time series prediction by using a connectionist network with internal delay lines," in Weigend, A.S. and Gershenfeld, N.A. (Eds.), *Time Series Prediction: Forecasting the Future and Understanding the Past*, Addison-Wesley, Reading, MA, pp. 195-217.

[33] Yingwei, L., Sundararajan, N., and Saratchandran, P. (1998), "Performance evaluation of a sequential minimal radial basis function (RBF) neural network learning algorithm," *IEEE Trans. Neural Networks*, vol. 9, pp. 308-318.

[34] Zemel, R.S. and Mozer, M.C. (1998), "Localist attractor networks," *Proc. NIPS 12*, MIT Press, 1999.

[35] Ziemer, R.E. and Peterson, R.L. (1992), *Introduction to Digital Communication*, Macmillan Publ. Co., New York.

Chapter 2

A Hyperrectangle-Based Method that Creates RBF Networks

M. Kubat

Radial-basis function networks have been successfully applied to many realistic pattern-recognition tasks. One of the problems faced by a designer of this kind of classifier is the need to determine the number of neurons and their parameters: Gaussian centers and variances. To this end, a recently developed method employs decision trees that partition the instance space into relatively homogeneous hyperrectangular regions. Each region is then associated with one RBF neuron. The technique is robust against irrelevant attributes and against the problem of disparate attribute scaling.

1   Introduction

Radial-basis function (RBF) networks rank among the most popular tools for function approximation. Building on geometrical properties analyzed a few decades ago, they were cast into the neural network paradigm in the late eighties [5]. The main asset of RBF networks is the availability of algorithms for their induction from examples. These induction techniques are much faster than those needed for some other tools such as multilayer perceptrons.

An important special case of the function-approximation task is *two-class pattern recognition* where the goal is to identify attribute vectors as positive or negative examples of a given class. The input of the attendant learning procedure consists of the *training set* of pairs $[\mathbf{x}, c(\mathbf{x})]$, where the vector $\mathbf{x} = [x_1, x_2, \ldots, x_n]$ describes an *example* that is labeled with $c(\mathbf{x}) = 1$ for positive examples, and with $c(\mathbf{x}) = -1$ for negative examples. The variables x_i are called *attributes*. If the attributes

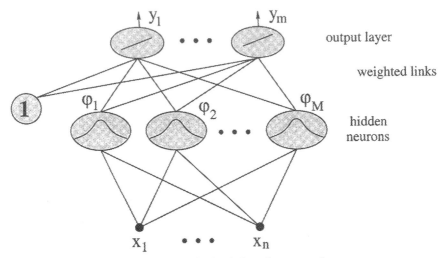

Figure 1. A radial-basis function network.

are numeric ($x_i \in R$), then $c(\mathbf{x})$ can be regarded as a binary function, $c : R^n \to \{-1, 1\}$. The induced *classifier*, a function $h : R^n \to \{-1, 1\}$ represented by a RBF network, should approximate c in a way that minimizes the probability of $h(\mathbf{x}) \neq c(\mathbf{x})$ for a randomly drawn $\mathbf{x}$. A more general classifier will label $\mathbf{x}$ with one out of several different classes, and can thus be formalized as a function $h : R^n \to L$, where L is the set of class labels.

Figure 1 depicts a RBF network. To determine the correct class of an attribute vector, $\mathbf{x}$, its elements, x_i, are applied in parallel to the hidden neurons. A hidden neuron then maps the input vector to a scalar that is weighted and forwarded to the output layer. The mapping function is known as a *transfer function*. Whereas the transfer functions of the output neurons are linear (each output neuron just returns the weighted sum of its inputs), the transfer function of the i-th hidden neuron is represented by the following Gaussian equation:

$$\varphi_i(\mathbf{x}) = \exp\{-\frac{||\mathbf{x} - \boldsymbol{\mu}_i||^2}{2\sigma_i^2}\} \tag{1}$$

where $\boldsymbol{\mu}_i$ is the *center* of the i-th Gaussian and σ_i^2 is this Gaussian's variance. Note that the larger the distance between $\mathbf{x}$ and $\boldsymbol{\mu}_i$, the smaller the value of $\varphi_i(\mathbf{x})$.

To decide which class label to assign to $\mathbf{x}$, the network first maps $\mathbf{x}$ to the M-dimensional vector $\boldsymbol{\varphi}(\mathbf{x}) = [\varphi_1(\mathbf{x}), \ldots, \varphi_M(\mathbf{x})]$. The value returned by the j-th output neuron is then calculated as $y_j = \sum_{i=0}^{m} w_{ij}\varphi_i(\mathbf{x})$, where w_{ij} is the weight of the link leading from the i-th hidden neuron to the j-th output neuron (the weights w_{0j} are connected to a fixed $\varphi_0 = 1$). The example is labeled with the j-th class if $y_j = \max_k(y_k)$.

The behavior of a RBF network depends on several parameters: the number of hidden neurons, the centers and variances of their associated Gaussian functions, and the weights of the connection links. Whereas optimum weights are quite easy to determine, adjusting the other parameters is not trivial. This chapter will describe a recent mechanism that solves the problem in a fairly unified way.

Section 2 specifies the learning task more formally and briefly surveys some popular solutions. Section 3 then provides detailed description of a method that defines the Gaussian functions with the help of hyperrectangles induced by a generator of decision trees. The technique was first published in [13]. Section 4 experimentally characterizes the behavior of this algorithm and Section 5 summarizes its merits.

2 Problem Definition

The weights of the output-layer neurons are relatively simple to train using the delta rule [25] or some more traditional statistical approach such as the pseudoinverse matrix [9]. What is more interesting is to investigate methods that seek to optimize the other parameters of RBF networks. In doing so, the following three research issues deserve particular attention.

1. First of all, the designer needs to know how to determine the coordinates of the Gaussian centers, $\boldsymbol{\mu}_i$, and how to decide how many neurons are needed if the classifier is to achieve reasonable classification accuracy not only on the training examples, but also on unseen data. The simplest approach draws inspiration from the theory of *kernel functions* [23] and identifies each center with the coordinates of one training example [20]. Unfortunately, in domains with large training sets, this approach leads to unmanageably large networks that are prone to overfit noisy training data. For this reason, Lee [16] and Lowe [17] suggest to pick just

a small random subset of examples. This may not be satisfactory in domains plagued with noise. Moreover, the designer can never be sure how large the subset should be.

Some researchers therefore prefer to pre-cluster the attribute vectors [18], [19] or to use an artificial-intelligence search algorithm with operators 'add a neuron' and 'delete a neuron' [6], [7]. By way of further improvement, techniques for tuning the coordinates of the centers were developed [10], [11], [24]. Although the classification accuracy achieved by the resulting RBF networks is more than encouraging, the main trouble is the computation tractability in hard domains with large training sets. For instance, the complexity of a typical clustering algorithm for N training examples is $O(N^2)$. This problem is to a great extent solved by the recently proposed technique [14] that selects complementary groups of examples.

2. The second problem is how to cope with the fact that each attribute can have a different scale. Surely the decision whether to measure the length of an object in inches or in miles will affect the geometry of the pattern-recognition problem. Saha and Keeler [22] suggest to use different variance for each attribute. Let μ_{ik} denote the k-th coordinate of μ_i and let σ_{ik}^2 denote the variance of the i-th Gaussian along the k-th attribute. Recall that $||\mathbf{x} - \mu_i||^2 = \Sigma_k(x_k - \mu_{ik})^2$ and that $e^{\Sigma x_i} = \prod e^{x_i}$. This means that, for the calculation of the output of the i-th hidden neuron in domains with n attributes, Equation 1 can be re-written as follows:

$$\varphi_i(\mathbf{x}) = \prod_{k=1}^{n} \exp\{-\frac{(x_k - \mu_{ik})^2}{2\sigma_{ik}^2}\} \qquad (2)$$

To mitigate the impact of disparate attribute scales, [22] proposes to set each σ_{ik}^2 to a value proportional to the distance (along the k-th attribute) between the center μ_{ik} of the i-th Gaussian function and the center of its nearest neighbor among the other neurons. Adaptation formulas that a machine can use to learn σ_{ik}^2 from training examples can be found in [12]. Again, the main difficulty is that the procedure tends to be computationally expensive.

3. The third research question asks how to address the fact that some attributes are not directly relevant to classification. For instance, the shoe

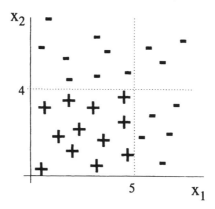

Figure 2. The relevance of attributes can vary in different parts of the instance space. If $x_1 > 5$, then the value of x_2 is irrelevant. If $x_2 > 4$, then the value of x_1 is irrelevant.

size of a patient visiting a dentist certainly has no bearing on the diagnosis of the cause of the toothache. Still, when included in the description of the training examples, such attributes affect the values returned by Equations 1 and 2 and can distort the results.

Machine learning literature has devoted considerable attention to the studies of algorithms for weeding out irrelevant attributes – for a good survey, see [3]. What is usually neglected is that the degree of relevance of the individual attributes can vary in different parts of the instance space. Figure 2 illustrates this point using a simple two-dimensional domain. The reader can see that, for $x_1 < 5$, both attributes are needed to determine the class label. On the other hand, in the subspace defined by $x_1 > 5$, the information about x_2 is totally irrelevant because all examples from this subspace belong to the same class. Conversely, the information about x_1 is irrelevant in the subspace $x_2 > 4$.

This aspect is rarely appreciated but still deserves attention [1]. For one thing, the classification accuracy can be improved if the classifier considers in each part of the instance space only information that is in some way important. Moreover, the size of the resulting RBF network, when expressed by the number of weighted links, can be reduced. This can be beneficial in hardware implementations of RBF networks on VLSI chips.

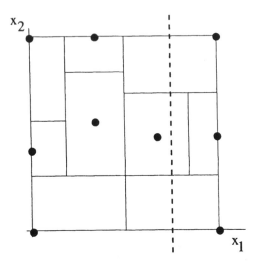

Figure 3. Two-dimensional instance space, decomposed into hyperrectangular regions. Black dots indicate the suggested positions of the Gaussian centers.

3   Solution

The simple technique described below was designed to address, in a fairly natural way, all of the three research issues raised in the previous section. The method was originally published in [13] and its essence rests on the idea to associate each neuron with some relatively pure (homogeneous) region in the instance space. A well-established method to create homogeneous regions of hyperrectangular shape uses generators of decision trees.

3.1   Hyperrectangular Regions of High Purity

Each neuron of a RBF network defines a specific region in the instance space. Ideally, each of these regions should be homogeneous in the sense that all examples in the region belong to the same class that will then be represented by a single neuron.

Let us ignore, for the time being, the question how to discover such regions, and focus rather on how to use them to define RBF neurons. Figure 3 illustrates the point using a simple two-dimensional domain where all training examples fall into a square delimited by the maximum and minimum values of attributes x_1 and x_2. The square has been decom-

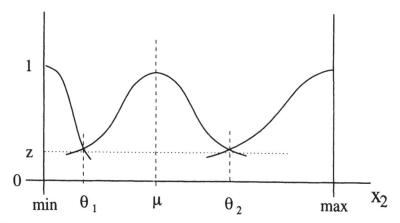

Figure 4. Gaussian bell functions placed over subintervals of an attribute's domain. Note that the functions have minimum values at the borders between pairs
of rectangles.

posed into small rectangles (for n attributes, the regions would be hyperrectangular), each containing a black dot that represents a neuron. More
precisely, each black dot marks the location of the center of a Gaussian
function. The idea is that the neuron will give the maximum output for
attribute vectors that find themselves in the dot's vicinity and that this
value will decrease with the growing distance from the dot. At the rectangle's border, the output is equal to some prespecified value, z, that is
the same for any neuron.

Note that only some of the rectangles in Figure 3 are surrounded by other
rectangles. In the "inside" rectangles, the black dots are placed at the geometric centers, whereas in the "outside" rectangles, this is not the case.
To see why, turn your attention to Figure 4. Here, the two-dimensional
instance space from Figure 3 is cut along the dashed line (along attribute
x_2). Points max and min are the maximum and minimum values of this
attribute as observed in the training set. The picture shows three Gaussian functions, each reaching its peak at the maximum distance from the
region's border. Depending on whether or not the given region is inside
the instance space, this maximum distance is either at the rectangle's geometric center or on its circumference.

This consideration gives rise to a simple algorithm that uses the "rectangular" decomposition to determine the coordinates of the Gaussian cen-

Table 1. Algorithm that associates Gaussian centers with hyperrectangles.

For each hyperrectangle, decide about the position of the associated Gaussian center, μ, using the following rules:

1. If one and only one side of the hyperrectangle lies on a border of the instance space, then place μ, in the geometrical center of this side.

2. If two or more adjacent sides of the hyperrectangle lie on the borders of the instance space, then place μ in the corner defined by these sides.

3. If the hyperrectangle borders on all sides with other hyperrectangles, then place μ in its geometric center.

ters, denoted here by the Greek letter, μ. The algorithm is summarized in Table 1. A "border of an instance space" is informally defined as the maximum or minimum value encountered for the given attribute in the training set.

Once the centers of the Gaussian functions have been defined, the next step is to determine their variances along the individual attributes. This, again, can be accomplished using the principle illustrated by Figure 4. Recall that variance determines how fast the value of the function $\varphi(\mathbf{x})$ decreases with the growing distance between $\mathbf{x}$ and μ. Reasonable value of this parameter will depend on the size of the hyperrectangle's k-th side because we want to make sure that $\varphi(\mathbf{x})$ is the same ($\varphi(\mathbf{x}) = z$) at each hyperrectangle's border.

Let I_{ik} denote the size of the k-th dimension of the i-th hyperrectangle (in Figure 4, this value for the Gaussian centered at μ will be $I_k = \theta_2 - \theta_1$). To simplify our notation, we will introduce a new parameter, α, such that $\alpha^2 = I_{ik}^2/\sigma_{ik}^2$. The fact that α has the same value for all attributes, k, and for all neurons, i, guarantees that the ratio between I_{ik}^2 and σ_{ik}^2 will be constant at all inter-region boundaries. The output of the i-th neuron is then calculated by the following formula that is obtained by substituting $\sigma_{ik}^2 = I_{ik}^2/\alpha^2$ in Equation 2:

$$\varphi_i(\mathbf{x}) = \prod_{k=1}^{n} \exp\{-\frac{\alpha^2(x_k - \mu_{ik})^2}{2I_{ik}^2}\} \qquad (3)$$

The described technique demonstrates that any method that decomposes the instance space into hyperrectangular regions can in principle be extended by a mechanism that determines the parameters of RBF networks. The next section will describe a simple technique that accomplishes this decomposition.

3.2   Decision-Tree Based Initialization of RBF Networks

A well-established method to create highly homogeneous regions is induction of decision trees, a field that received significant attention in the eighties and early nineties [4], [21]. This section will show that a decision tree with single-attribute tests defines a set of homogeneous hyperrectangles that are easy to turn into a RBF network.

Figure 5 shows a decision tree that decomposes a two-attribute instance space into the regions that were depicted in Figure 3. Each branch of the tree consists of a series of binary single-attribute tests and ends in a leaf that contains a class label (in the picture, only two classes, positive and negative, are considered). To determine the class of an attribute vector, **x**, the classifier will subject **x** to these tests, starting at the root, the result of each test deciding whether to continue down the left or right branch. When **x** reaches a leaf, the tree assigns it the class label associated with this leaf. The fact that each test imposes a threshold on a single attribute guarantees the axis-parallel rectangular shapes of the induced regions.

A study of the various methods that induce decision trees from data is beyond the scope of this text. Suffice it to say that most of the existing algorithms use a recursive procedure that, at each step, searches for a test that divides the training set in two subsets in a manner that maximizes their homogeneity. Today, powerful software packages accomplishing this task are available, the most popular perhaps being Quinlan's C4.5 [21] and its derivatives. It should be noted that a decision tree, once induced, usually has to be pruned. In the process of pruning, some of its subtrees are either just removed from the tree, or replaced with smaller subtrees.

In multidimensional domains, a single branch of the decision tree will

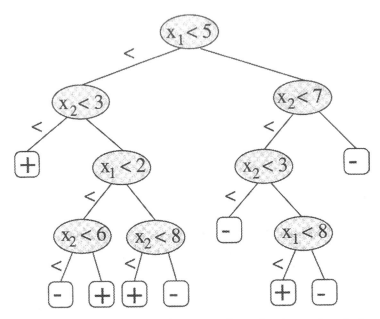

Figure 5. A decision tree that partitions a two-dimensional space into the hyper-rectangles from Figure 3.

often test only a subset of the attributes. As the other attributes are in the given subspace deemed irrelevant, it is enough to calculate Equation 3 only for those values of the index k that correspond to attributes tested in this branch. For instance, the rightmost branch of the decision tree from Figure 6 characterizes a rectangle defined by $x_1 \in [0, 5]$ and $x_4 \in [0, 7]$ (provided that zero is the minimum value of attributes x_1 and x_4). Denoting the rectangle by index 5, we see that $I_{51} = 5$ and $I_{54} = 7$. Using $\alpha = \sqrt{2}$ (so that $\alpha^2/2 = 1$), the transfer function of the corresponding neuron will be defined by the following equation:

$$\varphi_5(\mathbf{x}) = \exp\{-\frac{(x_1 - 0)^2}{25}\} \cdot \exp\{-\frac{(x_4 - 0)^2}{49}\} \qquad (4)$$

The last thing to be determined are the output-layer weights, w_{ij}. If all these weights are set to 1, then the RBF network classifies any vector $\mathbf{x}$ in exactly the same manner as the original decision tree. However, the very fact that the weights are trainable provides the network with additional degrees of freedom that facilitate further "post-tuning" of the classifier. The RBF network can therefore in many applications be expected to out-perform the original decision tree in terms of classification accuracy. An

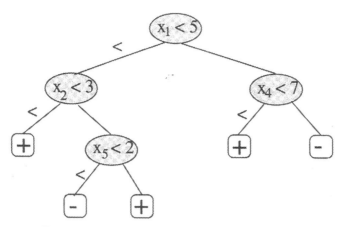

Figure 6. A decision tree in a 5-dimensional space.

intuitive explanation can be found in the geometry of the decision surfaces separating the individual classes. Whereas in decision trees, the
decision surface is piecewise axis-parallel (which limits the tree's accuracy in domains where the separation between the two classes is highly
non-linear), the Gaussian functions in the RBF networks, together with
the trainable weights, provide additional source of flexibility.

A simple method to determine the weights uses a statistical tool called
pseudoinverse matrix. Suppose the transformed training examples have
been arranged in a matrix, $\mathbf{X}$, such that each row represents one example
and the i-th column contains the value of φ_i for this example. A zeroth
attribute, whose value is always set to 1, will represent φ_0. Let $\mathbf{C}$ denote
the *classification matrix* where each column stands for one class label: if
the r-th example is labeled with the j-th class, then the j-th field in the
r-th row of $\mathbf{C}$ contains 1 and all other fields in this row contain -1.

Given $\mathbf{X}$ and $\mathbf{C}$, the task is to find the weight matrix, $\mathbf{W}$, that will minimize the mean square error defined as $\mathbf{X} \cdot \mathbf{W} - \mathbf{C}$. This is accomplished
by means of the pseudoinverse-matrix, $\mathbf{X}^{\mathbf{P}}$, using the well-known fact
[9] that the mean square error is minimized when:

$$\mathbf{W} = (\mathbf{X}^{\mathbf{T}}\mathbf{X})^{-1}\mathbf{X}^{\mathbf{T}}\mathbf{C} = \mathbf{X}^{\mathbf{P}}\mathbf{C} \qquad (5)$$

Many software packages have a standard function for the calculation of
pseudoinverse matrices, so the implementation of a program that determines the weights is trivial. In general, the concrete method employed to

Table 2. The algorithm of TB-RBF

---

1. Decompose the instance space into highly homogeneous hyperrectangular regions. This can be accomplished with a generator of decision trees.

2. Associate each region with one RBF neuron whose parameters depend on the location and dimensions of the hyperrectangle.

3. Organize the neurons in a single layer and create a neural network around them. Determine the output-layer weights.

---

obtain **W** does not seem to be critical for the system's performance. An alternative approach would use the gradient-descent rule [25].

This concludes the description of the algorithm that uses a generator of decision trees to create a RBF network. Table 2 summarizes the entire procedure, referring to it by the acronym TB-RBF (tree based RBF network). The first step decomposes the instance space into highly homogeneous hyperrectangular regions (each region is dominated by one class). This decomposition can be carried out by any commercial generator of decision trees. Once the hyperrectangles have been defined, each of them is assigned a neuron whose parameters depend on the region's geometry. Finally, the output-layer weights are determined by a mechanism that maximizes the network's classification accuracy on the training set.

3.3   Discussion

What does the algorithm of TB-RBF offer to the general paradigm of RBF networks? To answer this question, we will examine whether the technique successfully addresses the research issues postulated by Section 2.

1. *Computation costs.* In TB-RBF, the Gaussian centers are determined by the hyperrectangles created by a decision-tree generator. For N training examples and n attributes, the costs associated with the decision-tree induction are upper bounded by $O(nN \log N)$ [21]. Compared to, say, the $O(N^2)$ complexity of clustering techniques, this is a clear improvement. The computation needed to determine

the output-layer weights can be accomplished at costs that are linear in the number of examples if the gradient-descent rule is used [25].

2. *Attribute scaling*. The dimensions of the hyperrectangles define the variations of the Gaussians separately for each attribute. Changed scale entails different hyperrectangles. As the algorithm guarantees that the Gaussians will have the same value at the borders of the hyperrectangles, the sensitivity of TB-RBF to changed scales is drastically reduced.

3. Also vulnerability to *irrelevant attributes* is greatly diminished because decision-tree generators usually weed them out, especially when pruning is applied. TB-RBF also addresses the frequently neglected peculiarity that, in different parts of the instance space, the relevance of the individual attributes can vary. Each branch of a decision tree contains tests on attributes that are relevant in the corresponding subspace.

An important advantage of TB-RBF is that the number of user-set parameters is significantly reduced compared to most methods for induction of RBF networks. In particular, the entire set of variances, σ_{ik}^2, is replaced by a single parameter, α. Experimental experience indicates that the technique is rather insensitive to the choice of α as long as this parameter finds itself in the interval $\alpha \in (0.5, 4)$. The only remaining parameter that the user has to worry about (apart from α) is the extent of decision-tree pruning.

4   Classification Accuracy

Induction of RBF networks clearly benefits from the TB-RBF technique. However, this is not enough. What is important is to make sure that the resulting network outperforms, in terms of classification accuracy, also the decision tree that determines the network's architecture, or else the merits of turning the tree into RBF network would be dubious.

To test and compare the performance of their algorithms, machine learning researchers usually experiment with publicly available benchmark domains so that their colleagues can replicate their results. A widely accepted source of benchmark data is the repository assembled by the de-

Table 3. Characteristics of the benchmark domains used for experimentation.

	#attributes	# classes	# examples	majority
bupa	6	2	345	58.0
diab	8	2	768	65.1
glass	9	6	214	35.5
vowels	10	11	990	9.1
vehicles	18	4	846	28.3
kr2	15	7	931	32.4

partment of computer science of the University of California at Irvine [2].

To demonstrate the classification accuracy of TB-RBF, the benchmark data used for our experimentation have to be selected with great care. The primary claim to be verified is that TB-RBF has a performance edge in domains where the decision surfaces are highly non-linear and where the data is known to be noisy. Moreover, the technique has been developed for applications where the examples are described by numeric attributes. Implementational convenience (the use of pseudoinverse matrix) further limited the experiments to domains with no more than a thousand examples.

With this in mind, the following domains were selected: bupa, diab, glass, vowels, and vehicles. Another file, kr2, was borrowed from the research reported in [15] because it is known to be very difficult for most pattern-recognition algorithms. Essential information about the data files is summarized in Table 3: the number of attributes, the number of examples, and the number of classes. The rightmost column gives the percentage of examples that belong to the majority class. This number gives the performance that would be achieved if the system consistently labeled all testing examples with the most frequent class.

The hypothesis to be verified is that TB-RBF outperforms the original decision tree in terms of classification accuracy. Statistical significance of such comparisons is customarily evaluated by the t-test. However, this methodology is known to be unreliable in domains with limited numbers of examples. For this reason, [8] suggests a modified methodology, called the "5x2cv" test. As its details cannot be discussed here, suffice it to say that the original data file is randomly split into two subsets of equal size, S_1 and S_2. The learner uses S_1 for training and S_2 for testing, and then swaps them, using S_2 for training and S_1 for testing. This is repeated for 5 different splits into training and testing subsets so that, in effect, the approach implements 5 different 2-fold cross-validations whose results are then compared to a theoretical distribution. For the needs of this particular study, the confidence level of 95% was requested.

TB-RBF was implemented as indicated in Table 2. For the induction of the decision tree, Quinlan's C4.5 was used, with the pruning constant set at the default value. Auxiliary experiments (not reported here) showed that the classifier's performance is only marginally affected when much stronger pruning (leading to smaller trees and, as a result, more compact RBF networks) was used. The parameter that controls the variances of the Gaussian functions was in all domains set to $\alpha = 1$.

The performance aspects are visualized by Figure 7 that compares classification accuracies achieved by TB-RBF to those of the original decision tree. The reader can see that TB-RBF outperforms C4.5 in all domains, sometimes by a wide margin (by 10% in vowels and in vehicles, and by 5% in kr2). The 5x2cv test showed that, with the exception of the glass domain, the observed performance edge was statistically significant.

Another useful point about TB-RBF is illustrated by Figure 8 that shows the reduction of the number of links between the input layer and the hidden layer. While the number of RBF neurons is equal to the number of branches of the decision tree, the number of links leading to any hidden neuron is given by the number of attributes tested in the corresponding tree-branch. The bar chart compares the number of links in our RBF network to the number that would be necessary (for the same number of neurons) if the hidden neurons were fully interconnected with the attributes presented at the network's input. Note that this reduction was achieved even for the relatively mild default pruning. As already mentioned, much stronger pruning can be used without detriment to classification accuracy.

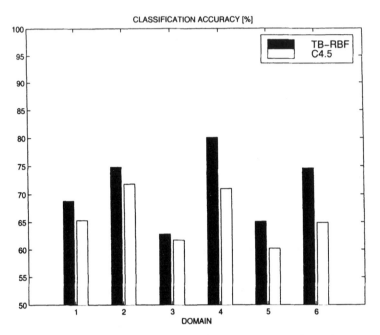

Figure 7. TB-RBF outperforms a decision tree generator, C4.5, in terms of classification accuracy on unseen data. With the exception of the third domain (glass), this claim is statistically significant.

5   Conclusion

This chapter described a simple method that designs a RBF network using a generator of decision trees. The technique is simple and its implementation is straightforward. Induction of decision trees is a domain that has been thoroughly investigated, especially during the eighties and early nineties [4], [21]. Today, advanced software packages that induce decision trees in a computationally efficient manner are ubiquitous.

TB-RBF has three main advantages over more classical techniques. First, the size of the RBF network is determined automatically, and also the parameters of the hidden neurons are obtained directly from the decision tree. Second, the method is capable of dealing with the difficulties caused by the fact (fairly common in realistic domains) that the individual attributes can be measured along disparate scales. Third, the issue of irrelevant attributes is addressed: each RBF neuron considers only attributes relevant in the corresponding region. Moreover, the set of relevant attributes can differ in each region.

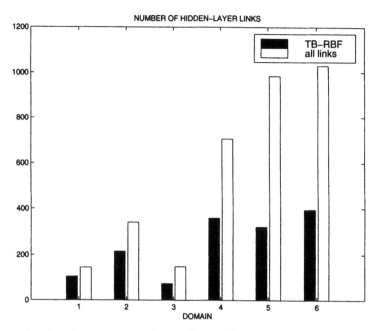

Figure 8. The chart compares the numbers of links actually used in the RBF network with the numbers of links that would be necessary if the neurons were fully interconnected with the input.

As for the classification accuracy of TB-RBF, practical experiments are indicative of synergy that results from the combination of two well-established methods. For one thing, the RBF paradigm benefits from the simple initialization offered by the decision-tree paradigm. On the other hand, the classification accuracy of the resulting network outstrips the original decision tree in domains characterized by non-linear decision surfaces and noise.

The reader is reminded that, in simple tasks that are easy for decision trees, no increase in accuracy can reasonably be expected from mapping the tree to a RBF network. TB-RBF can only be expected to outperform C4.5 in domains with highly non-linear decision surfaces.

References

[1] Andrew, C., Kubat, M., and Pfurtscheller, G. (1995), "Trimming the inputs of RBF networks," *European Symposium on Artificial Neural Networks*, Brussels, Belgium.

[2] Blake, C.L. and Merz, C.J. (1998), "UCI Repository of machine learning databases," University of California Irvine, Department of Information and Computer Science, http://www.ics.uci.edu /~mlearn/MLRepository.html.

[3] Blum, A. and Langley, P. (1997), "Selection of relevant features and examples in machine learning," *Artificial Intelligence*, pp. 245-271.

[4] Breiman, L., Friedman, J., Olshen, R., and Stone, C.J. (1984), *Classification and Regression Trees*, Wadsworth International Group, Belmont, CA.

[5] Broomhead, D.S. and Lowe, D. (1988), "Multivariable functional interpolation and adaptive networks," *Complex Systems*, vol. 2, pp. 321-355.

[6] Chen, S., Cowan, C.F.N., and Grant, P.M. (1991), "Orthogonal least squares learning algorithm for radial basis function networks," *IEEE Transactions on Neural Networks*, vol. 2, pp. 302-309.

[7] Cover, T.M. and Hart, P.E. (1967), "Nearest neighbor pattern classification," *IEEE Transactions on Information Theory*, IT-13, pp. 21-27.

[8] Dietterich, T.G. (1996), "Statistical tests for comparing supervised classification learning algorithms," Technical Report, Department of Computer Science, Oregon State University.

[9] Duda, R.O. and Hart, P.E. (1973), *Pattern Classification and Scene Analysis*, John Wiley & Sons, New York.

[10] Fritzke, B. (1993), "Supervised learning with growing cell structures," in Cowan, J., Tesauro, G., and Alspector, J. (Eds.), *Advances in Neural Information Processing Systems 6*, San Mateo, CA:Morgan Kaufmann, pp. 255-262.

[11] Fritzke, B. (1994), "Fast learning with incremental RBF networks," *Neural Processing Letters*, vol. 1, pp. 2-5.

[12] Haykin, S. (1994), *Neural Networks, a Comprehensive Foundation*, Maxmillan College Publishing Company, New York.

[13] Kubat, M. (1998), "Decision trees can initialize radial-basis function network,". *IEEE Transactions on Neural Networks*, vol. 9, pp. 813-821.

[14] Kubat, M. and Cooperson Jr., M. (1999), "Initializing RBF-networks with small subsets of training examples," *Proceedings of the 16th National Conference on Artificial Conference, AAAI-99*, Orlando, FL, pp. 188-193.

[15] Kubat, M., Pfurtscheller, G., and Flotzinger D. (1994), "AI-based approach to automatic sleep classification," *Biological Cybernetics*, vol. 79, pp. 443-448.

[16] Lee, Y. (1991), "Handwritten digit recognition using k-nearest-neighbor, radial-basis function, and backpropagation neural networks," *Neural Computation*, vol. 3, pp. 440-449.

[17] Lowe, D. (1989), "Adaptive radial basis function nonlinearities and the problem of generalization," *1st International Conference on Artificial Neural Networks*, London, U.K., pp. 171-175.

[18] Moody, J.E. and Darken, C.J. (1989), "Fast algorithms in networks of locally-tuned processing units," *Neural Computation*, vol. 1, pp. 282-294.

[19] Musavi, M.T., Ahmed, W., Chan, K.H., Faris, K.B., and Hummels, D.M. (1992), "On the training of radial basis function classifiers," *Neural Networks*, vol. 5, pp. 595-603.

[20] Poggio, T. and Girosi, F. (1990), "Regularization algorithms for learning that are equivalent to multilayer networks," *Science*, vol. 247, pp. 987-982.

[21] Quinlan, J.R. (1993), *C4.5: Programs for Machine Learning*, Morgan Kaufmann, San Mateo.

[22] Saha, A. and Keeler, J.D. (1990), "Algorithms for better representation and faster learning in radial basis function networks," in Touretzky, D.S. (Ed.), *Advances in Neural Information Processing Systems 2*, San Mateo, CA, Morgan Kaufmann, pp. 482-489.

[23] Schölkopf, B., Burges, C.J.C., and Smola, A.J. (Eds.) (1990), *Advances in Kernel Methods: Support Vector Learning*, MIT Press, Cambridge, MA.

[24] Wettschereck, D. and Dietterich, T.G. (1992), "Improving the performance of radial basis function networks by learning center locations," in Moody, J.E., Hanson, S.J., and Lippmann, R.P. (Eds.), *Advances in Neural Information Processing Systems 4*, San Mateo, CA: Morgan Kaufmann, pp. 1133-1140.

[25] Widrow, B. and Hoff, M.E. (1960), "Adaptive switching circuits," *IRE WESCON Convention Record*, pp. 96-104.

Chapter 3

Hierarchical
Radial Basis Function Networks

N.A. Borghese

Hierarchical Radial Basis Functions (HRBF) Networks are constructed stacking grids of Gaussians, at decreasing scale, one over the other. The Gaussians are inserted only in those grid crossings where the residual error is greater than the noise on the input data. This allows to achieve a uniform reconstruction error over all the input space. Moreover, it can be shown that HRBF can be regarded as a Riesz basis and that they offer a Multi-Scale Analysis which is different from Wavelet decomposition. Thanks to the local operations involved, the algorithm can be easily parallelised and potentially work in real-time. HRBF Networks are suitable to a wide range of applications, where the local density of the input data is related to the local frequency content of the surface. An interesting application, illustrated here, is 3D scanner, where a continuous surface has to be reconstructed from a set of noisy points sampled over the surface.

1   Introduction

In the last decade, the learning problem in Neural Netwoks has been related to multi-variate approximation [1], [2]. Learning is seen as the reconstruction of a continuous smooth function from sparse, not equally sampled, data points for which a model of the noise, introduced by the sampling process, is available; the function comes out from a trade-off between a perfect interpolation of the data points and a smoothness constraint which penalises brisk oscillations [1], [3]. In the framework of regularisation theory, the function $z(x)$, is such that:

$$z(x): \underset{\min\{w\}}{H(z(w;x))} = \sum_k \left(z(w;x_k) - z_k\right)^2 + \lambda\omega(z(w;x_k)) \qquad (1)$$

where $\omega(.)$ is the regularizer which enforces the smoothness constraint, w are a set of parameters which define the actual shape of $z(.)$ and $\{P(z_k, x_k)\}$ are the sampled points. When the functional $\omega(.)$ assumes a form in which the integral of the derivatives of every order are taken into account, the general solution of Equation (1) is represented by a Gaussian Radial Basis Function Network [3]:

$$z(x) = \sum_{k=1}^{M} w_k g(x; c_k; \Sigma_k) \qquad (2)$$

where the following parameters are considered: the number M and the position $\{c_k\}$ of the Gaussians, their covariance $\{\Sigma_k\}$ and the coefficients $\{w_k\}$. Unfortunately, a computability algorithmic solution for Equation (2) is not available and the parameters have to be determined numerically through a global search in the solution space. Moreover, regularisation does not give an explicit control over the residual error which comes out from the interaction of the regularisation process with the input data. The residual will be unknown in amplitude and will vary from region to region of the input domain. The introduction of techniques like cross-validation to set a proper value for the regularisation term [4] allows to achieve a desired mean residual error but, as $\omega(.)$ affect the whole input domain, it does not guarantee its uniformity in all the regions of the input space.

A different strategy is pursued in Hierarchical Radial Basis Function (HRBF) Networks which are based on the combination of linear filtering theory and Multi Scale Analysis. A simple criterion to set a proper value of Σ_k, M and the Gaussian spacing Δx_c can be derived, considering the Gaussian units equally spaced [5], [6]; and the weight, $\{w_k\}$, can be estimated directly from local sub-sets of data points. Finally the Gaussian units are allocated incrementally to obtain a uniform residual error. Results on the reconstruction of Human Faces are reported and discussed.

2   The HRBF Network

For the sake of simplicity, the analysis will be carried out in the 1-dimensional space. The results are general and can be extended to multi-dimensional spaces by observing that multi-dimensional Gaussians can be obtained by factorisation of 1-D Gaussians. When the Gaussians have the same value of σ, Equation (2) becomes:

$$z(x) = \sum_{k=1}^{M} w_k g(x;c_k;\sigma) = \sum_{k=1}^{M} w_k \frac{e^{-\frac{(x-c_k)^2}{\sigma^2}}}{\sqrt{\pi}\sigma} \tag{3}$$

Let us assume that the Gaussians are placed at the crossings of a regular grid ($c_k - c_{k-1} = \Delta x_c, \forall k$) and that the function to be reconstructed, $z(x)$, has been sampled in the grid crossings: $S = \{z_k = z(x_k) \mid k \in 0,1,2,...,M\}$. Under these assumptions, it can be shown [6], [7] that Equation (3) is equivalent to the convolution of the sequence of the weights, $\{w_k\}$, with the Gaussian kernel $g(x; c_k; \sigma)$; which is equivalent to the filtering of the weights sequence with the Gaussian filter. By substituting in Equation (3) the product of the data points $\{z_k\}$ times the sampling interval Δx_c, to the weights $\{w_k\}$, we obtain:

$$\tilde{z}(x) = \sum_{k=1}^{M} z_k g(x;x_k;\sigma)\Delta x_c = \frac{\Delta x_c}{\sqrt{\pi}\sigma} \sum_{k=1}^{M} z_k e^{-\frac{(x-x_k)^2}{\sigma^2}} \tag{4}$$

which is the basic equation of each grid of the HRBF network [6]. Let us analyse Equation (4) as a linear filter to find which are the conditions which g(.) has to satisfy to get $\tilde{z}(x)$ close to the real function $z(x)$.

2.1   The Gaussian Filter

A linear filter has two main characteristics: it should approximate a certain function from a finite number of samples and it should clean the noise. These two tasks can be specified in the frequency domain. Let us call $h(x)$ our filter with frequency content, $H(v)$, obtained through its Fourier transform: F $(h(x)) = H(v)$. When $h(x)$ is a low-pass filter, like in the Gaussian case, the amplitude of $H(v)$ will be negligible over a certain v_{Max}. This means that when the filter $h(x)$ is applied to a given function, $z(x)$, the frequency components of $z(x)$, which constitute its spectrum, will be reproduced only up to v_{Max}. It follows that an ideal low-pass filter should have amplitude equal to one for all the frequencies inside the spectrum of $z(x)$, that is below v_{Max} (*Pass Band*), and equal to zero above v_{Max} (*Stop Band*). Unfortunately, such a filter is not physically realisable: the transition from the Pass Band to the Stop Band cannot be a step edge and the Pass and the Stop Bands cannot be flat. Some approximation has to be negotiated. In the following a filter will be characterised as follows [8].

2.2   Definition of a Real Linear Filter

The *Pass Band* of the real filter $h(x)$ is defined as the frequency range for which $|H(v)|$ is bounded between $[\delta_1, 1]$:

$$\delta_1 \le |H(v)| \le 1 \qquad 0 \le v \le v_{cut-off} \tag{5a}$$

where $v_{cut-off}$ is the frequency at which $|H(v)| = \delta_1$. The Stop Band of $h(x)$ is defined as the frequency range for which $|H(v)|$ is bounded between $[0\ \delta_2]$:

$$0 \le |H(v)| \le \delta_2 \qquad v_{Max} \le v < +\infty \tag{5b}$$

where v_{Max} is the frequency at which $|H(v)| = \delta_2$. $0 \le \delta_2 \ll \delta_1 \le 1$ holds. As $v_{cut-off} < v_{Max}$, a third Band (*Transition Band*), in which the frequencies which constitute $z(x)$ are progressively attenuated, is also defined. These considerations can now be applied to the Gaussian filter (Equation (3)), whose Fourier Transform is itself a Gaussian:

$$G(v;\sigma) = F(g(x;\sigma)) = e^{-\pi^2\sigma^2 v^2} e^{-2\pi j v x_c} \tag{6a}$$

whose modulus is:

$$|G(v;\sigma)| = e^{-\pi^2\sigma^2 v^2} \tag{6b}$$

Equation (6b) allows to relate the values of $v_{cut-off}$ and v_{Max} to σ.

$$\begin{cases} e^{-\pi^2\sigma^2 v_{cut-off}^2} = \delta_1 \\ e^{-\pi^2\sigma^2 v_{Max}^2} = \delta_2/2 \end{cases} \Rightarrow \begin{cases} v_{cut-off} = \dfrac{\sqrt{-\ln\delta_1}}{\pi\sigma} \\ v_{Max} = \dfrac{\sqrt{-\ln(\delta_2/2)}}{\pi\sigma} \end{cases} \tag{7}$$

δ_2 has been divided by two because at $v = v_{Max}$ the Gaussian spectrum receives equal contributions from the Gaussian centred in $v = 0$ and from that centred in $v = v_s$. In the following, δ_1 will be chosen equal to $\frac{1}{2}\sqrt{2}$, a common choice in Linear Filtering, which corresponds to a maximum attenuation in the Pass Band of 3dB [13]. δ_2 will be chosen equal to 0.01 which corresponds to an attenuation in the Stop Band of -40dB. From Equation (7), the following relationships between $v_{cut-off}$, v_{Max} and σ is found:

$$v_{cut-off} = \frac{0.1874}{\sigma} \tag{8a}$$

$$v_{Max} = \frac{0.7327}{\sigma} \tag{8b}$$

$$v_{cut-off} = 0.2558\, v_{Max} \tag{8c}$$

We explicitly remark here that different values of δ_1 and δ_2 modify the constants in Equation (8) but the underlying process on which HRBF Networks are based still holds.

2.3   Computing Δx_c, M and σ

$\tilde{z}(x)$ will be close to $z(x)$ as far as Equations (8a-8c) are satisfied. These can be reformulated as:

$$v_M < v_{cut-off} < 0.2558\,(v_s/2) \tag{9a}$$

where v_M is the maximum frequency content of $z(x)$ and v_s is the sampling frequency: $v_s = 1/\Delta x_c$. Equivalently,

$$\frac{v_M}{0.2558} < v_{Max} < v_s/2 \tag{9b}$$

where v_{Max} is the maximum frequency content of g(.) defined through the approximation described in Section 2.1. From Equations (9a-9b) the following constraint on σ is obtained:

$$\sigma_{min} = \frac{1.465}{v_S} = 1.465\, \Delta x_p \leq \sigma \leq \frac{0.1874}{v_M} = \sigma_{Max} \tag{10}$$

which (10) prescribes a range of possible values of σ. If σ is too small, there will be aliasing which produces a jerky reconstruction; if σ is too large, some of the details of $z(x)$ will be lost (filtered out).

Equation (10) gives a condition on σ which is more restrictive than the empirical criterion suggested by the Parzen window-based density estimators [9], [10]; the difference is meaningful as the amount of overlap between two consecutive Gaussians increases from 68.2% to 73.3%. On the other side, the criterion suggested by Equation (10) is consistent with the heuristic proposed in [11] where the spread parameter, σ, is set equal to twice the average spacing between the centres of not-equally spaced Gaussian units.

By rearranging Equations (9a-9b), the following relationship between v_s and v_M can be obtained:

$$v_S = 2\frac{v_M}{0.2558} \cong 7.8 v_M \tag{11}$$

which tells that the function $z(x)$ should be over sampled at least by a factor 3.9 with respect to the Shannon theorem to get a true reconstruction through RBF. In fact, the Gaussian cannot be considered an optimal low-pass filter as its Transition Band is large (cf. Equation 8c). Although other functions have been proposed to interpolate between neighbour grid crossings, like Butterworth or Tchebichev filters or splines [1], Gaussians are used here for two main reasons: they are claimed to constitute a processing module common in the human nervous system [12] and they have a straightforward simple implementation in parallel hardware [13] which makes them particularly attractive for real-time network implementations.

Summarising: the algorithm starts with a certain spacing between the Gaussians which reflects a hypothesis on the minimum frequency content over all the input space (Equation (10)). In line with the Occam's razor which prescribes to choose the simplest possible representation, the value of σ is set to the maximum allowed by Equation (10), that is σ_{Max}. This in fact minimises the number of adopted Gaussian units, M, which is obtained subdividing the input range by the inter-Gaussian distance or grid side:

$$M = \frac{(x_{max} - x_{min})}{\Delta x_c} \qquad (12)$$

where $[x_{min} \ x_{max}]$ is the input range.

2.4   Computing the $\{w_k\}$

At this stage the weights $\{w_k\}$ are the only parameters in Equation (3) to be computed. These assume value of $z(x)$ in the grid crossings: $\{z_k\}$ (cf. Equation (4)). To this scope we consider that in the real case the number of sampled points, N, is much larger than that of the Gaussian units: N >> M. Moreover, the samples are in general not equally spaced. A straightforward solution would be to regard Equation (4) as a linear system of N equations (one for each data point) in M unknowns (the weights associated to each Gaussian). This can be solved by linear algebra computing the pseudo-inverse with techniques like the Singular Value Decomposition [14]. Better schemas, which allow the elimination of the outliers, are based on a modified distance which weights little points which are too distant from the surface [15].

However, these techniques are computationally demanding and may cause memory allocation and numerical stability problems for large networks. For this reason a local schema which is based on surface restoration [16] has been developed in HRBF [6]. It is based on the observation that, if a function is smooth, it will assume close values in close points; therefore, the value of a function in a certain point can be obtained by an average of the neighbourhood points weighted by a function of their distance from the point. If we chose a Gaussian weighting function, the following estimator is obtained:

$$z_c = \frac{\displaystyle\sum_{r \in RF} z_r e^{-\frac{(x_r - x_c)^2}{\sigma_w^2}}}{\displaystyle\sum_{r \in RF} e^{-\frac{(x_r - x_c)^2}{\sigma_w^2}}} \tag{13}$$

where σ_w is a scale parameter, set equal to that of the Gaussians in the network. RF is the neighbourhood region of x_k and it defines a Receptive Field for the Gaussian centred in x_k. In the following, somehow arbitrary, its amplitude, A_{RF}, has been assumed equal to $\pm 2\Delta x_c$. Equation (13) is used in kernel-regression models [2] and in Maximum-A-Posteriori Estimate [16]. It maximises the probability to get a true value of z_k given a random error distributed over the data points considered in the estimate. For equally spaced sampled points, coincident with the Gaussian centres, the choice $A_{RF} = xc \pm \Delta x_c$ is equivalent to use 5^D points in the estimate; As, in the real case, $N \gg M$, the number of sampled points will be much larger.

2.5   Building the Hierarchy of RBFs

When σ in Equation (4) is chosen such as to satisfy Equation (10), it will guarantee the reconstruction of the finest details of $z(x)$. Unfortunately this choice may cause a waste of resources when the highest frequency content of the target function is concentrated (localised) in narrow regions of the input space. In this case, fewer Gaussians with a larger scale would be sufficient in those input regions where the frequency content is lower. Moreover, these regions could easily have been sampled less densely with the result that there may be not enough data points (the sampling step cannot be small enough) to get a reconstruction with the smallest scale (in these regions, the interval of Equation (10) would turn out empty).

The solution proposed in the HRBF model is to resort to Multi Scale Analysis [17]. We start with a first basic layer of Gaussian RBF, featuring a larger scale. This layer will be complete (each grid crossing contains one Gaussian) and outputs the bulk part of the surface to be reconstructed (cf. Fig. 2a). A hierarchy of processing layers is then constructed with the aim of reconstructing what is missing of the surface. These grids will feature a progressively smaller scale and do not need to contain Gaussian units in every grid crossing. The reconstruction of the surface becomes:

$$\tilde{z}(x) = \sum_{l=1}^{L}\sum_{k=1}^{M} z_{kl}\, g(x; x_{kl}; \sigma_l)\Delta x_{cl} = \frac{\Delta x_{pl}}{\sqrt{\pi}\sigma_l}\sum_{l=1}^{L}\sum_{k=1}^{M} z_{kl}\, e^{-\frac{(x-x_{kl})^2}{\sigma_l^2}} \qquad (14)$$

where L is the number of grids. z_{kl} represents the height of the surface in the grid crossings of the first grid, while it represents the residual in the crossings of the higher grids. The Gaussians in each of these higher grids will therefore approximate the residual of the surface at the lower grid. This is defined as the set $\{r(x_m)\}$ constituted of the following elements:

$$r(x_m): \left(\sum_{l=1}^{L_1}\sum_{k=1}^{M} z_{kl}\, g(x_m; x_{kl}; \sigma_l)\Delta x_{cl} - z_m(x_m)\right) \qquad (15)$$

where $(z_m(x_m))$ is the set of sampled data points and L_1 is the number of grid used. The Gaussian units in the higher layers are inserted only when the local mean residual error, R_{kl}, is over threshold. This is evaluated inside the receptive field RF_{kl} of the corresponding Gaussian at the lower scale as:

$$R_{kl} = \frac{\sum_{r \in RF_{kl}} |r(x_r)|}{C_{kl}} \qquad (16)$$

where C_{kl} is the number of data points sampled inside the receptive field RF_{kl}. It has been shown in [18] that HRBF networks do employ Riesz bases and can approximate at any degree of approximation all the functions which have compact support, belong to C^∞ and have equilimited derivatives. Most real surfaces belong to this class of functions. Moreover, with respect to Multi Scale analysis carried out through Wavelet decomposition, approximation spaces represented by the different layers of HRBF have a smaller angle which guarantees a better match of a given approximation error.

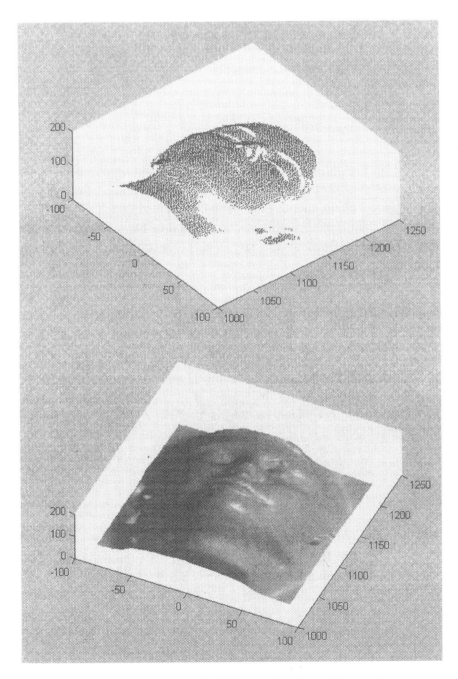

Figure 1. On top, the ensemble of 9,370 data point collected by the Autoscan 3D digitiser; at the bottom, the surface reconstructed by a four layers HRBF Network (cf. Table 1 for the parameters adopted).

3   Reconstruction of 3D Surfaces from Range Data

HRBF can find application in many real problems where the reconstruction of continuous surfaces, with space-varying frequency content has to be performed from not equally spaced data. One of these applications is the reconstruction of 3D surfaces from range data (3D scanning). This is typically a two step procedure: in the first step a sufficient number of 3D points over the surface is sampled (digitisation); in the second step, these points are transformed into a 3D surface, cleaning the noise introduced by the digitisation process. One of the most interesting surfaces is the Human Face. This in fact, shows a high frequency content in the regions of the lips, eyebrows and nose, and much lower content in the cheeks and fore-head.

The range data are sampled through Autoscan [19], a flexible and portable 3D scanner with a high accuracy. It collects the 3D position of a set of spots (points) created on the surface by a commercial laser pointer operated manually. This adds a further reason to use HRBF networks to reconstruct the surface. Manual scanners, in fact, collect more points in the most difficult regions (the ones which show the highest frequency content) and less points in the others. The net effect is that, if Gaussians with the lowest scale are used everywhere, there might not be enough data points and Equation (10) would be empty in the regions with the lowest frequency content. The use of Hierarchical construction avoids this.

In Figure 1a, a typical set of data collected by Autoscan is plotted. It is constituted of $N = 9,370$ data points with a measurement noise (due to instrument error and head small movements) can be evaluated around 1mm. This value is used as a threshold on the mean residual error in the process of inserting Gaussians in the higher grids. In this case a HRBF of four layers has been used. The highest frequency content has been evaluated in 0.1Hz which requires a value of $\sigma = 1.875$mm and of $\Delta x_c = 1.275$mm. We have chosen to double the scale σ every grid; from which it follows that the first basic layer feature a grid spacing of $\Delta x_c = 10.2$mm (cf. Table 1). The first grid contains a total of $M_1 = 18 \times 21$ Gaussians and its output is reported in Figure 2a. It reproduces only a

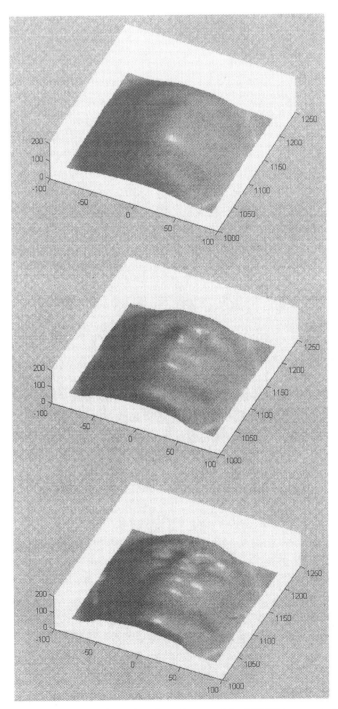

Figure 2. The output of the first three layers of the HRBF is reported here.

rough description of the surface which is refined in the following layers (cf. Figures 2b-2c). The final result is reported in Figure 1b.

Table 1. Parameters of the HRBF network. R_m is the mean value of the residual R.

Grid #	Δx_c [mm]	σ [mm]	$v_{cut-off}$ [Hz]	R_m [mm]	#Gauss/ total
1	10.2	15	0.0125	10.68	249/378
2	5.1	7.5	0.025	4.08	1014/1435
3	2.55	3.75	0.05	2.02	3435/5520
4	1.275	1.875	0.1	1.05	9101/21646

4   Conclusion

The HRBF Network presented here is constructed with local operations carried out on sub-sets of data points. Therefore, the algorithm complexity does not increase with the cardinality of the input set and it is fully parallelisable and it can be easily implemented in real-time on a parallel machine. It is suitable to a large range of applications where the density of sampled data points is a function of the difficulty of the surface to be reconstructed as shown by the example of the reconstruction of Human Faces from range data.

References

[1] Girosi, F., Jones, M., and Poggio, T. (1995) "Regularization theory and neural networks architectures," *Neural Computation*, vol. 7, pp. 219-269.

[2] Baraldi, A. and Borghese, N.A. (1988), "Learning from data: general issues and special applications of radial basis function network," Technical Report, TR-98-028, ICSI, Berkeley, CA.

[3] Poggio, T. and Girosi, F. (1990), "Regularization algorithms for learning that are equivalent to multilayer networks," *Science*, vol. 247, pp. 978-981.

[4] Wahba, G. (1985), "A comparison of GCV and GML for choosing the smoothing parameter in the generalised splines smoothing problem," *Ann. Statist.*, vol. 13, pp. 1378-1402.

[5] Orr, M.J.L. (1995), "Regularization in the selection of radial basis function centres," *Neural Computation*, vol. 7, no. 3, pp. 606-623.

[6] Borghese, N.A. and Ferrari, S. (1998), "Hierarchical RBF networks in function approximation," *Neurocomputing*, vol. 19, pp. 259-283.

[7] Marchini, S. and Borghese, N.A. (1994), "Optimal local estimation of RBF parameters," *Proc. of ICAN94.*

[8] Oppenheim, A.V. and Schafer, R.W. (1994), *Digital Signal Processing*, Prentice-Hall, Englewood Cliffs, N.J., U.S.A.

[9] Specht, D.F. (1990), "Probabilistic neural networks," *Neural Networks*, vol. 3, pp. 109-118.

[10] Xu, L., Krzyzak, A., and Yuille, A. (1994), "On radial basis function nets and kernel regression: statistical consistency, convergence rates, and receptive field size," *Neural Networks*, vol. 7, no. 4, pp. 609-628.

[11] Bishop, C.M. (1995), *Neural Networks for Pattern Recognition*, Clarendon Press, Oxford, U.K.

[12] Poggio, T. (1990), "A theory of how the brain might work," *Cold Spring Harbor Symp. Quantitative Biology*, pp. 899-910.

[13] Poggio, T., Torre, V., and Koch, C., (1985), "Computational vision and regularization theory," *Nature*, vol. 317, pp. 314-319.

[14] Press, W.H., Vetterling, W.T., Teukolsky, S.A., and Flannery, B.P. (1992), *Numerical Recipes in C*, Cambridge University Press.

[15] Sanchez, D.V. (1995), "Robustization of a learning method for RBF networks," *Neurocomputing*, vol. 9, pp. 85-94.

[16] Marroquin, J.L., Mitter, S., and Poggio, T. (1987), "Probabilistic solution of ill-posed problems in computational vision," *J. Am. Stat. Assoc.*, vol. 82, pp. 76-89.

[17] Strang, G. and Nguyen, T. (1996), *Wavelets and Filter Banks*, Wellesley – Cambridge Press.

[18] Borghese, N.A., Maggioni, M., and Ferrari, S. (2000), "Multi-scale approximation with hierarchical radial basis functions networks," *IEEE Trans. Neural Networks*. (Submitted.)

[19] Borghese, N.A., Ferrigno, G., Baroni, G., Savarè, R., Ferrari, S., and Pedotti, A. (1998), "AUTOSCAN: a flexible and portable scanner of 3D surfaces," *IEEE Computer Graphics & Applications*, May/June, pp. 38-41.

Chapter 4

RBF Neural Networks with Orthogonal Basis Functions

This chapter introduces the minimal spectral RBF neural networks. The method of calculation of these neural networks is similar to the method of support vector machine neural networks, but it uses a natural prior. We describe how to build the natural prior associated to the data in the context of a given basis function class through the construction of the associated spectrum of the data. We show how to apply the general method if the class of basis functions has some orthogonal structure. We describe the construction of spectral neural networks with orthogonal basis functions that are minimal orthogonal representations of the true minimal model of the data. We discuss some practical application issues, too.

1   Introduction

The theory and practice of approximation with artificial neural networks was revolutionized in the last years by the application of the Bayesian analysis framework [2], [7], [8], [16]. The methodology of support vector machine neural networks [14], [15] is the most advanced technique in this line of results. The Bayesian analysis offers an integrating framework for theories and techniques about minimal neural network models, such as general regularization [10], complexity regularization [1], and various pruning methods [11]. The theory of support vector machine neural networks is built on foundations provided by the Bayesian analysis framework and gives a rigorous way to determine the minimal neural network models given a set of data.

While the Bayesian analysis works in general with any kind of prior distribution over the parameter space for the neural networks, its realizations

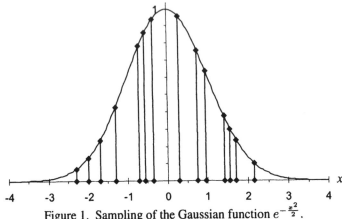

Figure 1. Sampling of the Gaussian function $e^{-\frac{x^2}{2}}$.

in the form of Bayesian regularization [1], [16] and the support vector machine method [14], [15] work with special kinds of prior distributions that are formed by sums of Dirac-δ distributions [6]. More specifically, the prior distribution that is considered in the context of these methods is a mixture of Dirac-δ distributions centered at the input vectors of the given data set. As a result, the solutions given by these methods are minimal models with respect to the neural network space determined by the basis functions parameterized by the given data. Of course, in this way we may not get the true minimal model of the data with respect to the neural network space corresponding to the full class of the basis functions.

To see the essence of the above problem, we consider the approximation of the Gaussian function $f(x) = e^{-\frac{x^2}{2}}$, with given data: $D = \{(x_i, y_i); i = 1, \ldots, m\}$, $y_i = f(x_i)$, $x_i \in [-3, 3]$, $|x_i| > \varepsilon > 0$, for every $i = 1, \ldots, m$ (see Figure 1). Constructing the minimal model of the data with basis functions of the form $g_c(x) = e^{-\frac{(x-c)^2}{2}}$ and with the support vector machine method leads to a neural network of the following form:

$$\widehat{f}(x) = \sum_{i \in SV} a_i e^{-\frac{(x-x_i)^2}{2}} \tag{1}$$

where $SV \subset \{1, \ldots, m\}$ is the set of indices corresponding to the support vectors. Notice that the generated minimal model is more complex than the true function that was approximated. Moreover, the complexity of the resulted model increases as the value of ε increases, i.e., more basis functions are included in the approximation of the true function.

So, as demonstrated by the above simple example, even the most developed neural network method can fail in providing a truly minimal approximation. The reason for this is that we restrict ourselves to priors made by combinations of Dirac-δ distributions centered at the given data vectors. The question naturally arises, what can we do to have a more natural prior that can lead us to the true minimal solution.

An attempt to provide an answer to this problem is to use the method of sparse approximation [3], [5]. The variations of this method (e.g., best orthogonal basis, basis pursuit [3]) try to solve the problem by considering all basis functions, but as it is pointed out in Chen [3] many times they fail to provide a really minimal solution. The basis pursuit method proposed by Chen [3] is equivalent to the support vector machine solution [5] and in consequence it has the same problem, i.e., the solution corresponds to a prior made by combination of Dirac-δ-s centered at the given data vectors.

Our objective is to find a minimal RBF neural network model of a given data that corresponds to a more natural prior than the one considered implicitly in the case of support vector machines. In this way we aim to provide more minimal models than those provided by the support vector machine method.

We propose an alternative method for the calculation of the minimal neural network model of given data. Our method continues the direction of the support vector machines, but it corresponds to a more natural prior over the network parameters than the prior made by the Dirac-δ-s centered at the given data vectors. The idea is that we try to find the optimal prior for a given class of basis functions. We introduce the concept of the associated spectrum of the data with respect to the chosen class of basis functions. The associated spectrum is used to determine the solution that corresponds implicitly to the natural prior. This is associated to the data in the context of approximation with a given class of basis functions. We call minimal spectral neural network the obtained neural network. We show how to find the associated spectrum of the data if the class of basis functions has a simple or generalized orthogonal structure. Finally, we describe how to calculate minimal RBF neural networks with orthogonal basis functions that approximate the true minimal model, obtainable by using general optimization with the natural prior.

The structure of the chapter is as follows. Section 2 contains the formulation of the problem. In Section 3, we interpret the problem in the context of orthogonal basis functions. Section 4 provides an example, the case of the Fourier approximation. In Section 5, we describe the orthogonalization of classes of basis functions. In Section 6, we present the orthogonalization of the class of Gaussian basis functions. Section 7 contains practical considerations with respect to the application of the proposed method. Finally, in Section 8, we draw the conclusions.

2   Problem Formulation

In this section we present the basic formulation of our approximation problem in the context of mutual information of functions. Our formulation starts from the concept of 'minimum description length' and we end up with a formulation that is structurally related to the problem formulation of the support vector machines.

Suppose we would like to approximate a function $f : R^n \to R$ by a linear combination of some basis functions $g_i \in G$.

We start from the concept of 'minimum description length' [12], and we intend to find a minimal description of the approximated function f in terms of our dictionary consisting of the basis functions $g_i \in G$. In information related formulation this is equivalent to the finding of a minimal description of the approximated function that contains as much as possible of the information contained in the approximated function. Going forward we may reformulate this by saying that we look for a minimal description in the terms of the basis function dictionary that has maximal mutual information with the approximated function. Generally, we may consider any convenient measure of mutual information between the functions.

To be more explicit, let us consider that the function f contains the information about how the values of it differ from the zero. In other words, we pick the identically zero function as the reference basis and we consider the information content of a function to be the information about the differences of the function f from the identically zero function. In this context we can easily see, that the identically zero function contains no information or zero information, as it does not differ in any way from itself.

Now we can formulate our criteria about the optimality of the approximation. Assume that f is the approximated function and g is the combination of the selected basis functions. We would like to have that the difference between the two functions, i.e., f and g, is the identically zero function. We write this objective, using the concept of mutual information introduced before, as

$$< f - g, f - g >= 0 \qquad (2)$$

where by $< \cdot, \cdot >$ we denoted the mutual information operator.

Considering the mutual information operator as an internal product operator we can define the corresponding norm by

$$||f||^2 =< f, f > \qquad (3)$$

(i.e., we consider that the mutual information of a function with itself is positive). Generally, this norm should be equivalent with the usual $|| \cdot ||_p$ norms (i.e., Cauchy, Euclidean, Tschebishev, Minkowski norms) in order to achieve approximation in the sense of the usual norms as well.

The optimization problem for our mutual information based approximation is as follows

$$\min_{g \in \overline{G}} ||f - g||^2 \qquad (4)$$

where by $\overline{G}$ we denoted the linear closure of the set of basis functions. We may rewrite this formula as

$$\min_{g \in \overline{G}} \left(\frac{1}{2}||f||^2 + \frac{1}{2}||g||^2 - < f, g > \right) \qquad (5)$$

Consider the expanded form of g, which is

$$g = \sum_{k=1}^{m} a_k g_{w^k} \tag{6}$$

where $a_k \in R$ and $w^k \in \Omega$ are the parameters of the basis functions, and Ω is the set of these parameters. Therefore we have

$$\min_{\theta} \left(\frac{1}{2}\|f\|^2 + \frac{1}{2}\sum_{i=1}^{m}\sum_{j=1}^{m} a_i a_j < g_{w^i}, g_{w^j} > - \sum_{i=1}^{m} a_i < g_{w^i}, f > \right) \tag{7}$$

where $\theta = (w^1, \ldots, w^m, a_1, \ldots, a_m) \in \Omega^+ \times R^+$, and by the star sets we denoted $\Omega^+ = \bigcup_{m \geq 1} \Omega^m$ and $R^+ = \bigcup_{m \geq 1} R^m$.

Obviously, in many cases we may arrive to infinite solutions. In such cases, the best approximation of f is $g = \lim_{m \to \infty} g^m$, where by g^m we denote the solution of the optimization for a fixed m, i.e., for $\theta \in \Omega^m \times R^m$. In order to impose a complexity regularization on the solution (i.e., on the number of the basis functions included in the best approximation) we introduce the concept of ε-insensitive minimum, defined using the concept of ε-insensitive error

$$E_\varepsilon(x) = \begin{cases} |x| - \varepsilon & if \quad |x| > \varepsilon \\ 0 & if \quad |x| \leq \varepsilon \end{cases} \tag{8}$$

In this way, the formula for minimization turns to be

$$\min_{\theta} E_\varepsilon \left(\frac{1}{2}\|f\|^2 + \frac{1}{2}\sum_{i=1}^{m}\sum_{j=1}^{m} a_i a_j < g_{w^i}, g_{w^j} > - \sum_{i=1}^{m} a_i < g_{w^i}, f > \right) \tag{9}$$

and

$$m^* = \arg\min_{m} E_\varepsilon \left(\frac{1}{2}\|f\|^2 + \frac{1}{2}\sum_{i=1}^{m}\sum_{j=1}^{m} a_i^{*m} a_j^{*m} < g_{w^{*mi}}, g_{w^{*mj}} > \right.$$

$$\left. - \sum_{i=1}^{m} a_i^{*m} < g_{w^{*mi}}, f > \right) \tag{10}$$

where by a_i^{*m} and w^{*mi} we denote the optimal values of the parameters calculated for m. In other words, we take the smallest m for which the calculated mutual information of $f - g$ with itself is smaller than ε.

We observe that the resulting optimization problem has a similar structure as the support vector machine problem [14], [15] (i.e., the dual problem of the primary support vector machine problem). The major difference is that here the kernel function does not appear explicitly. Instead, we have the internal products representing the mutual information of the functions. Another important difference is that here the regularization condition is imposed directly with respect to the number of the basis functions, while in the case of support vector machines this is imposed implicitly by restricting the values of the a_i-s to be positive.

We emphasize that our optimization problem is a Bayesian regularization problem. It corresponds to a natural prior over the space of the parameters. This prior fits to the data of the problem, i.e., f, and the solution context of the problem, that is G, through the appropriate selection of the mutual information operator.

3 The Problem in Orthogonal Context

We continue by presenting our approximation problem with mutual information minimization in the context of orthogonal basis functions. The advantage of the orthogonal context is that the internal product that defines the orthogonal structure of the class of basis functions can be used naturally as the mutual information operator.

Let us consider G to be a class of basis functions that has an orthogonal basis. This means that there exists $G_\perp \subset G$ such that $G \subset \overline{G_\perp}$ and

$$< g_{w^1}, g_{w^2} > = \begin{cases} c_w^2 & if \quad w^1 = w^2 = w \\ 0 & otherwise \end{cases} \tag{11}$$

for every $g_{w^1}, g_{w^2} \in G_\perp$. $G_\perp$ is called the orthogonal basis of G. If we have that $c_w = 1$ for every w such that $g_w \in G_\perp$, then we say that G has an orthonormal basis. We say that G has a simple orthogonal structure if it has an orthogonal basis.

If the class of the basis functions has a simple orthogonal structure, then we can write every function $g_w \in G$ as a linear combination of the functions from the orthogonal basis. Consequently, the problem of approximation reduces to the problem of approximation in terms of the members of the orthogonal basis.

By applying equation (11), we rewrite the minimization problem from equations (9) and (10) as follows

$$\min_\theta E_\varepsilon \left(\frac{1}{2}||f||^2 + \frac{1}{2}\sum_{i=1}^m a_i^2 c_{w^i}^2 - \sum_{i=1}^m a_i < g_{w^i}, f > \right) \tag{12}$$

$$m^* = \arg \min_m E_\varepsilon \left(\frac{1}{2}||f||^2 + \frac{1}{2}\sum_{i=1}^m a_i^{*m2} c_{w^{*mi}}^2 \right.$$

$$\left. - \sum_{i=1}^m a_i^{*m} < g_{w^{*mi}}, f > \right) \tag{13}$$

Continuing the transformation of equation (12) we get

$$\min_\theta E_\varepsilon \left(\frac{1}{2}||f||^2 + \frac{1}{2}\sum_{i=1}^m a_i^2 c_{w^i}^2 - \sum_{i=1}^m a_i < g_{w^i}, f > \right.$$

$$\left. + \frac{1}{2}\sum_{i=1}^m \frac{1}{c_{w^i}^2} < g_{w^i}, f >^2 - \frac{1}{2}\sum_{i=1}^m \frac{1}{c_{w^i}^2} < g_{w^i}, f >^2 \right)$$

$$= \min_\theta E_\varepsilon \left(\frac{1}{2}||f||^2 - \frac{1}{2}\sum_{i=1}^m \frac{1}{c_{w^i}^2} < g_{w^i}, f >^2 \right.$$

$$\left. + \frac{1}{2}\sum_{i=1}^m \left(a_i c_{w^i} - \frac{1}{c_{w^i}} < g_{w^i}, f > \right)^2 \right) \tag{14}$$

Optimizing formula (14) separately for a_i yields

$$a_i = \frac{1}{c_{w^i}^2} < g_{w^i}, f > \tag{15}$$

Using this last result, we write the optimization formula as

$$\min_{\theta_w} E_\varepsilon \left(||f||^2 - \sum_{i=1}^{m} \frac{1}{c_{w^i}^2} < g_{w^i}, f >^2 \right) \tag{16}$$

where by θ_w we denoted the parameter vector $(w^1, \ldots, w^m)$. This minimization has sense, hence we have the Bessel inequality for the case of orthogonal approximation [13]

$$\sum_{i \in I} \frac{1}{c_{w^i}^2} < g_{w^i}, f >^2 \leq ||f||^2 \tag{17}$$

where I is the index set associated with the orthogonal basis of the class of basis functions.

Thus, our minimization problem means that we look for the minimal set of orthogonal basis functions for which we get

$$\left|\left| f - \sum_{i \in I} \frac{1}{c_{w^i}^2} < g_{w^i}, f > g_{w^i} \right|\right|^2 \leq \varepsilon \tag{18}$$

We can find these basis functions by the δ-limited maximization of

$$\sum_{i \in I} \frac{1}{c_{w^i}^2} < g_{w^i}, f >^2 \tag{19}$$

which we write as

$$\max_{\theta_w} \sum_{i \in I} E_\delta \left(\frac{1}{c_{w^i}^2} < g_{w^i}, f >^2 \right) \tag{20}$$

where we choose δ appropriately in the function of ε.

We call the associated spectrum of the function f with respect to the class of the basis functions G the function defined as

$$\eta_f(w) = \frac{1}{c_w^2} < g_w, f >^2 \tag{21}$$

If the class of basis functions has a simple orthogonal structure, our optimization problem means that we search for the most important peaks of the associated spectrum of the approximated function.

The following theorems hold for the associated spectrum of a function. The proofs are based on standard results from orthogonal approximation theory [13].

Theorem 1 *Let f be the approximated function, and let $G_\perp = \{g_{w^i} \mid i \in I\}$, $I \subset \mathbb{Z}$, be the orthogonal basis of the class of basis functions. The associated spectrum of f with respect to $G = \overline{G_\perp}$ has the following properties*

a. $\sum_{i \in I} \eta_f(w^i) \le ||f||^2$;

b. $\lim_{|i| \to \infty} \eta_f(w^i) = 0$, if $\infty \in I$.

Theorem 2 *Let f be the approximated function, and let $G_\perp = \{g_{w^i} \mid i \in I\}$, such that $|I| > |\mathbb{N}|$, be the orthogonal basis of the class of basis functions. The associated spectrum of f with respect to $G = \overline{G_\perp}$ has the following properties*

a. $\int_I \eta_f(w^i) dw^i \le ||f||^2$;

b. $\lim_{|i| \to i_\infty} \eta_f(w^i) = 0$, where $i_\infty \in \overline{I} - I$, with the condition that $\overline{I} - I \ne \emptyset$.

In view of the above theorems, if the class of basis functions has a simple orthogonal structure, the optimization reduces to the search for the most important peaks of the associated spectrum function within a finite (when I is countable) or bounded (when I is innumerable) set of peaks.

The minimal spectral neural network is a neural network with a single hidden layer. The neurons of this network have as activation function the basis functions corresponding to the selected peaks of the associated spectrum. The synaptic weights between the hidden layer neurons and the linear output neuron are calculated by the above described optimization method.

4 An Example: the Fourier Approximation

As a simple example, we consider the Fourier approximation of continuous one-dimensional functions [13]. We assume in this section that the approximated function f has a Fourier approximation that converges to this function. This class of functions contains most of the usual functions (see [13] for the general conditions on functions to have a converging Fourier approximation).

The Fourier spectrum of the function f is calculated as

$$\widehat{f}(\theta) = \frac{1}{2\pi} \int\limits_{-\pi}^{\pi} f(x)e^{-i\theta x} dx \qquad (22)$$

Using the Fourier spectrum, we get the general approximation formula for the function f in the form [4]

$$f(x) = \int\limits_{-\infty}^{\infty} \widehat{f}(\theta)e^{i\theta x} d\theta \qquad (23)$$

Here, the $e^{i\theta x}$ functions are the basis functions, which have the extended form of $\cos\theta x + i\sin\theta x$. So, the resulted approximation is build by a combination of sine and cosine functions.

We can view the Fourier spectrum as a natural prior over the space of the parameters (i.e., the θ-s). To be formally correct (i.e., unit integral over the definition domain), we consider the function $\widehat{f}^*(\theta) = \frac{1}{A}|\widehat{f}(\theta)|$, $A = \int_{-\infty}^{\infty} |\widehat{f}(\theta)| d\theta$; we know that $0 < A < \infty$. This natural prior distribution determines the weight of each basis function in the composition of the approximated function. Note that we made abstraction of the sign of $\widehat{f}(\theta)$, so this means that $\widehat{f}^*(\theta)$ is distribution value corresponding to $e^{i\theta x}$ if the sign of $\widehat{f}(\theta)$ is positive, and it corresponds to $-e^{i\theta x}$ if the sign of $\widehat{f}(\theta)$ is negative.

Using this prior distribution, we can find the minimal representation of the approximated function in terms of the basis functions (i.e., the sine and cosine functions). This remains true even if we have only a sample from the approximated function. In this case we can construct the approximation of the Fourier spectrum by doing Monte Carlo integration. So, contrary to the example presented in the introduction, if we have a sample from a basis function, e.g., $\cos x$, sampled at points x_i, $|x_i| > \varepsilon > 0$, we can approximate the Fourier spectrum and find the true minimal approximation (i.e., $\cos x$) of the function.

Furthermore, we know that the Fourier basis functions have an orthogonal basis, i.e., the functions $\sin nx$ and $\cos nx$, where n is an integer. So, instead of an approximation using all basis functions, we can approximate a function by using only the member functions of the orthogonal basis. We can write the approximation of the function f by the orthogonal basis functions in the form

$$f(x) = \sum_{n=-\infty}^{\infty} \widehat{f}(n) \cdot (\cos nx + i \sin nx) \tag{24}$$

As we observed in the previous section, in the case of orthogonal approximation only a limited number of the basis functions have a significant contribution to the approximation. Hence, in the case of the Fourier approximation we look for the most significant basis function components that can be detected by analyzing the square of the Fourier spectrum, i.e., $\widehat{f}^2(\theta)$. Practically, we search for the important peaks of the squared Fourier spectrum to find the most important basis functions.

We note that the theory of Fourier analysis shows that the orthogonal Fourier approximation gives an arbitrarily correct approximation of the true function. So, by using the orthogonal approximation we find the minimal orthogonal model of the function in terms of the orthogonal basis functions. This minimal orthogonal model is not as minimal as the one obtainable by applying general Fourier approximation (e.g., $\cos(0.12x)$ is approximated by a linear combination of several orthogonal Fourier basis functions, while it is in fact one of the general Fourier basis functions), but it is the approximation of this true minimal model and the minimal orthogonal representation of it.

We can see that the natural prior over the parameter space is characteristically associated to the approximated function in the context of the class of basis functions. Our example also points to the link between the associated spectrum (i.e., in the example the square of the Fourier spectrum) and the natural prior (i.e., the Fourier spectrum).

5 Orthogonalizing the Class of Basis Functions

In the previous sections we discussed how to use in general the approximation framework based on the mutual information and we also illustrated the advantages of the orthogonal structure of the class of basis functions. In fact, this latter case brings us closer to the practical application of the general ideas. The fundamental question is how to define the mutual information of the functions. If we can find an appropriate internal product that provides the orthogonal structure of the class of basis functions, then we can use this internal product to define the mutual information of two functions. In order to apply an internal product as measure of the mutual information, the norm defined using the internal product should be compatible with the usual norms used in the context of approximation (i.e., the $\|\cdot\|_p$ norms).

Let us consider the class of basis functions G, $G = \{g_w \mid w \in \Omega\}$, where Ω is the space of the parameters of the basis functions. First, we look for a subclass of the basis functions, $G_\perp \subset G$, such that for every $g_{w^1}, g_{w^2} \in G_\perp$ we have that

$$< g_{w^1}, g_{w^2} >_\perp = \begin{cases} c_w & if \quad w^1 = w^2 = w \\ 0 & otherwise \end{cases} \quad (25)$$

for an appropriately chosen internal product. In addition we require that $G = \overline{G_\perp}$, where the closure is understood as linear closure. We call the subclass $G_\perp$ together with the internal product $< \cdot, \cdot >_\perp$ the simple orthogonalizer of G. If $c_w = 1$ for every w such that $g_w \in G_\perp$, we say that this pair of subclass and internal product is an orthonormalizer of the class of basis functions. If we manage to find an orthogonalizer of the class G we can apply the technique described in the Section 3.

The more problematic case is when there is no orthogonalizer of the class G. In this case we try to find a set of subclasses $G_{\perp k} \subset G$, such that for every $G_{\perp k}$ we have an internal product $<\cdot,\cdot>_{\perp k}$, with respect to which the subclass is orthogonal, and we have that $G = \overline{\bigcup_{k\in K} G_{\perp k}}$, where K is the index set of the subclasses. If we can find a set of such subclasses we call them together with their associated internal products a general orthogonalizer of the class G. We call the individual pairs of basis function subclasses together with their internal product partial orthogonalizers. We say that the class G has a multiple orthogonal structure.

Let us consider this latter case. Let $f \in \overline{G}$ be a function that we try to approximate. We write f in the form

$$f = \sum_{k\in K} f_k \tag{26}$$

where $f_k \in \overline{G_{\perp k}}$. This is possible because $f \in \overline{G}$ and $G = \overline{\bigcup_{k\in K} G_{\perp k}}$. The sum sign in equation (26) is interpreted as integration if K has a continuous structure.

For each f_k we can use the spectrum-based orthogonal approximation method described in Section 3. The problem is that it is not guaranteed that

$$< f_{k_1}, f_{k_2} >_{\perp k_1} = < f_{k_1}, f_{k_2} >_{\perp k_2} = 0 \tag{27}$$

and not even that

$$< f_{k_1}, f_{k_2} >_{\perp k_1} = < f_{k_1}, f_{k_2} >_{\perp k_2} \tag{28}$$

To handle the problem we write a new optimization problem as

$$\min_{K'} \sum_{k,h\in K';\, k\neq h} \left(< f_k, f_h >_{\perp k}^2 + < f_k, f_h >_{\perp h}^2 \right) \tag{29}$$

where we minimize with respect to the index sets $K' \subset K$. By considering the sum of squares, we obtain a general minimization irrespective of the sign of the internal products.

Of course the problem (29) is not really friendly, because we do not know the functions f_k. The next step is to write the optimization in the terms of the orthogonal basis functions. First we write the generic form of the

f_k functions

$$f_k = \sum_{w^k \in \Omega_k} \frac{1}{c_{w^k}^2} \cdot < g_{w^k}, f >_{\perp^k} g_{w^k} \qquad (30)$$

where Ω_k is the parameter sub-space corresponding to $G_{\perp^k}$(i.e., $w \in \Omega_k$ if and only if $g_w \in G_{\perp^k}$). Then we have that

$$< f_k, f_h >_{\perp^k} = \sum_{w^k \in \Omega_k} \sum_{w^h \in \Omega_h} \pi(w^k, w^h, f) \qquad (31)$$

where

$$\pi(w^k, w^h, f) = \frac{1}{c_{w^k}^2} \cdot \frac{1}{c_{w^h}^2} \cdot < g_{w^k}, f >_{\perp^k} \cdot < g_{w^h}, f >_{\perp^h} \cdot < g_{w^k}, g_{w^h} >_{\perp^h} . \qquad (32)$$

Calculating all components for the minimization formula (29) we can use it to effectively handle the problem of minimal orthogonal approximation. Observe that for this optimization problem, the selection of the important peaks of the associated spectrum of each partial orthogonalizer can be used as a preprocessing step to reduce the number of the considered basis functions. This is so because values of the associated spectrum appear as multiplicative factors in the components of the to be optimized sums.

We end this section by emphasizing that by finding a simple or general orthogonalizer of the class of the basis functions, we can apply the mutual information-based approximation framework to find the minimal length descriptions of the approximated function.

6   Orthogonalizing the Class of Gaussian Functions

In this section, we show how to orthogonalize one of the most common classes of radial basis functions, namely the class of Gaussian functions. In order to do this, we analyze the Gaussian functions, we construct the internal products, and we show that we have to extend the class of Gaussian functions with the so-called complementary Gaussian functions in order to have a complete orthogonalization with a norm system that is compatible with the usual norms (i.e., the $|| \cdot ||_p$ norms).

6.1   Orthogonal Gaussian Functions

We note by $g_{c,r}$ the Gaussian functions centered at c and with width r, i.e., the functions with the form $e^{-\frac{(x-c)^2}{r^2}}$. Let us consider the simplest Gaussian function $g_{0,1}(x) = e^{-x^2}$. We write the Taylor expansion of this function

$$e^{-x^2} = (e^{-x^2})(0) + \frac{(e^{-x^2})'(0)}{1!}x + \ldots + \frac{(e^{-x^2})^{(n)}(0)}{n!}x^n + \ldots \qquad (33)$$

where we denoted by $(e^{-x^2})^{(n)}(0)$ the value at 0 of the n-th derivative of the function $g_{0,1}$. Writing the Taylor expansion explicitly, we get

$$e^{-x^2} = 1 - x^2 + \frac{x^4}{2!} - \frac{x^6}{3!} + \ldots + (-1)^n \frac{x^{2n}}{n!} + \ldots \qquad (34)$$

Observe that

$$\frac{(e^{-x^2})^{(2n)}(0)}{(2n)!} = (-1)^n \frac{1}{n!} \qquad (35)$$

and

$$\frac{(e^{-x^2})^{(2n+1)}(0)}{(2n+1)!} = 0 \qquad (36)$$

Now we write the Taylor expansion for the $\cos x$ function, that is

$$\cos x = 1 - \frac{x^2}{2!} + \frac{x^4}{4!} - \frac{x^6}{6!} + \ldots + (-1)^n \frac{x^{2n}}{(2n)!} + \ldots \qquad (37)$$

Equivalently we write

$$\cos x = \frac{0!}{0!} \cdot 1 - \frac{1!}{2!} \cdot x^2 + \frac{2!}{4!} \frac{x^4}{2!} - \frac{3!}{6!} \frac{x^6}{3!} + \ldots + \frac{n!}{(2n)!} \cdot (-1)^n \cdot \frac{x^{2n}}{n!} + \ldots \qquad (38)$$

or in a more compressed form

$$\cos x = \sum_{n=0}^{\infty} \frac{n!}{(2n)!} \cdot \frac{(e^{-x^2})^{(2n)}(0)}{(2n)!} \cdot x^{2n} \qquad (39)$$

Using the last result we define the operator

$$L_c f = \sum_{n=0}^{\infty} \frac{n!}{(2n)!} \cdot \frac{f^{(2n)}(c)}{(2n)!} \cdot (x - c)^{2n} \qquad (40)$$

We observe immediately that

$$L_0(g_{0,1}) = \cos x \tag{41}$$

and in general that

$$L_c(g_{c,r}) = \cos \frac{x-c}{r} \tag{42}$$

Define an internal product for each operator L_c by

$$< f, g >_c = \int_{c-\pi}^{c+\pi} L_c f(x) \cdot L_c g(x) dx \tag{43}$$

The orthogonality properties of the cosine functions imply

$$< g_{c,\frac{1}{n}}, g_{c,\frac{1}{m}} >_c = \begin{cases} 2\pi & if \quad n = m = \infty \\ \pi & if \quad n = m \neq \infty \\ 0 & if \quad n \neq m \end{cases} \tag{44}$$

where n and m are integer numbers.

In this way, we obtain a partial orthogonalizer for each $c \in R$ that is comprised by the set $G_c = \{g_{c,r} \mid r \in R\} \subset G$ and the internal product $< \cdot, \cdot >_c$, where $g_{c,r} = e^{-\frac{(x-c)^2}{r^2}}$. At the same time, we note that $G = \bigcup_{c \in R} G_c$ and consequently $\overline{G} = \overline{\bigcup_{c \in R} G_c}$. So, the set of the partial orthogonalizers makes up a complete general orthogonalizer.

Clearly, the L_c operators are linear, i.e., $L_c(\alpha f + \beta g) = \alpha L_c f + \beta L_c g$, and they are invertible within the set of even functions centered at c (i.e., $f(c - x) = f(c + x)$), permitting the inverse operator

$$L_c^{-1} f = \sum_{n=0}^{\infty} \frac{f^{(2n)}(c)}{n!} \cdot (x - c)^{2n} \tag{45}$$

We define the associated Gaussian spectrum of a function f as

$$\eta_G(c, r; f) = < g_{c,r}, f >_c^2 = \left(\int_{c-\pi}^{c+\pi} L_c f(x) \cdot \cos \frac{x-c}{r} dx \right)^2 \tag{46}$$

Having the invertibility of the L_c operators with respect to the even functions centered at c, the approximation of the transformed functions with cosine functions can be converted back into the approximation of the original function by Gaussian functions. In other words, if we have $f = \sum_{c \in R} f_c$ such that the f_c-s are even functions centered at c, and we have the approximation of the $L_c f_c$ functions by cosine functions in the form $L_c f_c \simeq \sum_{r \in R} a_{c,r} \cos \frac{x-c}{r}$, then we can approximate the functions f_c in the form $f_c \simeq \sum_{r \in R} a_{c,r} \cdot e^{-\frac{(x-c)^2}{r^2}}$. Consequently, using the orthogonality of the basis functions, we can get the minimal approximation of these functions in terms of Gaussian basis functions by applying the method described in Section 3.

Note that, similarly as in the case of the Fourier approximation, we can identify the natural prior over the parameter space associated with the approximated function as the distribution defined by $\frac{1}{A_c} | < L_c f, L_c g_{c,r} >_c |$ for the parameter pair (c, r), where $A = \int_{C \times R} | < L_c f, L_c g_{c,r} >_c | dc dr$, and C and R are the considered definition domains of c and r.

6.2   Completing the Class of Gaussian Functions

We note that we may have to deal with odd functions too (i.e., $f(-x) = -f(x)$, or in general $f(c - x) = -f(c + x)$), and in this case we cannot apply properly the above framework for approximation. In order to solve this problem we observe that the odd functions are approximated by the sine components in the context of the Fourier approximation. So, we look for a complementary class for the class of the Gaussian functions, such that the members of the complementary class provide the corresponding functions of the sine functions. If we can find them, then we can use the Fourier approximation for the approximation of functions with Gaussian and complementary Gaussian functions through the corresponding operators.

The Taylor expansion of the $\sin x$ function is

$$\sin x = x - \frac{x^3}{3!} + \frac{x^5}{5!} + \ldots + (-1)^{n+1} \frac{x^{2n-1}}{(2n-1)!} + \ldots \quad (47)$$

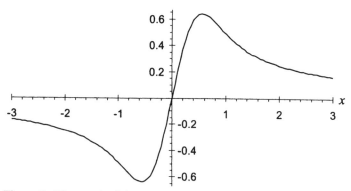

Figure 2. The graph of the complementary Gaussian function $\tilde{g}_{0,0.5}$.

The function $1 - g_{0,1} = 1 - e^{-x^2}$ has the Taylor expansion

$$1 - e^{-x^2} = x^2 - \frac{x^4}{2!} + \frac{x^6}{3!} + \ldots + (-1)^{n+1}\frac{x^{2n}}{n!} + \ldots \qquad (48)$$

Further, we define the complementary Gaussian function $\tilde{g}_{0,1} = \frac{1}{x}(1 - g_{0,1}) = \frac{1}{x}(1 - e^{-x^2})$ with the Taylor expansion

$$\tilde{g}_{0,1}(x) = x - \frac{x^3}{2!} + \frac{x^5}{3!} + \ldots + (-1)^{n+1}\frac{x^{2n-1}}{n!} + \ldots \qquad (49)$$

We have

$$\frac{(1 - e^{-x^2})^{(2n-1)}(0)}{(2n-1)!} = (-1)^{n+1}\frac{1}{n!} \qquad (50)$$

and

$$\frac{(1 - e^{-x^2})^{(2n)}(0)}{(2n)!} = 0 \qquad (51)$$

where $(1 - e^{-x^2})^{(n)}$ denotes the n-th derivative of $\tilde{g}_{0,1}$. We also note that the function $\tilde{g}_{0,1}$ is continuous and derivable at $x = 0$, having the values $\tilde{g}_{0,1}(0) = 0$ and $\tilde{g}'_{0,1}(0) = 1$. Figure 2 shows an example of the complementary Gaussian functions.

We write the Taylor expansion of $\sin x$ in the equivalent form

$$\sin x = \frac{1!}{1!} \cdot x - \frac{2!}{3!} \cdot \frac{x^3}{2!} + \frac{3!}{5!} \cdot \frac{x^5}{3!} + \ldots + \frac{n!}{(2n-1)!} \cdot (-1)^{n+1}\frac{x^{2n-1}}{n!} + \ldots \qquad (52)$$

or in compressed form

$$\sin x = \sum_{n=1}^{\infty} \frac{n!}{(2n-1)!} \cdot \frac{(1-e^{-x^2})^{(2n-1)}(0)}{(2n-1)!} \cdot x^{2n-1} \tag{53}$$

Let

$$\tilde{L}_c f = \sum_{n=1}^{\infty} \frac{n!}{(2n-1)!} \cdot \frac{f^{(2n-1)}(c)}{(2n-1)!} \cdot (x-c)^{2n-1} \tag{54}$$

Then

$$\tilde{L}_0(\tilde{g}_{0,1}) = \sin x \tag{55}$$

In general, we define complementary Gaussian functions as $\tilde{g}_{c,r}(x) = \frac{1}{x-c}(1 - g_{c,r}(x)) = \frac{1}{x-c}(1 - e^{-\frac{(x-c)^2}{r^2}})$ and we have

$$\tilde{L}_c(\tilde{g}_{c,r}) = \sin \frac{x-c}{r} \tag{56}$$

We define the internal product for each operator $\tilde{L}_c$ by

$$\widetilde{<f,g>}_c = \int_{c-\pi}^{c+\pi} \tilde{L}_c f(x) \cdot \tilde{L}_c g(x) dx \tag{57}$$

We define the complementary Gaussian spectrum as

$$\tilde{\eta}_G(c,r;f) = \widetilde{<g_{c,r},f>}_c^2 = \left(\int_{c-\pi}^{c+\pi} \tilde{L}_c f(x) \cdot \sin \frac{x-c}{r} dx \right)^2 \tag{58}$$

Similarly as in the case of the Gaussian functions we can approximate the odd functions by the complementary Gaussian functions using the Fourier approximation and the $\tilde{L}_c$ operators that are linear and invertible with respect to the set of odd functions centered at c.

We know that the continuous functions are decomposable in the sum of an odd and an even function [13]. We use this property by choosing as center any $c \in R$, and applying the operators L_c and $\tilde{L}_c$ to calculate the minimal approximation of functions with Gaussian and complementary

Gaussian functions. To unify the two parts, i.e., the Gaussian and complementary Gaussian approximation, we define the unified operators

$$L_c^* f = L_c f + i\widetilde{L}_c f \qquad (59)$$

where $i = \sqrt{-1}$. This operator transforms the unified basis functions $g_{c,r}^* = g_{c,r} + \widetilde{g}_{c,r}$ into the Fourier basis functions centered at c, i.e., $e^{i\frac{x-c}{r}} = e^{i\theta(x-c)}$, where $\theta = \frac{1}{r}$. We define the associated general Gaussian spectrum of the function f as

$$\eta_G^*(c, r; f) = < g_{c,r}, f >_c^2 + < \widetilde{g}_{c,r}, f >_c^2$$

$$= \left(\int_{c-\pi}^{c+\pi} L_c f(x) \cdot \cos\frac{x-c}{r} dx \right)^2 + \left(\int_{c-\pi}^{c+\pi} \widetilde{L}_c f(x) \cdot \sin\frac{x-c}{r} dx \right)^2 \qquad (60)$$

The Fourier approximation is compatible with the approximation in the sense of the usual norms (i.e., the $\| \cdot \|_p$ norms). The approximation of $L_c^* f$ with the Fourier basis functions is equivalent with the approximation of f with Gaussian and complementary Gaussian basis functions. Consequently, we get that the latter approximation is compatible with approximation in the sense of usual norms too.

In this way we arrive at the conclusion that the approximation based on the associated general Gaussian spectrum is equivalent with approximation with respect to the usual norms. By applying the method described in Section 3, we can find the minimal approximation of a function in terms of Gaussian and complementary Gaussian basis functions. This approximation corresponds to the natural prior defined by the associated general Gaussian spectrum. The combination of orthogonal Gaussians and complementary Gaussians approximates the true minimal model. This can be obtained by applying the optimization over the full class of Gaussian and complementary Gaussian basis functions. The orthogonal combination is the minimal orthogonal representation of the true minimal model.

6.3   How Does This Work?

One may say that these things seem to work, theoretically, but it seems counterintuitive that the flatter Gaussians can be approximated by combination of sharper Gaussians, e.g., how can we approximate $e^{-0.25x^2}$ with

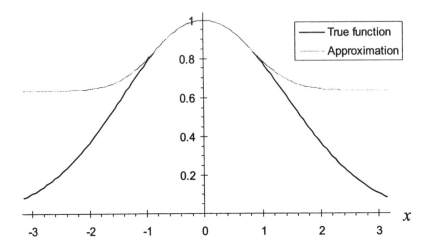

Gaussians like e^{-x^2}, e^{-4x^2}, e^{-9x^2}. The same observation applies to the corresponding complementary Gaussian functions.

The fact is that we can do the approximation because we have as basis function the constant 1 function, which corresponds to $e^{-0x^2} = e^{-0} = 1$. It is also true that the approximation of the Gaussians outside the orthogonal subsets is not exact on the whole definition domain. Figure 3 shows the approximation of $e^{-0.25x^2}$ by the combination of the corresponding orthogonal Gaussians (i.e., the orthogonal Gaussians centered at 0).

We see that the approximation is good in a certain interval around 0, but not good outside this interval. Looking at the maximum approximation error in the approximation of the functions $e^{-\frac{(x-c)^2}{r^2}}$ with the corresponding orthogonal Gaussian functions (i.e., those centered at c) we see that it varies periodically as we increase $\frac{1}{r}$ (see Figure 4). It has its local maxima at the $\frac{1}{r} = n + \frac{1}{2}$ values, where $n \in N$, and the local maxima have a descending tendency as $\frac{1}{r}$ increases.

In order to find a predictive value for the maximum error we look at the sum of the weights of the considered orthogonal Gaussians. As we can see in Figure 5, this varies also periodically, having the maxima at the $n + \frac{1}{2}$ values. In addition we note that if $\frac{1}{r} \in [n - \frac{1}{2}, n + \frac{1}{2})$, the most

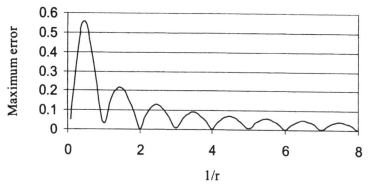

Figure 4. The variation of the maximum approximation error as $\frac{1}{r}$ increases.

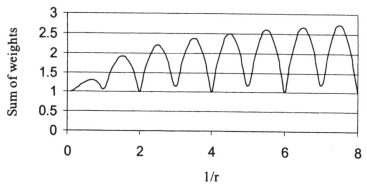

Figure 5. The variation of the sum of weights as $\frac{1}{r}$ increases.

important orthogonal component is $e^{-n^2(x-c)^2}$ for the Gaussians $e^{-\frac{(x-c)^2}{r^2}}$.

Combining the two measures, i.e., the maximum error and the sum of weights, we obtain the graph presented in Figure 6. We see that the sum of weights together with the $\frac{1}{r}$ value of the most important orthogonal component can be used as a good predictor of the expected maximum error.

Also, we observe that the radius of the good approximation interval varies inversely proportional with the maximum error. This is shown in Figure 7. This relationship can be used in practice to determine the radius of the good approximation intervals. This radius is where we should truncate the Gaussian basis functions in order to obtain precise approximation of the target functional relationship (i.e., in the worst case, the good approximation radius is $R \simeq 1$, according to our calculations).

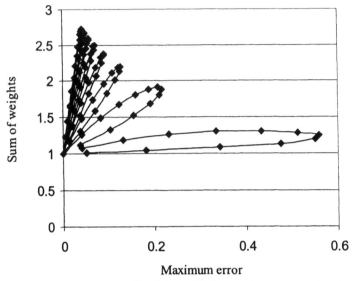

Figure 6. Variation of the sum of weights with the maximum approximation error.

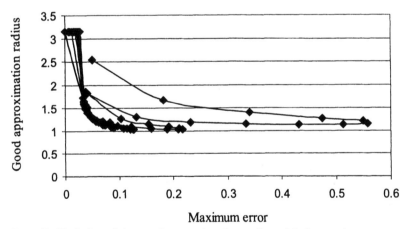

Figure 7. Variation of the good approximation radius with the maximum error.

This indicates that high precision approximation of all Gaussian functions is possible by combinations of the corresponding orthogonal Gaussian functions. We note that the Gaussian functions are truncated at the limits of the good approximation interval. The same is true for the orthogonal complementary Gaussian functions with respect to all complementary Gaussian functions. To determine the radius of good approximation we use the relationship between this radius and the maximum error. This depends on the measurable sum of weights and the $\frac{1}{r}$ value with the maximal weight. Having these latter two we can give a good estimate of the truncation radius that we should use to limit the effect of the considered basis functions.

The class of Gaussian functions has the universal approximation property [9]. Thus, every continuous and bounded function can be approximated with arbitrarily small error by combination of orthogonal Gaussian functions. If we fix an approximation error tolerance ε, we can find a corresponding minimal orthogonal Gaussian approximation of these functions, which is exactly what our previous theoretical analysis shows. The use of complementary Gaussian functions reduces the complexity of the minimal solutions even more, as these functions can be seen as a kind of representation of the difference of two Gaussians.

The approximation with a combination of orthogonal Gaussian and complementary Gaussian basis functions is simpler than the approximation with a combination of general Gaussians and complementary Gaussians. This is due to the fact that in the former case we search for the minimal model only over the grid of orthogonal basis functions instead of the full space of all basis functions. The search over the grid determined by the orthogonal basis functions is based on the natural prior associated with the data. The generated model in most cases will not be as minimal as it would be if all basis functions would be considered in the search for the minimal model. The resulting model is the orthogonal representation of the true minimal model.

We conclude that the minimal model obtained by search over the combinations of orthogonal Gaussians and complementary Gaussians is better than the one which can be obtained by the SVM methodology. The reason is that the basis functions corresponding to the support vectors do not have the universal approximation property in every case.

7 Practical Considerations

In practical applications, often we do not know the exact form of the approximated functions (this is the usual case). In such situations we can approximate the values of the associated spectrum by Monte Carlo approximation, i.e., considering a sufficiently large number of randomly selected values of the approximated functions. After having the approximate associate spectrum we can use this to do the optimization in order to get the minimal representation of the approximated function in the terms of basis functions. This representation is interpreted as a minimal neural network model of the approximated function.

Another use of the associated spectrum is to see whether functions from a given class F can be approximated or not with small size neural networks having hidden neurons with activation functions from a given class G of basis functions. To see this we can calculate theoretically or test practically the associated spectrum of the functions from the class F. If we find that the associated spectra have a small number of important peaks than we may assume that small size neural networks with basis functions form the class G can approximate well the functions from the class F. On the contrary, if the spectra have many similar size important peaks over large regions of the parameter space we may conclude that the approximation of functions from the class F is hard with neural networks having basis functions from the class G.

Finally, if the parameter space of the basis functions has high dimensionality, then we may encounter storage problems with the calculation of the associated spectrum. This may lead to the impossibility of the calculation of the complete associated spectrum. In such cases we can make a raw approximation of the spectrum to see whether it has a relatively small or high number of similar size important peaks. Calculating several spectra for different basis function classes, these raw spectrum approximations may serve as the basis for choosing the basis functions that are used as activation functions in the hidden neurons of the neural network that we want to use to approximate the objective function.

8   Conclusions

We presented the methodology of minimal spectral neural networks. We calculate the minimal neural network models using a natural prior distribution over the parameter space. The natural prior that we use is associated with the data in the context of the class of basis functions that we use. We use the natural prior implicitly by constructing the associated spectrum of the data. We call the obtained neural network the minimal spectral neural network.

We showed how to use this method when the class of basis functions has an orthogonal structure. In this case, the orthogonal structure of the class of basis functions provides us a straightforward way to calculate the natural prior by using the internal product that defines the orthogonal structure. We also discussed the general case of multiple orthogonal structure, when the class of basis functions has many partial orthogonalizers.

We showed how to find the proper orthogonalization for the most common radial basis function class, the class of Gaussian functions. Our analysis indicates that for the sake of completeness (in the sense of approximation) we need to augment the class of Gaussian functions with the complementary Gaussian functions (i.e., functions of the form $\frac{r}{||x-c||} \cdot (1 - e^{-\frac{||x-c||^2}{r^2}})$).

We discussed how to use the method practically and we pointed out that the obtained minimal spectral neural network with orthogonal Gaussian and complementary Gaussian functions corresponds to the natural prior. Although this model is not necessarily the truly minimal one, it is guaranteed that it approximates the true minimal model that would result by applying the methodology to the whole class of the considered basis functions. In comparison, in the case of the SVM methodology this is not guaranteed, so we conclude that the minimal spectral neural networks with orthogonal basis functions are better (i.e., closer to the true minimal model) than those obtained by applying the SVM methodology.

References

[1] Barron, A.R. (1991), "Minimum complexity density estimation," *IEEE Transactions on Information Theory*, vol. 37, pp. 1034-1054.

[2] Buntine, W.L. and Weigend, A.S. (1991), "Bayesian back-propagation," *Complex Systems*, vol. 5, pp. 604-643.

[3] Chen, S. (1995), *Basis Pursuit*, Ph.D. Thesis, Department of Statistics, Stanford University.

[4] Gelfand, I.M. and Vilenkin, N.I. (1985), *Generalized Functions. Applications of the Harmonic Analysis*, Editura Ştiinţifică şi Enciclopedică, Bucharest (in Romanian).

[5] Girosi, F. (1998), "An equivalence between sparse approximation and support vector machines," *Neural Computation*, vol. 10, pp. 1455-1481.

[6] Van de Laar, P. and Heskes, T. (1999), "Pruning using parameter and neuronal metrics," *Neural Computation*, vol. 11, pp. 977-994.

[7] MacKay, D.J.C. (1992), "Bayesian interpolation," *Neural Computation*, vol. 4, pp. 415-447.

[8] MacKay, D.J.C. (1992), "A practical Bayesian framework for back-propagation networks," *Neural Computation*, vol. 4, pp. 448-472.

[9] Park, J. and Sandberg, I.W. (1991), "Universal approximation using radial-basis function," *Neural Computation*, vol. 3, pp. 246-257.

[10] Poggio, T. and Girosi, F. (1990), "Networks for approximation and learning," *Proceedings of IEEE*, vol. 78, pp. 1481-1497.

[11] Reed, R. (1993), "Pruning algorithms - a survey," *IEEE Transaction on Neural Networks*, vol. 4, pp. 740-747.

[12] Rissanen, J. (1978), "Modeling by shortest data description," *Automatica*, vol. 14, pp. 465-471.

[13] Rudin, W. (1978), *Principles of Mathematical Analysis*, Muszaki Kiado, Budapest (in Hungarian).

[14] Schölkpof, B., Burges, C.J.C., and Smola, A.J. (Eds.) (1999), *Advances in Kernel Methods. Support Vector Learning*, MIT Press, Cambridge, MA.

[15] Vapnik, V.N. (1995), *The Nature of Statistical Learning Theory*, Springer-Verlag, New York.

[16] Williams, P.M. (1995), "Bayesian regularization and pruning using a Laplace prior," *Neural Computation*, vol. 5, pp. 140-153.

Chapter 5

On Noise-Immune RBF Networks

S.-T. Li and E.L. Leiss

Radial basis function networks (RBFNs) have recently attracted interest, because of their advantages over multilayer perceptrons as they are universal approximators but achieve faster convergence since only one layer of weights is required. The least squares method is the most popularly used in estimating the synaptic weights which provides optimal results if the underlying error distribution is Gaussian. However, the generalization performance of the networks deteriorates for realistic noise whose distribution is either unknown or non-Gaussian; in particular, it becomes very bad if outliers are present. In this chapter, we propose high noise-immune RBFNs by applying the least trimmed squares approach in robust regression such that assumptions about or estimation of the error distribution are avoidable. The resulting network is capable of accommodating the tradeoff between requirements and robustness for outliers and efficiency for Gaussian noise. Moreover, given a training set and a fixed-complexity RBFN, we establish an upper bound of the percentage of gross errors characterized by the robustness that the network can tolerate. Comprehensive experimental results are illustrated and analyzed to validate the effectiveness of the proposed network. The superiority in controlling bias and variance of the network when gross errors are present is also demonstrated by conducting a simple Monte Carlo process.

1   Introduction

Radial basis function networks (RBFNs), introduced by Broomhead and Lowe [1], also known as networks with locally-tuned overlapping receptive fields [2], have increasingly attracted interest for engineering and business applications. RBFNs have salient features over traditional multilayer perceptrons, namely faster convergence, smaller extrapolation errors, less sensitivity to the order of presenting training data, and higher reliability against noisy data. More importantly, RBFNs having one hidden layer are capable of universal approximation [3]. The radial basis function network is a class of single hidden layer feedforward networks where the activation functions for hidden units are defined as radially symmetric basis functions φ such as the Gaussian function:

$$\varphi(r) = \exp\left(\frac{-r^2}{\sigma^2}\right). \tag{1}$$

Given an N_D-observation data set $D = \{(\mathbf{x}_i, y_i) \mid i = 1, \cdots, N_D\}$, an RBFN can be regarded as a function approximator which estimates an unknown functional mapping:

$$\lambda : \Re^{N_I} \to \Re \tag{2}$$

such that

$$y_i = \lambda(\mathbf{x}_i) + \varepsilon_i, \qquad i = 1, \cdots, N_D, \tag{3}$$

where λ is the regression function and the error term ε_i is a zero-mean random variable of disturbance.

Each hidden unit in an RBFN forms a localized receptive field in the input space X, whose centroid is located on $\mathbf{c}$. The fraction of overlap between each hidden unit and its neighbors is decided by the width σ so that a smooth interpolation over the input space is allowed. Therefore, unit i gives a maximal response for input stimuli close to $\mathbf{c}_i$. The hidden layer performs a nonlinear vector-valued mapping ϕ from the input space X to an N_H-dimensional "hidden" space Φ spanned by the transformed vector set $\{\phi(\mathbf{x}_i) \mid i = 1, \cdots, N_D\}$,

$$\phi(\mathbf{x}) : \Re^{N_I} \to \Re^{N_H} \tag{4}$$

such that

$$\phi(\mathbf{x}) = \left[\phi_1(\mathbf{x}), \cdots, \phi_{N_H}(\mathbf{x})\right]^T. \tag{5}$$

Each nonlinear basis function $\phi_i(\mathbf{x})$ is defined by some radial basis function φ

$$\phi_i(\mathbf{x}) = \varphi(\|\mathbf{x} - \mathbf{c}_i\|), \tag{6}$$

where $\|\cdot\|$ denotes the Euclidean norm on $\Re^{N_I}$.

The output layer performs a biased linear combination of the nonlinear basis function ϕ_i to generate the function approximation by $\hat{\lambda}$:

$$\hat{\lambda}(\mathbf{x}, D) = w_0 + \sum_{i=1}^{N_H} w_i \phi_i(\mathbf{x}). \tag{7}$$

In general, training RBFNs involves two phases [2]: the first phase is to apply self-organized learning (clustering) on the hidden layer to determine centroids $\mathbf{c}_i$ and width σ_i of all N_H receptive fields in the training data set. This phase plays a key role for achieving good approximation precision, where the choice of the RBFs is not crucial for the performance of networks [4]. One commonly used method in determining cluster centroids is the classic K-means algorithm which finds K receptive field centroids and assigns each data point to the cluster with the nearest centroid. One hidden unit is allocated for each fixed receptive field centroid. Once the cluster centroids are determined, the width of each cluster also needs to be established. By setting appropriate widths, a certain amount of overlap between each cluster and its neighbors can be achieved so that a smooth interpolation over those regions of the input space is allowed [2]. Therefore, each data point falling into a certain cluster has to activate more than one hidden unit to some degree. In other words, the width should be selected to be sufficiently small in order to keep the locality of receptive fields and to be large enough so that overlapping is allowed. One popular way of determining the width is to apply the p-nearest neighbor heuristic:

$$\sigma_i = \frac{1}{p}\left(\sum_{j=1}^{p} \|\mathbf{c}_i - \mathbf{c}_j\|^2\right)^{\frac{1}{2}}, \tag{8}$$

where the c_j are the p-nearest neighbors of the centroid i. In this work, $p = 2$ is assumed, as suggested in [2].

After determining the parameters of centroids and widths, supervised learning is applied to train the output layer to estimate the connection weights $\mathbf{w}$. Note that the output simply implements a multiple linear regression[1] and the objective of training is to minimize the average squared error (ASE), defined as follows:

$$\mathcal{E}_{ase}(\mathbf{w}) = \frac{1}{N_D} \sum_{i=1}^{N_D} \left(y_i - \hat{\lambda}(\mathbf{x}_i, \mathbf{w}) \right)^2 . \tag{9}$$

Due to its linearity in nature, this problem can be solved by applying the Singular Value Decomposition procedure or by iterative gradient descent methods like least mean squares (LMS)[2].

2   The Need for Noise-Immune RBFNs

Training RBFNs based on the LS method provides an asymptotically optimal solution with minimum variance under the assumption that the error distribution ε is identically independent and Gaussian. However, this assumption usually fails to hold in real-world applications since either *a priori* information about the error distribution is generally unavailable or the data are contaminated by non-Gaussian noise whereby some data points fall far outside of the majority of the data so that outliers are encountered. This leads to the problems of reliability and stability of an LS-based network since training RBFNs is interpolative in nature.

Outliers may be introduced in different ways. For example, in computer version, they may be the result of clutter, large measurement errors, or impulse noise corrupting the data [5]. In general, there are two kinds of outliers, namely, leverage points and vertical outliers. Leverage points (often called horizontal outliers) result from contamination in the input space X due to some of the inputs $\mathbf{x}$ failing to obey the environmental probability rule $p(\mathbf{x})$. Contamination in the output space Y leads to vertical outliers due to the output y failing to obey the conditional

---

[1] It will be a multivariate multiple linear regression if multi-output nodes are required.
[2] The plain RBFN is referred to as the LS-based network, henceforth.

probability rule $p(y \mid \mathbf{x})$. Both anomalies in the training set D may result in an aberrant and biased estimator since the RBFN is trained to fit these significant fluctuations by interpolation instead of approximating the underlying model in an attempt to compensate for outliers with least squared residuals. That is, the RBFN is greatly sensitive to the presence of outliers.

Without doubt, outliers corresponding to large residuals should be filtered out during the training process. The problem is, given an N_D-element observation set D and an RBFN with N_W weights, how can one decide what percentage of outlying observations should be filtered? Choosing this percentage too low can make the estimator tune to the gross errors in D (overfitting), whereas choosing the percentage too high may cause some good observations to be left out (loss of efficiency). Both situations will diminish the RBFN's generalization performance and training efficiency. Therefore, it is of great importance to justify a trade-off between robustness and efficiency and determine the upper bound of gross errors that RBFNs can handle.

In the past decades, the theory of robust regression has provided a sound basis for dealing with deviations from the general assumption on the distribution of errors; see for example [6] and [7]. A brief review of robust regression is given in the following section to establish the foundation of our work.

3   The Theory of Robust Estimates

According to [6] and [7], a robust estimator should be able to fit a regression to the majority of the data, detect the outliers which posses large residuals, and provide a bounded bias and variance estimate. Alternative robust estimators have been proposed based on different ways of evaluating their robustness, namely, influence function, break-down point, and efficiency.

The influence function ψ of an estimator gives a local accurate assessment of the influence of a single outlying observation. It is defined to be the first derivative of the loss function,

$$\psi(r) = \rho'(r). \tag{10}$$

Generally, the robustness of an estimator can be ensured by defining a bounded and continuous influence function. It is easy to see that the LS method is not robust owing to the use of an unbounded influence function. Determining a precise form of the loss function (and hence its influence function) is crucial for obtaining a satisfactory estimation since it provides a meaningful measure of error distribution due to the estimation result. However, selecting an appropriate loss function is in turn dependent on the error distribution. This leads to a "catch22" problem as discussed in [8].

In contrast, the breakdown point of an estimator, without being confined to any assumed distribution of errors, gives a global measure of stability in terms of the fraction of outlying data it can tolerate. Clearly, the maximal breakdown point of a robust estimator is about 50% since there is no way to distinguish uncontaminated data from gross errors beyond it. The higher the breakdown point is, the more robustness the estimator achieves. The least trimmed squares (LTS) approach, proposed by Rousseeuw and Leroy, is one of estimators having the highest possible breakdown point [7]. The LTS estimator only considers the sum of the smallest ordered squared residuals up to the rank h,

$$\min_{\theta} \sum_{i=1}^{h} r_{(i)}^2 , \qquad (11)$$

where $r_{(1)}^2 \leq \cdots \leq r_{(h)}^2 \leq \cdots \leq r_{(n)}^2$ are obtained by squaring the residuals first, and then ordering them.

Finally, most robust estimators provide a conservative approach to enhancing the robustness against outliers at the price of low efficiency under minor Gaussian perturbations.

4   The Noise-Immunity of RBFNs

In this work, we adopt the approach of breakdown point to deal with the presence of gross errors. The ultimate goal is to develop a high noise-immune RBFN. For this, a formal definition of finite sample noise-immunity for RBFNs is defined as follows [7]:

Definition 1 Given an N_D-element training set D, the finite sample noise-immunity ξ^* of an estimator $\hat{\lambda}$ defined by an RBFN is

$$\xi^*_{RBFN}(\hat{\lambda}, D) = \min_{\kappa}\left\{\frac{\kappa}{N_D}\middle| B_{max}(\kappa; \hat{\lambda}, D, \mathbf{u}) = \infty\right\}, \tag{12}$$

where

$$B_{max}(\kappa; \hat{\lambda}, D, \mathbf{u}) = \sup_{D'}\left|\hat{\lambda}(\mathbf{u}, D') - \hat{\lambda}(\mathbf{u}, D)\right| \tag{13}$$

is the maximal bias for any fixed input $\mathbf{u}$ in D, taken over all possible contaminated data sets D' obtained by replacing any κ of the good data in D by arbitrarily large values. $\hat{\lambda}(\mathbf{u}, D')$ is the estimator based on D'.

Remark 1 Definition 1 states that ξ^*_{RBFN} is the smallest fraction of outliers that can make $\left|\hat{\lambda}(\mathbf{u}, D')\right|$ unbounded. In other words, the maximal number of gross errors that can be handled by RBFN is $\kappa - 1$.

In this definition, one can choose which observations are replaced, as well as the magnitude of the outliers, in the least favorable way. One notes that the noise-immunity does not depend on the distribution of good observations since there is no probability distribution involved in this definition. From the definition, it can be seen that RBFNs are noise-immune against horizontal outliers since RBFs are bounded in general.

Theorem 1 RBFNs are noise immune against any number of horizontal outliers (that is, where the $\mathbf{x}_i$ are being replaced while the corresponding y_i remain fixed).

Proof: It suffices to show that $\left|\hat{\lambda}(\mathbf{u}, D')\right|$ at a fixed input point $\mathbf{u}$ in D cannot exceed all bounds when all data $(\kappa = N_D)$ in D are contaminated by arbitrarily large horizontal outliers (the worst case).

Let $D' = \{(\mathbf{x}_i + \mathbf{d}_i, y_i) \mid i = 1, \cdots, N_D\}$ be any possible corrupted set of D, where $\mathbf{d}_i$ is an N_I-dimensional vector with arbitrarily large real number components.

Then $D'_X = \{(\mathbf{x}_i + \mathbf{d}_i) \mid i = 1, \cdots, N_D\}$ constructs an entirely different feature space far away from the original one spanned by $D_X = \{\mathbf{x}_i \mid i = 1, \cdots, N_D\}$ and hence a new layout of receptive fields is formed with new centroids $\mathbf{c}'_i$ and widths σ'_i.

Because of the limited width σ'_i of each receptive field[3], the responses from all receptive fields created by D'_X are nearly zero for any point $\mathbf{u}$ in D_X, i.e.,

$$\forall i, \quad 1 \le i \le N'_H, \quad \phi'_i(\mathbf{u}) = \exp\left(-\frac{\|\mathbf{u} - \mathbf{c}'_i\|^2}{(\sigma'_i)^2}\right) \tag{14}$$

$$\approx 0.$$

Therefore,

$$\hat{\lambda}(\mathbf{u}, D') = w'_0 + \sum_{i=1}^{N'_H} w'_i \phi'_i(\mathbf{u}) \tag{15}$$

$$\approx w'_0,$$

where w'_0 is the weight between the output and bias units in the new network learning from D'.

From this, we conclude that $\left|\hat{\lambda}(\mathbf{u}, D') - \hat{\lambda}(\mathbf{u}, D)\right|$ cannot take on arbitrarily large values. □

RBFNs are noise-immune against horizontal outliers; however, they do diminish the approximation accuracy because significant residuals are produced. In the general case in which moderate horizontal outliers occur in D, the impact of such outliers will depend on the fields where they scatter. If they are scattered in other existing fields, the approximation results in such fields are interpolated except that the number of correct data in the fields is comparatively large. On the other hand, if outliers are sufficient to form a separate cluster, the prediction result at the uncontaminated data point close to that cluster will be misled as shown in the above proof.

In contrast to horizontal outliers, RBFNs are greatly sensitive to vertical outliers, due to the linear combinations in the output layer.

---

[3] assuming σ'_i is suitably defined and is not arbitrarily large.

Theorem 2 The noise-immunity ξ^*_{RBFN} based on the LS method is $1/N_D$ in the presence of vertical outliers.

Proof: It is clear that $\left|\hat{\lambda}(\mathbf{u}, D')\right|$ will be forced outside an arbitrary range for any

$$D' = \{(\mathbf{x}_l, y_l + d)\} \cup \{(\mathbf{x}_i, y_i)| i = 1, \cdots, N_D, \ i \neq l\} \qquad (16)$$

obtained by altering one observation (say, the l-th observation) in the original set D with an arbitrary value d.

Then the residual at $\mathbf{x}_l$

$$\begin{aligned} \left|r_l^1\right| &= \left|y_l - (y_l + d)\right| \\ &= \left|d\right| \end{aligned} \qquad (17)$$

leads $\|\mathbf{w}\|$ to be out-of-bound[4]. Therefore, a single outlier in any possible set D' can make the estimator $\hat{\lambda}$ wrong, *i.e.*,

$$\left|\hat{\lambda}(\mathbf{u}, D') - \hat{\lambda}(\mathbf{u}, D)\right| = \infty, \qquad (18)$$

assuming that $\mathbf{u}$ is in the same cluster as the l-th point in D.   □

One notes that this noise-immunity goes asymptotically to 0, reflecting the extreme sensitivity of RBFNs to vertical outliers.

5   High Noise-Immune RBF Networks

In order to keep RBFNs robust against vertical outliers and improve the approximation accuracy in the presence of horizontal outliers, the least trimmed squares (LTS) method [7], known as an estimator with the highest possible breakdown point, is applied in estimating weights in the output layer. This results in a high noise immune RBFN, R^2BFN. Instead of minimizing the average of all squares residuals, R^2BFN only considers the average of the smallest ordered squared residuals up to the rank q by minimizing the cost function of the average-trimmed-squared error (ATSE):

---

[4] Recall that, for the least squares method, weight updates are proportional to residuals.

$$\mathcal{E}_{atse}(\mathbf{w}) = \tfrac{1}{2}\sum_{i=1}^{q} r_{(i)}^2 , \tag{19}$$

where $r_i = y_i - \hat{\lambda}_i$ and $r_{(1)}^2 \leq \cdots \leq r_{(q)}^2 \leq \cdots \leq r_{(N_D)}^2$ are ordered squared residuals and q is the number of residuals that needs to be taken into account at the true weight vector $\mathbf{w}$.

Selecting an appropriate q is definitely of crucial importance. Choosing this number too high can cause the estimator to overfit whereas choosing the number too low may cause loss of efficiency. Differing from [9], where $q \approx N_D/2$ is used, the capability of R^2BFN in handling outliers indicated by its noise-immunity is related to finite resources, i.e., the finite number of data and weights imposed on the network [10]. Before deriving the noise-immunity ξ^* and the optimal q for R^2BFN, we first give the original theorem for the LTS estimator and the definition of general position [7].

Theorem 3 (Rousseeuw & Leroy) Consider the linear regression model:

$$Y = X_1\theta_1 + X_2\theta_2 + \cdots + X_m\theta_m + \varepsilon \tag{20}$$

in terms of the observed data, the model is

$$Y_i = X_{i1}\theta_1 + X_{i2}\theta_2 + \cdots + X_{im}\theta_m + \varepsilon_i \quad \text{for } i = 1;\cdots,n. \tag{21}$$

If any subset of m vectors in the set $Z_X = \{[X_{i1};\cdots,X_{im}] \mid i = 1;\cdots,n\}$ is linearly independent, i.e., any m-element subset in the observation set $Z = \{([X_{i1};\cdots,X_{im}], Y_i) \mid i = 1;\cdots,n\}$ determines a unique nonvertical hyperplane in the $(m+1)$-dimensional space spanned by observations in Z or uniquely determines an estimate θ, the LTS estimator reaches its best possible breakdown point

$$\frac{\left\lfloor \dfrac{n-m}{2} \right\rfloor + 1}{n} \quad \text{when} \quad h = \left\lfloor \dfrac{n}{2} \right\rfloor + \left\lfloor \dfrac{m+1}{2} \right\rfloor,^5$$

where m is the number of parameters in the model.

---

[5] (see Equation (11))

Remark 2 The following is an obvious generalization of the model in Equation (20) with an intercept term θ_0,

$$Y = X_1\theta_1 + X_2\theta_2 + \cdots + X_m\theta_m + \theta_0 + \varepsilon. \tag{22}$$

The new model achieves the breakdown point of

$$\frac{\left\lfloor \dfrac{n-(m+1)}{2} \right\rfloor + 1}{n} \quad \text{when} \quad h = \left\lfloor \dfrac{n}{2} \right\rfloor + \left\lfloor \dfrac{(m+1)+1}{2} \right\rfloor$$

as long as any $|m+1|$ rows in the design matrix

$$\begin{bmatrix} X_{11} & \cdots & X_{1m} & 1 \\ \vdots & \ddots & \vdots & \vdots \\ X_{n1} & \cdots & X_{nm} & 1 \end{bmatrix} \tag{23}$$

will uniquely determine $\theta_1, \cdots, \theta_m, \theta_0$.[6]

Therefore, the definition of general position is given as follows.

Definition 2 Let $D_X = \{[x_{i1}; \cdots, x_{iN_I}]^T \mid i = 1; \cdots, N_D\}$ be a set of N_I-dimensional vectors $(N_D > N_I)$. The set D_X is said to be in general position if and only if no subset of N_I+1 points lies on an affine hyperplane.[7]

The concept of general position can be extended to Φ space without loss of generality by following [11]:

Definition 3 Given the vector set D_X defined previously, let ϕ be the vector-valued measurement function which maps each x in the N_I-dimensional input space X into the N_H-dimensional Φ space such that $\phi(x) = [\phi_1(x); \cdots, \phi_{N_H}(x)]^T$. Then D_X is in ϕ-general position in X space if there is no ϕ surface in the pattern space containing N_H+1 or more vectors of D_X.

---

[6] That is, any $|m+1|$ rows are linearly independent, or equivalently there is no subset of $m+1$ vectors in Z_X which lie on an $(m-1)$-dimensional hyperplane.

[7] An affaine hyperplane is a subspace of dimension $N_I - 1$ translated over an arbitrary vector, so it needs not pass through zero.

With the concepts of general position and ϕ-general position and using Theorem 3, the noise-immunity and the optimality of q for R^2BFNs can be stated as follows.

Theorem 4 If the N_D-element set D_X is in ϕ-general position in X space, R^2BFN reaches its optimal noise-immunity given by

$$\xi^*_{R^2BFN}(\hat{\lambda}, D) = \frac{\left\lfloor \dfrac{\left| N_D - N_W \right|}{2} \right\rfloor + 1}{N_D} \tag{24}$$

when

$$q = \left\lfloor \frac{N_D}{2} \right\rfloor + \left\lfloor \frac{N_W + 1}{2} \right\rfloor,$$

where $N_W = N_H + 1$ is the number of weights including the one between the biased unit and the output unit.

Proof: It is obvious that the training process of R^2BFNs involving estimating the weights between the hidden and the output layers is essentially the same as the special model as shown in Remark 2. Therefore, one has only to prove that the corresponding N_D-element set, $D_H = \{\phi(\mathbf{x}_i) \mid i = 1; \cdots, N_D\}$, is in general position in Φ space. This argument is implicit in Definition 3 which states that every $(N_H + 1) \times (N_H + 1)$ submatrix of the $(N_H + 1) \times N_D$ matrix

$$\begin{bmatrix} \phi_1(\mathbf{x}_1) & \phi_1(\mathbf{x}_2) & \cdots & \phi_1(\mathbf{x}_{N_D}) \\ \phi_2(\mathbf{x}_1) & \phi_2(\mathbf{x}_2) & \cdots & \phi_2(\mathbf{x}_{N_D}) \\ \vdots & \vdots & \ddots & \vdots \\ \phi_{N_H}(\mathbf{x}_1) & \phi_{N_H}(\mathbf{x}_2) & \cdots & \phi_{N_H}(\mathbf{x}_{N_D}) \\ 1 & 1 & \cdots & 1 \end{bmatrix} \tag{25}$$

has a nonzero determinant. Matrix (25) can be interpreted so that the vector set D_H is in general position in Φ space. In other words, if the set D_X is in ϕ-general position in X, the corresponding set D_H is in general position in Φ space. Figure 1 illustrates this concept. Thus, the noise-immunity of $\xi^*_{R^2BFN}(\hat{\lambda}, D)$ in X space will be equal to the one of LTS in the Φ surface, as expressed in Remark 2. $\square$

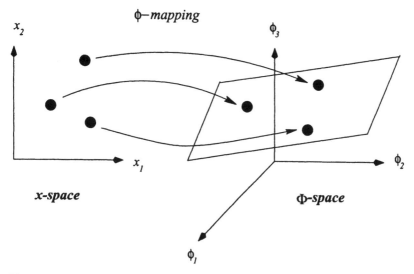

Figure 1. Points that are in general position in Φ-space are also in ϕ-general position in X-space since Φ-space is spanned by $\{\phi(\mathbf{x}_i)\,|\,i = 1;\cdots,N_D\}$ and continuous Gaussian radial units are used.

Remark 3 From the definition of noise-immunity, Theorem 4 indicates that the upper bound of the fraction of arbitrarily large vertical outliers that R^2BFN can withstand is

$$\frac{\left\lfloor \dfrac{N_D - N_W}{2} \right\rfloor}{N_D}.$$

In other words, at least[8]

$$\left\lfloor \frac{N_D + N_W + 1}{2} \right\rfloor$$

training data should be uncontaminated by arbitrarily large outliers in order to keep the estimator from failing. Note that q is the largest number of residuals that need to be considered during training since

$$\left\lfloor \frac{N_D}{2} \right\rfloor + \left\lfloor \frac{N_W + 1}{2} \right\rfloor \le \left\lfloor \frac{N_D + N_W + 1}{2} \right\rfloor.$$

---

[8] $N_D - \left\lfloor \dfrac{N_D - N_W}{2} \right\rfloor = \left\lfloor \dfrac{N_D + N_W + 1}{2} \right\rfloor$

It is worth noting that for the problem of function approximation in which the components of input vectors are in general generated from a continuous random distribution, with probability 1 the set D_X will be in general position. Furthermore, due to the use of continuous Gaussian radial units, the event that D_X is in ϕ-general position also has probability 1 [12]. However, the condition of general position is often violated for binary inputs, redundant observations, and sparsity of inputs, which lead to D_X being in reduced position [13]. A new robust estimator, the so-called D-estimator, has been recently proposed for dealing with this case [13].

6   Adaptive Noise-Immune RBFNs

The training of R^2BNFs can be performed by the standard steepest descent method since ordering squared residuals is required to decide what proportion needs to be involved in weight updating. That is, the weight update is following the negative direction of the weight gradient:

$$\Delta \mathbf{w} = -\eta \nabla_w \mathcal{E}_{atse}(\mathbf{w}) = -\eta \frac{\partial \mathcal{E}_{atse}(\mathbf{w})}{\partial \mathbf{w}}, \tag{26}$$

where η is the learning rate. The weight between output unit j and hidden unit i is thus updated by

$$\Delta w_{ji} = \eta \sum_{k=1}^{q} r_j^{(k)} \phi_i^{(k)}, \tag{27}$$

where $r_j^{(k)} = \left(y_j^{(k)} - \hat{\lambda}_j^{(k)} \right)$ is the k-th smallest squared residual and $\phi_i^{(k)}$ is the corresponding output of hidden unit i.

To assess the learning performance, the popular criterion normalized root-mean-squared error (NRMSE) is calculated on the training set D:

$$NRMSE_{train}(\mathbf{w}) = \sqrt{\frac{\sum_{i=1}^{N_D} \left(y_i - \hat{\lambda}(\mathbf{x}_i, \mathbf{w}) \right)^2}{\sum_{i=1}^{N_D} (y_i - E[y])^2}}, \tag{28}$$

where $E[\cdot]$ is the expectation operator over the set D. $NRMSE_{test}$ is similarly defined on an uncontaminated N_V-element validation set V independently constructed for measuring the generalization capability of networks. The measurement $NRMSE_{test}$ is more useful than the former one in evaluating the learning achievement since V is clean.

As mentioned earlier, a satisfactory robust estimator should be able to mitigate the relative instability in the presence of small fluctuations as well as protect it against gross errors. However, there is a conflict between achieving these goals. The LTS method has been shown to suffer from low efficiency when the errors are really normally distributed [7]. In addition, the overhead of additional computation time for ordering the squared residuals takes $O(N_D \log N_D)$. Therefore, it is desirable to modify the R^2BF learning rule to effect a tradeoff between efficiency and robustness. Moreover the objective function for the LTS method, as for most high breakdown estimators is non-convex and can have several local minima [14]. In this work, two modifications have been adopted that result in a new learning rule, namely the adaptive R^2BF learning rule (AR^2BF rule for short).

First, in order to reduce the sorting overhead, the task of training is accelerated by a "normalized" steepest descent method, called ABP, proposed in [15]. By defining the learning rate η as a specific function of $\mathcal{E}_{atse}$ and introducing a gradient norm term

$$\left\| \frac{\partial \mathcal{E}_{atse}(\mathbf{w})}{\partial \mathbf{w}} \right\|^2,$$

the ABP method has been shown to result in improved performance in terms of learning speed and probability of convergence without adding more "tuning" parameters [15]. Our AR^2BF rule adopts the following weight update rule:

$$\Delta \mathbf{w} = -\eta \frac{\partial \mathcal{E}_{atse}}{\partial \mathbf{w}} \left/ \left\| \frac{\partial \mathcal{E}_{atse}}{\partial \mathbf{w}} \right\|^2 \right. . \tag{29}$$

The overhead of sorting can also be reduced by ordering residuals every few epochs, say 5, as proposed in [9]. This is based on the assumption that the q-pattern associated with the lowest residuals will remain the same over these epochs. Experimental simulation results show that the generalization quality is not very sensitive to this number as long as it is not chosen too large.

Second, the efficiency of the R^2BF rule when small perturbations are encountered can be improved by adaptively adjusting the number of residuals contributing to weight updates q. This is inspired by the observation that the more training data are involved in the beginning of training, the quicker the network can fit the underlying model [10]. Unlike the R^2BF rule, in which a specific value of q is fixed during training, the AR^2BF rule updates q at time t according to the following rule:

$$q(t+1) = \lfloor \tau(t)N_D \rfloor + \lfloor (1-\tau(t))(N_W + 1) \rfloor, \tag{30}$$

where $\tau \in [\frac{1}{2},1]$ is a free parameter that determines the proportion of observations involved in error backpropagation.

Therefore, a natural learning strategy, "fit-then-trim,"is adopted by the AR^2BF rule in which τ is a function of $NRMSE_{test}$, since it keeps track of the generalization ability of the network:

$$\tau(e) = 0.5\exp\left(-\frac{v}{e^2}\right) + 0.5, \tag{31}$$

where v is a small positive real number and e is NRMSE. At the very beginning of training, $\tau \approx 1$ due to large NRMSEs; if this were maintained constant, it would degenerate to the traditional RBF rule. On the other hand, if smaller NRMSEs are achieved, τ goes to $\frac{1}{2}$; a non-adaptive R^2BF rule based on the classic LTS method is obtained. Figure 2 compares the impact of different values for v on τ and suggests that before the network fits the underlying data trend implied by larger NRMSEs, it requires more training data to participate in training indicated by larger τ.

7   Experimental Results and Analysis

A number of experiments have been conducted to evaluate the effectiveness and stability against the presence of outliers for the proposed AR^2BFN. Experimental results using the aforementioned learning rules, namely RBF, R^2BF, and AR^2BF, on the problems of one-dimensional and two-dimensional function approximation are discussed in this section.

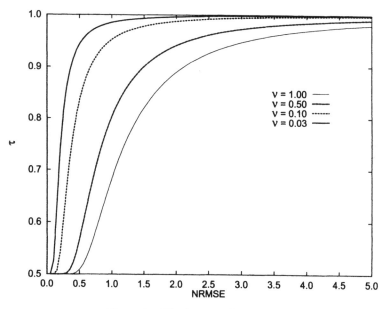

Figure 2.   The impact of v on τ.

7.1   One-Dimensional Function Approximation

First, we analyze various results on nonlinear one-dimensional function approximation in the presence of vertical outliers. The target function (regression function) to be estimated is

$$y = \sin(\pi x), \qquad x \in [-1, 1]. \tag{32}$$

The training set D and validation set V are composed of 31 points and 60 points evenly sampled from $[-1,1]$, respectively. For simplicity, the optimal complexity degree of networks is determined empirically with the number of hidden units being $N_H = 15$. Therefore, from Theorem 4,

$$\xi^*_{R^2 BFN}(\hat{\lambda}, D) = 0.290$$

when $q = 23$. In other words, the maximal number of outliers in D that the R^2BFN can handle is 7. The centroids $\mathbf{c}$ and their associated width σ are determined by k-means clustering on D and two-nearest neighbor heuristic, respectively. Then, 1-15-1 networks are trained by these learning rules with the same initial weights and learning rate for each error model.

7.1.1   Vertical Outliers

In order to bring in realistic vertical outliers, the error distribution is assumed to be the Cauchy distribution with location 0 and scale 0.1. Figure 3 illustrates the evolution of the $NRMSE_{train}$ and $NRMSE_{test}$ during training for RBF and AR^2BF rules, in which the "jumpy" behavior of the curves indicates that a local or global minimum is approached [15]. All curves drop sharply in the beginning, indicating that both networks have quickly tuned to the underlying trend in the data. One notes that the NRMSE curve on the test data for AR^2BFN consistently decreases because doubtful outliers are being filtered out. Obviously, RBFN converges with a higher NRMSE which reflects a poorer generalization performance.

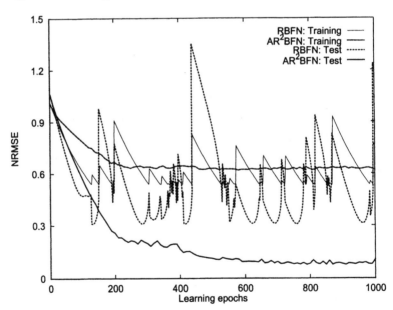

Figure 3.   Learning curves of the RBF and AR^2BF networks in the presence of vertical outliers, where $\eta = 0.05$ and $v = 0.06$.

The comparison of the generalization performances for both networks is depicted in Figure 4, where the training data are severely corrupted. One can see that the curve shape predicted by the RBFN is pulled toward the larger outliers due to the interpolative character of the network. On the other hand, seven major outliers having larger residuals have been successfully trimmed by the AR^2BFN.

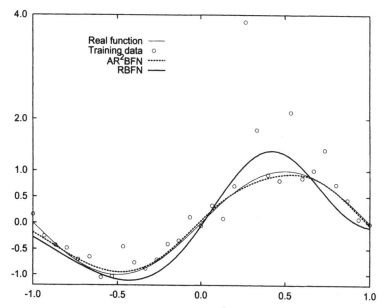

Figure 4. The contrast of the RBF and AR^2BF networks in generalization performance when vertical outliers are encountered.

As mentioned before, one motivation for developing AR^2BFN is the need for relieving the computational overhead for ordering residuals. Figure 5 shows that a decent speedup is made possible by AR^2BFN. One conjecture related to AR^2BFN is that the sooner the learning process gets fitted to the underlying curve, the more efficiency it can achieve. This is because the source of residuals cannot be identified prior to the sharp drop, and hence more training data will speed up the training process. Figure 6 depicts the evolution of the number of training data q, involved in training AR^2BFN. Compared to AR^2BFN, with more observations contributing to learning in the first 190 epochs, AR^2BFN achieves faster convergence. This approach is also different from [8], where an *ad hoc* approach was adopted in the initial estimation.[9]

---

[9] For example, an absolute number of learning epochs, say 1000, is required for the initial estimation.

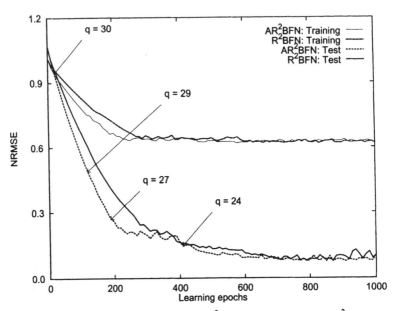

Figure 5.   The learning speed of the AR^2BFN in contrast to the R^2BFN.

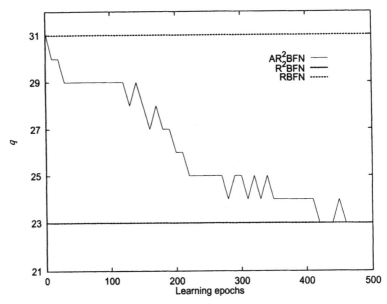

Figure 6.   The evolution of the number of training data involved in error backpropagation during training.

In order to take into account the influence of the parameter v which indirectly affects the learning epochs required, ten independent runs were carried out for each value of v considered. Table 1 illustrates the statistics for each case corresponding to the average, best, worst performance and associated standard deviation on the experiment of horizontal outliers. All trials are based on the 1-15-1 network structure and the same learning rate, $\eta = 0.05$. This comparison indicates that $v = 0.06$ has fewer average learning epochs and is more stable although the overall differences for the various values are small. Indeed, a suitable range between 0.005 and 0.4 is empirically suggested since the normalized performance criterion, NRMSE, is used. All experiments henceforth to be discussed are based on the value of v empirically determined.

Table 1.   The influence of v on the learning epochs required.

v	Learning Epochs			
	Mean	Best	Worst	Std. Dev.
1.00	918	785	1040	70.98
0.50	988	830	1335	181.95
0.10	893	785	1020	88.82
0.08	870	710	1130	116.01
0.06	764	725	815	39.80
0.04	724	650	820	56.70

7.1.2   Gaussian Noise

The proposed AR^2BFN and R^2BFN, as do most robust estimators, come at the expense of the loss of efficiency and relative instability in the presence of Gaussian noise or small fluctuations, such as rounding errors. Therefore, it is not surprising that RBFN converges faster than AR^2BFN in the presence of small perturbations as shown in Figure 7, where the error model is assumed to be N(0, 0.01). The loss of efficiency for AR^2BFN is due to the fact that some good data points have unavoidably been left out. On the other hand, AR^2BFN has demonstrated a significant improvement in learning speed and stability over R^2BFN (see Figure 8). This is because more useful sample points (representing information) have been definitely discarded by R^2BFN, therefore more epochs are needed to compensate for such a loss. Finally, as expected, the generalization performance of AR^2BFN is as good as that of RBFN; this is shown in Figure 9.

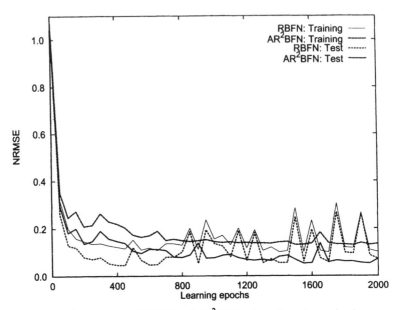

Figure 7. Learning curves of RBFN and AR^2BFN when Gaussian noise is present.

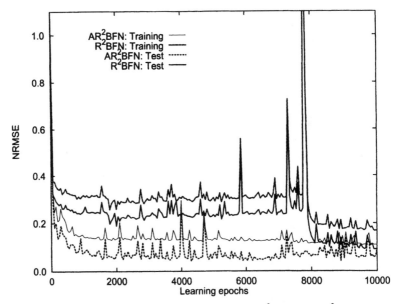

Figure 8. The comparison of learning speed for AR^2BFN and R^2BFN in the presence of Gaussian noise.

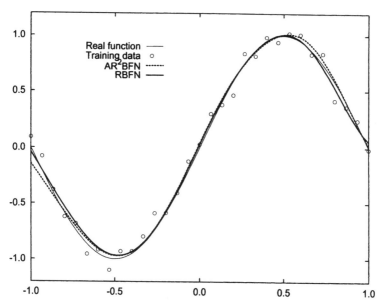

Figure 9.   The contrast of RBFN and AR^2BFN in generalization performance when Gaussian noise $N(0, 0.01)$ is encountered.

7.2   Two-Dimensional Function Approximation

In this experiment, the two dimensional function

$$y = \frac{4x_1 x_2}{4(x_1^2 + x_2^2) + 0.1} + 0.05 \qquad (33)$$

is approximated by AR^2BFN to illustrate the validity of the proposed learning rule for more complicated problems. The training set D and the evaluation set V are constructed by evenly spaced 35×35 and 36×36 grids on [−0.5, 0.5] × [−0.5, 0.5], respectively. In order to investigate the impact of vertical outliers on clusters (local receptive fields), eight synthetic outliers are injected into a corner of the original surface (see Figure 10).

The network is trained with the topology 2-140-1 determined empirically, initial weights randomly selected from [−0.1, 0.1], and a learning rate $\eta = 0.005$. All residuals are ordered after every 10 epochs and $v = 0.006$ is used. Figures 11 and 13 show the reconstructed surface and its corresponding residual surface by the plain RBF network, while Figures 12 and 14 depict the results by the proposed AR^2BF network. One notes that the significant residuals resulting from the synthetic outliers have only local impact on the approximation result as radial basis function networks are locally tuned in nature.

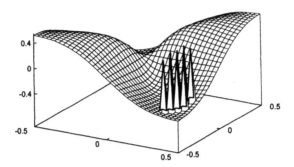

Figure 10.   The original surface contaminated by eight synthetic outliers.

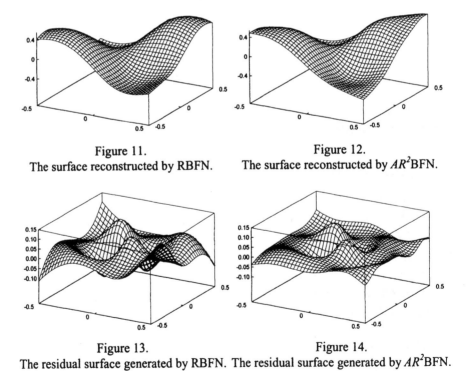

Figure 11.   Figure 12.
The surface reconstructed by RBFN.   The surface reconstructed by AR^2BFN.

Figure 13.   Figure 14.
The residual surface generated by RBFN. The residual surface generated by AR^2BFN.

7.3   Controlling Bias and Variance by AR^2BFN

The aim of training RBFNs is to obtain an appropriate estimator $\hat{\lambda}$ so that the discrepancy between the desired and predicted responses over all inputs in D is minimized. It is obvious that different fixed-size training sets yield different estimation results due to the stochastic error term ε in the sense that $\mathbf{w}$ is determined by the training set D; thus $\hat{\lambda}(\mathbf{x},\mathbf{w})$ can be rewritten as $\hat{\lambda}(\mathbf{x},\mathbf{w}(D))$. Therefore, the amount by which the average estimator differs from the regression function λ at a specific input $\mathbf{x}$ is the bias of the estimator $\hat{\lambda}(\mathbf{x}, D)$ at $\mathbf{x}$ [16]:

$$E_D\big[\hat{\lambda}(\mathbf{x},D)\big] - \lambda(\mathbf{x}) \tag{34}$$

while the variation among different estimators is the variance of the estimator $\hat{\lambda}$:

$$E_D\left[\big(\hat{\lambda}(\mathbf{x},D) - E_D\big[\hat{\lambda}(\mathbf{x},D)\big]\big)^2\right], \tag{35}$$

where E_D is the average over the ensemble of possible D with fixed size N_D. It has been established that both terms contribute to the mean-squared error (MSE) of $\hat{\lambda}$ [16] as an estimator of the regression function λ in Equation (3):

$$E_D\left[\big(\hat{\lambda}(\mathbf{x},D) - \lambda(\mathbf{x})\big)^2\right] =$$
$$\big(E_D\big[\hat{\lambda}(\mathbf{x},D)\big] - \lambda(\mathbf{x})\big)^2 + E_D\left[\big(\hat{\lambda}(\mathbf{x},D) - E_D\big[\hat{\lambda}(\mathbf{x},D)\big]\big)^2\right]. \tag{36}$$

Consequently, a single vertical outlier in any possible D is sufficient to result in a high bias and high variance estimator $\hat{\lambda}$ (since the $E_D[\hat{\lambda}(\mathbf{x}, D)]$ term may exceed any bound) and hence causes MSE to exceed any bound.

In order to demonstrate that AR^2BFN is capable of controlling both bias and variance when gross errors are present, we carry out a simple Monte Carlo process, similar to [16], on a one-dimensional function approximation. For simplicity, 20 independent contaminated training sets $D'_1, D'_2, \cdots, D'_{20}$ are generated from the regression model

$$y_i = \lambda(x_i) + \varepsilon_i, \qquad i = 1, ..., 31, \tag{37}$$

where x is evenly sampled over $[-1,1]$ and ε is Cauchy-distributed noise with location 0 and scale 0.1. $\lambda(x)$ is the regression function; it is $\sin(\pi x)$ in this simulation. Figure 15 plots the scatter diagrams for the 20 contaminated sets. The corresponding estimators formed by training the networks with these data sets are denoted by $\hat{\lambda}(x, D'_1); \cdot\cdot \ \hat{\lambda}(x, D'_{20})$. A clean 60-element validation set V is similarly constructed, without noise. The network topology and learning rate are empirically determined to be 1-15-1 and 0.01.

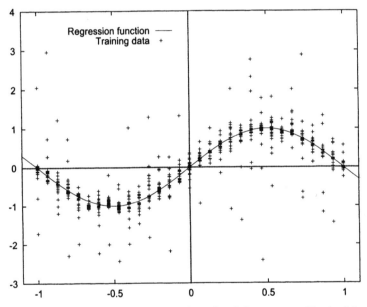

Figure 15.   The scatter plot of 20 contaminated training sets used in the Monte Carlo simulation.

The average response on input x is $E_{D'}[\hat{\lambda}(x, D')]$, which can be approximated by the function

$$\bar{\lambda}(x) = \frac{1}{20}\sum_{i=1}^{20} \hat{\lambda}(x, D'_i). \tag{38}$$

Then the estimated bias of $\hat{\lambda}$ at x indicating the disagreement between the average and the regression function is

$$\text{Bias}(x) = E_{D'}\left[\hat{\lambda}(x, D')\right] - \lambda(x)$$

$$\approx \bar{\lambda}(x) - \lambda(x).$$
(39)

On the other hand, the estimated variance of $\hat{\lambda}$ at x measuring the average difference among the 20 estimators is

$$\text{Variance}(x) = E_{D'}\left[\left(\hat{\lambda}(x, D') - E_{D'}\left[\hat{\lambda}(x, D')\right]\right)^2\right]$$

$$\approx \frac{1}{20}\sum_{i=1}^{20}\left(\hat{\lambda}(x, D_i') - \bar{\lambda}(x)\right)^2.$$
(40)

For comparison, the bias and variance indicated by standard deviation at each input x for $\hat{\lambda}_{RBFN}$ and $\hat{\lambda}_{AR^2BFN}$ are illustrated in Figures 16 and 17. The small circle in each error bar denotes the average response at that point x; the distance between this circle and the regression function is the bias for the estimator at the point; the error bar itself stands for the standard deviation of the estimator. It is obvious that the proposed AR^2BFN is superior in controlling the bias and variance in the presence of gross errors. It is worth mentioning that the larger variance for $\hat{\lambda}_{AR^2BFN}$ appearing close to both ends of the curve is fairly common for all network estimators. On the other hand, the RBFN estimator exhibits high variance but moderately controlled bias due to its interpolative nature and the Cauchy error distribution with location 0.

8   Conclusions

The work presented in this chapter is motivated by the need for developing a noise-immune RBFN that can handle more realistic noise in which outliers or gross errors may occur. Unlike most studies in robust learning in which the robustness requirement is attained by defining a globally bounded influence function, we adopt the breakdown point approach in developing noise-immune RBFNs such that neither *a priori* information about the error distribution nor estimating it is required. We propose a robust learning algorithm based on the least trimmed squares method in order to improve the robustness; as a result, a high noise-immune RBFN (R^2BFN) is obtained.

Furthermore, we bound the maximal number of outliers in terms of the number of training data and synaptic weights that R^2BFN can tolerate.

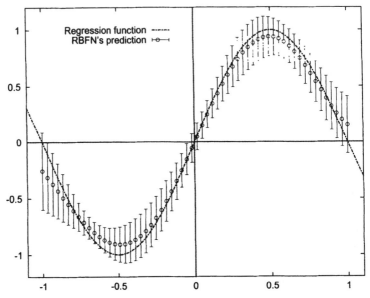

Figure 16. The bias and variance indicated by its standard deviation at each point x for the estimator RBFN.

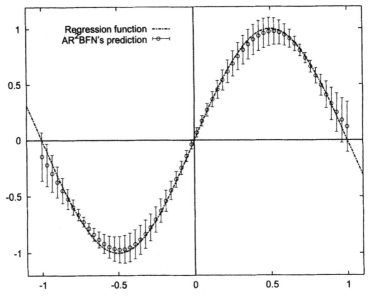

Figure 17. The bias and variance at each point x for the estimator AR^2BFN.

We further take into account the issues of efficiency and stability in the presence of Gaussian noise or minor errors; they constitute the price of robust estimators. For this, we derive an adaptive robust learning rule by applying a normalized steepest descent technique which allows faster convergence and higher probability in escaping local minima. We conduct extensive experiments on function approximation and compare the resulting network, AR^2BFN, with the plain RBFN and R^2BFN from the viewpoint of learning speed and generalization performance for diverse outliers. In this way, we show the superiority of AR^2BFN in noise-immunity, efficiency, and stability over similar models. We also perform a simple Monte Carlo simulation to confirm the ability of AR^2BFN in controlling variance and bias.

References

[1] Broomhead, D.S. and Lowe, D. (1988), "Multivariable functional interpolation and adaptive networks," *Complex Systems*, vol. 2, pp. 321-355.

[2] Moody, J.E. and Darken, C.J. (1989), "Fast learning in networks of locally-tuned processing units," *Neural Computation*, vol. 1, pp. 281-294.

[3] Park, J. and Sandberg, I.W. (1991), "Universal approximation using radial-basis function networks," *Neural Computation*, vol. 3, pp. 246-257.

[4] Powell, M.J.D. (1987), "Radial basis function approximations to polynomials," *Proceedings of the 12th Biennial Numerical Analysis Conference*, pp. 223-241.

[5] Meer, P., Mintz, D., Rosenfeld, A., and Kim, D.Y. (1991), "Robust regression methods for computer vision: a review," *International Journal of Computer Vision*, vol. 6, pp. 59-70.

[6] Hampel, F.R., Ronchetti, E.M., Rousseeuw, P.J., and Stahel, W.A. (1986), *Robust Statistics: the Approach Based on Influence Functions*, John Wiley & Sons, New York, NY.

[7] Rousseeuw, P.J. and Leroy, A.M. (1987), *Robust Regression and Outlier Detection*, John Wiley & Sons, New York, NY.

[8] Chen, D.S. and Jain, R.C. (1994), "A robust back propagation learning algorithm for function approximation," *IEEE Trans. on Neural Networks*, vol. 5, pp. 467-479.

[9] Joines, J.A. and White, M.W. (1992), "Improved generalization using robust cost functions," *Proceedings of the IEEE ICNN*, vol. 3, pp. 911-918.

[10] Li, S-.T. (1995), *Spatial and Stochasticity in Artificial Neural Networks*, Ph.D. Thesis, University of Houston, University Park.

[11] Nilsson, N.J. (1990), *The Mathematical Foundations of Learning Machines*, Morgan Kaufmann Publishers, San Mateo, CA, U.S.A.

[12] Haykin, S. (1994). Personal communication.

[13] Mili, L. and Coakley, C.W. (1993), "Robust estimation in structured linear regression," Technical Report No. 93-13, Department of Statistics, Virginia Polytechnic and State University, Blacksburg, VA, U.S.A.

[14] Rousseeuw, P.J. and Bassett Jr., G.W. (1991), "Robustness of the *p*-subset algorithm for regression with high breakdown point," in Stahel, W. and Weisberg, S. (Eds.), *Directions in Robust Statistics and Diagnostics Part II*, Springer-Verlag, New York, NY, pp. 185-194.

[15] Parlos, A.G., Fernandez, B., Atiya, A.F., Muthusami, J., and Tsai, W.K. (1994), "An accelerated learning algorithm for multilayer perceptron networks," *IEEE Trans. on Neural Networks*, vol. 5, pp. 493-497.

[16] Geman, S., and Bienenstock, E. (1992), "Neural networks and the bias/variance dilemma," *Neural Computation*, vol. 4, pp. 1-58.

Chapter 6

Robust RBF Networks

A.G. Borş and I. Pitas

We introduce training algorithms for Radial Basis Function (RBF) networks using robust statistics. The proposed training algorithms have two stages. The first stage rely on a robust learning vector quantization approach which estimates the hidden unit weights. The second stage employs backpropagation for the output weight calculation. We introduce the Median RBF (MRBF) training algorithm and Alpha-Trimmed Mean RBF. The efficiency of MRBF and classical training using learning vector quantization are compared in estimating overlapping Gaussian distributions. Applications to artificial data classification and object modeling are provided for the proposed algorithms.

1   Introduction

Radial Basis Functions (RBF) have been used in several applications for functional modeling and pattern classification. They have been found to have very good functional approximation capabilities. It has been proven that any continuous function can be modeled up to a certain precision by a set of radial basis functions [1]-[3]. RBFs have their fundamentals drawn from probability function estimation theory.

RBF network consists of a two layer feed-forward neural network. The hidden units implement functions which geometrically have a radial activation region similar to that of electric charges. Various types of functions have been considered for the hidden unit activation functions. Gaussian, thin-plate, multi-quadric, cubic radius or Cauchy basis function are among those proposed for modeling radial basis functions. Gaussian functions are considered in this study, because they are able to model the first and the second order statistics with their mean and covariance matrix. Modeling using mixtures of Gaussian functions has been considered in many fields of science.

The output layer implements a sum of hidden unit outputs. The network inputs have different meanings depending on the application. When modeling time series, the inputs represent data samples located at various time laps [4]-[8]. In a pattern recognition application each input corresponds to a feature entry [9]. The number of inputs determines the size of the hyper space in which the classification takes place. As a consequence of their functional approximation capabilities, RBF networks have been shown to approximate the Bayesian classifier [9], [10]. Usually, in the case of time-series approximation, only one network output is assumed, while in the case of pattern classification each network output is assigned to a class.

In order to model the functions implied in a specific problem, the parameters of the RBF neural network have to be estimated by means of a training algorithm. A large variety of training algorithms has been tested in RBF networks. Most of these training algorithms correspond to supervised training or to a joint unsupervised-supervised paradigm. Each data sample has been assigned a basis function in [15]. In such a case too many data samples are required. In a supervised problem a training set of input-output pairs is given. The estimation of the neural network parameters can be seen as finding a system of equations solution [16]. This task can be achieved by computing the inverse of a matrix corresponding to the RBF hidden unit outputs for a certain set of data samples. The product of this matrix with the vector of network outputs provides the solution of the system. The output unit weights are calculated correspondingly. A large computation time is required for calculating the inverse matrix in the case when the system of equations is large. Due to their functional approximation capabilities, RBF networks have been seen as a good solution to interpolation problems [17], [18]. A least squares solution has been found suitable for estimating the output parameters of the RBF networks [17]. Orthogonal least squares has been proposed in [19] for estimating the RBF weights. Gram-Schmidt orthogonalization is combined with a cluster merge condition for finding the parameters of the RBF networks in [20]. An adaptive solution is the use of a gradient descent algorithm. Backpropagation algorithm has been proposed for training RBF networks [3], [9], [10], [12], [21]. Backpropagation algorithm provides a near-optimal solution. However, according to the specific problem, it may require a large amount of iterations and training time. Expectation-maximization algorithm is proposed for training a generalized Gaussian network in [13]. Clustering algorithms, e.g., k-means [11] or its adaptive implementation represented by the LVQ [14], have been applied for estimating the hidden unit parameters. In such a case, the center of the basis function corresponds to the first order statistics of data samples from a certain cluster. The covariance matrix associated with a basis function models the second order statistics. The solutions offered by such training algorithms are sub-optimal. However, clustering-based algorithms can handle large amounts of data and they offer good solutions to a variety of problems.

The number of hidden units is chosen using either a criterion which compromises between the performance and the number of required parameters, as Akaike criterion does [19], or based on a condition of cluster merging [20]. Adding new hidden units when certain conditions are fulfilled is proposed in [9], [21]. Clustering merging-splitting [11] can be employed for selecting the number of hidden units when clustering algorithms are employed for training.

Radial Basis Functions have close connections with other classical pattern classification approaches as potential functions [11], [12] or clustering algorithms such as k-means [11] and Learning Vector Quatization [14]. They have interesting properties which make them attractive in very many applications. Chaotic-time series generated by dynamical systems have been modeled by RBFs in [4], [16]. RBF networks have good approximation capabilities when modeling time-series generated by Mackey-Glass differential equation [4]-[7]. Control modeling by RBF Networks has been employed in [18]. Equalization and detection problems in the case when assuming inter-symbol and co-channel interference have been solved using RBF Networks [9], [10], [19], [27]. RBF networks have been used for static speech classification [6], [9], [17]. Several applications of RBF networks have been done in image processing as well. In [13] the neural network is employed for image restoration when considering that the image is distorted by a non-linear distortion function. A face classification system successfully used an RBF network in [22]. Modeling 3-D shapes from shading has been employed based on

RBF networks in [23]. RBF networks have been used for modeling 3-D shapes in medical imaging [24], [25].

In this study we present some algorithms for training RBF networks using robust statistics. After introducing the structure of the RBF network and describing the training algorithms based on clustering in Section 2.1, we introduce the Median RBF Network and the Alpha-Trimmed Mean RBF Network in Sections 2.2 and 2.3 respectively. Section 3 provides the analysis of the bias in the case when RBF Networks are used to estimate a mixture of Gaussian functions. A comparison between the RBF network trained using classical estimation and robust statistics estimation is done in Section 3. Experimental results are provided in Section 4 when using the proposed algorithms in a 3-D object modeling application. The conclusions of this study are drawn in Section 5.

2   Estimation of RBF Parameters Using the LVQ Algorithm

In the approach adopted in this study, we consider Gaussian activation functions for the hidden units:

$$\phi_j(\mathbf{X}) = \exp\left[-(\mu_j - \mathbf{X})^T \Sigma_j^{-1}(\mu_j - \mathbf{X})\right], \; j = 1, \ldots, L \qquad (1)$$

where μ is the mean vector and Σ is the covariance matrix. Geometrically, μ represents the center and Σ the shape of the basis functions. A hidden unit function can be represented as a hyper-ellipsoid in the N-dimensional space.

The output layer implements a weighted sum of hidden-unit outputs:

$$\psi_k(\mathbf{X}) = \sum_{j=1}^{L} \lambda_{jk}\phi_j(\mathbf{X}) \qquad (2)$$

where $k = 1, \ldots, M$. L is the number of hidden units and M is the number of outputs. The weights λ_{kj} show the contribution of the hidden unit j for modeling the output k.

In pattern classification applications, the outputs are limited within the interval $(0,1)$ by a sigmoidal function:

$$Y_k(\mathbf{X}) = \frac{1}{1 + exp[-\psi_k(\mathbf{X})]} \tag{3}$$

2.1   Classical Statistics Estimation

A two-stage training algorithm has been employed in [6] considering the capabilities of basis functions to represent data clusters. This algorithm has a first unsupervised stage and a second supervised stage. In the first stage, the parameters of the basis function centers are estimated based on a self-organizing algorithm, *e.g.*, Learning Vector Quantization (LVQ) [14]. In the second stage, the algorithm estimates the parameters of the output weights λ based on the LMS algorithm [26]. Such an algorithm even though is not optimal provides a clear speed-up in the training time over other RBF training algorithms. In the first stage a set of centers are generated at random and the algorithm calculates the Euclidean distances between the data samples and the class centers. The closest center to the given data vector is chosen to be updated:

$$\|\mathbf{X} - \mu_k\| = \min_{i=1}^{L} \|\mathbf{X} - \mu_i\| \tag{4}$$

where μ_k is the closest center to the incoming data sample $\mathbf{X}$. The center is updated as follows:

$$\mu_k(t) = \mu_k(t-1) + \eta(\mathbf{X} - \mu_k(t-1)) \tag{5}$$

where η is the training rate and t is the iteration number. Similar algorithms have been used in [27] and [28]. The LVQ algorithm for minimum output variance [29] is obtained when we use the learning rate from (5) as in [28]:

$$\eta = \frac{1}{N_k(t-1)} \tag{6}$$

where $N_k(t-1)$ represents the number of data samples associated with the k-th hidden unit at iteration $t-1$ according to Equation (4). For the sake of simplicity, we will drop the t-dependency of N_k from now on.

For the covariance matrix, the on-line updating is:

$$\hat{\Sigma}_k(t) = \frac{N_k - 2}{N_k - 1}\hat{\Sigma}_k(t-1) + \frac{(\hat{\mu}_i(t-1) - \mathbf{X})(\hat{\mu}_i(t-1) - \mathbf{X})^T}{N_k - 1} \tag{7}$$

In some applications it is worth using the Mahalanobis distance instead of the Euclidean distance for the choice of the winner class. The Mahalanobis distance takes into consideration the covariance matrix for each basis function:

$$(\hat{\mu}_k - \mathbf{X}_i)^T \hat{\boldsymbol{\Sigma}}_k^{-1} (\hat{\mu}_k - \mathbf{X}_i) = \min_{j=1}^{L} (\hat{\mu}_j - \mathbf{X}_i)^T \hat{\boldsymbol{\Sigma}}_j^{-1} (\hat{\mu}_j - \mathbf{X}_i) \qquad (8)$$

However, at the start of the learning algorithm, an imprecision in estimating the covariance parameters can occur and this can lead to a singular covariance matrix. Thus, for the first few data samples we can use the Euclidean distance (4) and afterwards employ the Mahalanobis distance (8). The initial values for the center estimates $\hat{\mu}$ are randomly generated and the covariance matrix is initialized with $\mathbf{0}$.

The second layer is used in order to group the clusters, found in the unsupervised stage, in classes. We use the backpropagation algorithm for finding the output parameters [10]:

$$\lambda_{jk} = \sum_{\mathbf{X}} [F_k(\mathbf{X}) - Y_k(\mathbf{X})] Y_k(\mathbf{X}) [1 - Y_k(\mathbf{X})] \phi_j(\mathbf{X}) \qquad (9)$$

where $Y_k(\mathbf{X})$ is the output provided by the network (3) and $F_k(\mathbf{X})$ is the data target label for a supervised pattern classification problem.

2.2   Median RBF Networks

The approach described in the previous section corresponds to a classical (non-robust) statistics estimate of the mean and covariance matrix. In the training stage, it is desirable to avoid using outlying patterns which may cause bias in the estimation of the RBF network parameters. The patterns which do not correspond to the data statistics (noisy patterns) should be rejected rather than used in the training stage [30], [33]. Let us consider the ordering of data samples assigned to a hidden unit $X_{(1)} < X_{(2)} < \ldots < X_{(N_k)}$. A robust statistics estimate of a cluster center is given by [30]:

$$\hat{\mu}_k = \frac{\sum_{i=1}^{N_k} W_i X_{(i)}}{\sum_{i=1}^{N_k} W_i} \qquad (10)$$

where $W_i \in (0, 1)$ is the weight depending on the ranking of the respective data sample. The estimate of the covariance matrix can be calculated from

$$\hat{\Sigma}_k = \frac{\sum\limits_{i=1}^{N_k} W_i^2 (\mathbf{X}_{(i)} - \hat{\mu}_k(t-1))(\mathbf{X}_{(i)} - \hat{\mu}_k(t-1))^T}{\sum\limits_{i=1}^{N_k} W_i^2 - 1} \qquad (11)$$

where the weights $W_i \in (0, 1)$ depend on the ranking as well [31], [32]. If $W_i = 1$ for $i = 1, \ldots, N_k$ (Equations (10) and (11)), then the center and the covariance matrix are calculated as in classical statistics. The adaptive versions of these are provided in Equations (5) and (7).

If W_i in Equation (10) is replaced by a function which decreases with respect to the distance of the ordered sample $X_{(i)}$ from the central ordered data sample $X_{(\lfloor \frac{N_k}{2} \rfloor)}$, we obtain various robust statistics estimators [30]. Robust statistics-based algorithms are known to provide accurate estimates when data are contaminated with outliers or have long-tailed distributions. They are insensitive to extreme observations which make them attractive for parameter estimation. Such algorithms have been used in image processing for noise removal [33]. In the Marginal Median LVQ (MMLVQ) algorithm [34], data samples are marginally ordered and the centroid is taken as the marginal median [33]:

$$\hat{\mu}_j = \mathrm{med}\, \{\mathbf{X}_0, \mathbf{X}_2, \ldots, \mathbf{X}_{N_k-1}\} \qquad (12)$$

where $\mathbf{X}_{N_k-1}$ is the last pattern assigned to the cluster j. This corresponds to $W_i = 0$ for $i = 1, \ldots, \lfloor \frac{N_k}{2} \rfloor - 1, i = \lfloor \frac{N_k}{2} \rfloor + 1, \ldots, N_k$, and $W_i = 1$ for $i = \lfloor \frac{N_k}{2} \rfloor$ in Equation (10).

In order to avoid an excessive computational complexity, the median operation can be done on a finite data set, extracted through a moving window that contains only the last W data samples assigned to the hidden unit j:

$$\hat{\mu}_k = \begin{cases} \mathrm{med}\, \{\mathbf{X}_0, \mathbf{X}_1, \ldots, \mathbf{X}_{N_k-1}\} & \text{if } N_k < W \\ \mathrm{med}\, \{\mathbf{X}_{N_k-W}, \mathbf{X}_{N_k-W+1}, \ldots, \mathbf{X}_{N_k-1}\} & \text{if } N_k \geq W \end{cases} \qquad (13)$$

where $\mathbf{X}_i, i = N_k - W, \ldots, N_k - 1$ are the samples assigned to the k-th neuron according to (4). The size of the window W can be small if the statistics of the sample population changes rapidly in time and large if the sample statistics are relatively unchanged in time and a better estimation of the given population median is desired. Unlike in image filtering [33], where the window is rather small, a rather big window should be employed in most cases in order to have a good estimate of the median for a population of samples.

For the scale parameter associated with kernel functions we use the median of the absolute deviation from the median (MAD) estimator given by :

$$\hat{\sigma}_k = \frac{\text{med}\{|\mathbf{X}_0 - \hat{\mu}_k|, \ldots, |\mathbf{X}_{N_k-1} - \hat{\mu}_k|\}}{0.6745} \tag{14}$$

where 0.6745 is a scaling parameter in order to make the estimator Fisher consistent for the normal distribution [30], [33]. MAD calculation is performed along each data dimension independently. The same set of data samples are taken into consideration in Equation (14) and for the marginal median in Equation (13).

The cross-correlation members of the covariance matrix can be calculated based on MAD estimator [30]. We consider two arrays corresponding to the difference and the sum of each two different components for a data sample from the moving window:

$$Z_{i,hl}^{+} = X_i(h) + X_i(l) \tag{15}$$

$$Z_{i,hl}^{-} = X_i(h) - X_i(l) \tag{16}$$

for $i = N_k - W, \ldots, N_k - 1$. First the median of these new populations is calculated according to Equation (13). The squares of the corresponding MAD estimates (14) for the arrays Z_{hl}^{+} and Z_{hl}^{-} represent their variances and they are denoted as $\hat{V}_{k,hl}^{+}$ and $\hat{V}_{k,hl}^{-}$. The cross-correlations are derived as:

$$\hat{\sigma}_{k,hl}^{2} = \hat{\sigma}_{k,lh}^{2} = \frac{1}{4}(\hat{V}_{k,hl}^{+} - \hat{V}_{k,hl}^{-}). \tag{17}$$

In marginal median LVQ, both Euclidean (4) and Mahalanobis distances (8) can be used. In the case of Mahalanobis distance, a good estimation is desired for the covariance matrix in order to be appropriately used for the winner class selection. By using a robust estimation of the covariance matrix as in Equations (14) and (17), we can be more confident in the evaluation of the Mahalanobis distance. The order of updating the RBF network weights is well defined: first the kernel center, the covariance matrix (which uses the previously evaluated center) and afterwards the hidden unit to output weights are updated. For the last one we use Equation (9). MRBF network has been successfully used for simultaneous optical flow estimation and moving object segmentation [39], brush stroke and crack pixel classification for painting restoration [40] and data fusion in person authentification [41].

2.3   Alpha-Trimmed Mean RBF Networks

The α-trimmed Mean algorithm [30], [33] assigns $W_i = 1$ for $i = \alpha_k N_k, \ldots, N_k - \alpha_k N_k$, and $W_i = 0$ for the rest of the data samples in (10). α_k is the percentage of data samples to be trimmed away at each extreme of the k-th hidden unit data distribution.

The adaptive implementation of the algorithm updates the parameters of a basis function using only the data samples which are inside a certain range of ranked samples:

$$\hat{\mu}_{k,t} = \begin{cases} \hat{\mu}_{k,t-1} + \dfrac{\mathbf{X}_{(i)} - \hat{\mu}_{k,t-1}}{N_{k,t} - 2\alpha_k N_{k,t}} & \text{if } \alpha_k N_{k,t} < i < N_{k,t} - \alpha_k N_{k,t} \\ \hat{\mu}_{k,t-1} & \text{otherwise} \end{cases}$$

$$(18)$$

where $\hat{\mu}_{k,t}$ and $N_{k,t}$ denote the center estimate and the number of data samples assigned to the k-th basis function at the moment t. We can observe that for $\alpha_k=0$ we obtain the LVQ algorithm for minimum output variance [29].

The parameter α_k is chosen according to the data distribution. The following measure is used for estimating the tail of the data distribution [35], [36]:

$$Q = \frac{U[0.5] - L[0.5]}{U[0.05] - L[0.05]} \tag{19}$$

where $U[\beta]$, $L[\beta]$ represent the average of the upper and respectively the lower β percent from the total number of data samples assigned to a specific basis function. The number of data samples to be trimmed away relies directly on the value of Q:

$$\hat{\alpha}_k = \frac{1 - Q}{2}. \tag{20}$$

For long tailed distributions, the amount of data samples to be trimmed is large and for short tailed distributions less samples are trimmed away.

For the second order statistics, we order the data samples assigned to a basis function according to their Mahalanobis distance from the estimated center $\hat{\mu}_k$, starting with:

$$\mathcal{M}_{(0)} = \min_{i=1}^{N_k} [(\mathbf{X}_i - \hat{\mu}_k)^T \hat{\mathbf{\Sigma}}_k^{-1} (\mathbf{X}_i - \hat{\mu}_k)]. \tag{21}$$

After ordering the data samples assigned to the k-th basis function according to this measure $\mathbf{X}_{(0),\mathcal{M}} < \ldots < \mathbf{X}_{(N_k),\mathcal{M}}$, the estimate of the covariance matrix is obtained using ellipsoidal trimming [37]:

$$\hat{\mathbf{\Sigma}}_k = \frac{\sum_{i=0}^{N_k - \alpha_{k,\mathcal{M}} N_k} (\mathbf{X}_{(i),\mathcal{M}} - \hat{\mu}_k) (\mathbf{X}_{(i),\mathcal{M}} - \hat{\mu}_k)^T}{N_k - \alpha_{k,\mathcal{M}} N_k} \tag{22}$$

where $\mathbf{X}_{(i),\mathcal{M}}$ denotes the i-th ordered data sample according to the Mahalanobis distance (21) and $\alpha_{k,\mathcal{M}}$ is the trimming percentage in this case. As with Equation (18), this formula can also be implemented in an adaptive form. Equation (22) corresponds to peeling off observations in shells using a sequence of convex hulls. Equations (18) and (22) make up the Alpha-Trimmed Mean RBF training algorithm. An Alpha-Trimmed Mean RBF network has been applied for segmenting 3-D medical images [43].

3   Theoretical Assessment

In order to compare the results provided by the RBF network training algorithm based on classical statistics and those provided by the algorithms relying on robust statistics we estimate a function made up from overlapping Gaussian functions. Mixture of Gaussians are used for data modeling in many fields. We have chosen the MRBF algorithm as a representative robust training algorithm in order to be compared with the classical RBF network.

The marginal median operates independently on each data axis. Therefore, the performance analysis can be done for the one-dimensional (1-D)
case without loss of generality. We shall use mixtures of 1-D normal distributions and we shall estimate the center and the dispersion for each
Gaussian function by using robust techniques compared against the classical ones. We shall perform an asymptotic analysis of performance, i.e.,
when we have a sufficiently large number of observations for each class.

Let us consider a *pdf* function $f(X)$ being a mixture of L one-
dimensional normal distributions $N(\mu_j, \sigma_j)$ each of them with *a priori*
probability ε_j:

$$f(X) = \sum_{j=1}^{L} \frac{\varepsilon_j}{\sqrt{2\pi}\sigma_j} \exp\left[-\frac{(X-\mu_j)^2}{2\sigma_j^2}\right] \tag{23}$$

$$\sum_{j=1}^{L} \varepsilon_j = 1 \tag{24}$$

The second equation represents the normalization relationship for the *a
priori* probabilities. We can assume that each distribution in the mixture
(23) corresponds to one data class. Our aim is to separate each class j by
choosing appropriate thresholds T_j, T_{j+1}. We have to consider the overlap among different distributions in estimating the components of Equation (23). The normalized data distribution after thresholding is given by

$$g(X) = \frac{f(X)}{\int_{T_j}^{T_{j+1}} f(X)dx} \tag{25}$$

where T_j and T_{j+1} are the optimal boundaries of the j-th function with
its neighboring functions.

The expected value of the center can be obtained from:

$$E[\hat{\mu}_j] = E[X | X \in [\hat{T}_j, \hat{T}_{j+1})] = \frac{\int_{\hat{T}_j}^{\hat{T}_{j+1}} X f(X)dX}{\int_{\hat{T}_j}^{\hat{T}_{j+1}} f(X)dX} \tag{26}$$

where $\hat{T}_j$ and $\hat{T}_{j+1}$ are the estimates of the decision boundaries for the
j-th Gaussian kernel and $f(X)$ is given in Equation (23).

In a parameter estimation problem, the bias represents the difference between the estimated parameter value and the optimal one. It is desirable
to obtain a small bias. The bias of the boundary estimation between two
classes is directly related to the estimation of the class probabilities. If
these probabilities are well estimated, the bias is small. If not, the bias is
larger.

When $\hat{\mu}_j$ is evaluated as in classical LVQ (5), the stationary value of the
estimate for the jth Gaussian kernel center is given by:

$$
E[\hat{\mu}_{j,LVQ}] = \frac{\left\{ \sum_{i=1}^{L} \varepsilon_i \left\{ \mu_i \left[\operatorname{erf}\left(\dfrac{\hat{T}_{j+1} - \mu_i}{\sigma_i} \right) - \operatorname{erf}\left(\dfrac{\hat{T}_j - \mu_i}{\sigma_i} \right) \right] + \dfrac{\sigma_i}{\sqrt{2\pi}} \left\{ \exp\left[-\dfrac{(\hat{T}_j - \mu_i)^2}{2\sigma_i^2} \right] - \exp\left[-\dfrac{(\hat{T}_{j+1} - \mu_i)^2}{2\sigma_i^2} \right] \right\} \right\} \right\}}{\sum_{i=1}^{L} \varepsilon_i \left[\operatorname{erf}\left(\dfrac{\hat{T}_{j+1} - \mu_i}{\sigma_i} \right) - \operatorname{erf}\left(\dfrac{\hat{T}_j - \mu_i}{\sigma_i} \right) \right]}
$$

(27)

where the erf function is [38] :

$$
\operatorname{erf}(X) = \frac{1}{\sqrt{2\pi}} \int_0^X exp\left(-\frac{t^2}{2} \right) dt
$$

(28)

In the case of median estimator (12) the *pdf* for $N = 2i + 1$ independent
and identically distributed data is given by [33]:

$$
f_{i+1}(X) = N \binom{N-1}{i} F^i(X)[1 - F(X)]^i f(X)
$$

(29)

where $F(X)$ is the cumulative distribution function (*cdf*) for the data
whose *pdf* is given in Equation (23). If we replace Equation (29) in Equation (26), we obtain the expected value of the median estimator assuming
N data samples.

The median is located where the *pdf* of the given data samples is split in
two equal areas [33]:

$$
\int_{\hat{T}_j}^{E[\hat{\mu}_{j,Med}]} f(X)dX = \int_{E[\hat{\mu}_{j,Med}]}^{\hat{T}_{j+1}} f(X)dX
$$

(30)

The stationary value of the estimate for the center of the jth Gaussian distribution using the median can be obtained after replacing Equation (23) in Equation (30):

$$\sum_{i=1}^{L} \varepsilon_i \, \text{erf}\left(\frac{E[\hat{\mu}_{j,Med}] - \mu_i}{\sigma_i}\right) =$$
$$\sum_{i=1}^{L} \frac{\varepsilon_i}{2} \left[\text{erf}\left(\frac{\hat{T}_{j+1} - \mu_i}{\sigma_i}\right) + \text{erf}\left(\frac{\hat{T}_j - \mu_i}{\sigma_i}\right)\right] \tag{31}$$

In the case when we want to find the expectation for the variance estimator $\hat{\sigma}_j^2$, we can use a similar approach. The expected value for $\hat{\sigma}_j^2$ using the estimator (7) is

$$E[\hat{\sigma}_j^2] = E[(X - \hat{\mu}_{j,LVQ})^2 | x \in [\hat{T}_j, \hat{T}_{j+1})]) =$$
$$\frac{\int_{\hat{T}_j}^{\hat{T}_{j+1}} (X - E[\hat{\mu}_{j,LVQ}])^2 f(X) dX}{\int_{\hat{T}_j}^{\hat{T}_{j+1}} f(X) dX} \tag{32}$$

where $f(X)$ is given by Equation (23) and $E[\hat{\mu}_{j,LVQ}]$ is evaluated in Equation (27).

When MAD is used as dispersion estimator (14), its expected value is given by

$$E[\hat{\sigma}_{j,MAD}] = \frac{\int_{\hat{T}_j}^{\hat{T}_{j+1}} |X - E[\hat{\mu}_{j,Med}]| \, f(X) dX}{c \, \int_{\hat{T}_j}^{\hat{T}_{j+1}} f(X) dX} \tag{33}$$

where $c = 0.6745$.

By taking into account the median property of splitting the data distribution into two equal areas as in Equation (30), we have

$$\int_{E[\hat{\mu}_{j,Med}] - cE[\hat{\sigma}_{j,MAD}]}^{E[\hat{\mu}_{j,Med}] + cE[\hat{\sigma}_{j,MAD}]} f(X) dX = \frac{1}{2} \int_{\hat{T}_j}^{\hat{T}_{j+1}} f(X) dX \tag{34}$$

where $E[\hat{\mu}_{j,Med}]$ is calculated in Equation (31) and $f(X)$ is obtained by replacing Equation (23) in Equation (29). For MAD, the expected stationary value can be found from

$$
\sum_{i=1}^{L} \varepsilon_i \left[\mathrm{erf}\left(\frac{E[\hat{\mu}_{j,Med}] - \mu_i + cE[\hat{\sigma}_{j,MAD}]}{\sigma_i} \right) - \right.
$$
$$
\left. \mathrm{erf}\left(\frac{E[\hat{\mu}_{j,Med}] - \mu_i - cE[\hat{\sigma}_{j,MAD}]}{\sigma_i} \right) \right]
$$
$$
= \frac{1}{2} \sum_{i=1}^{L} \varepsilon_i \left[\mathrm{erf}\left(\frac{\hat{T}_{j+1} - \mu_i}{\sigma_i} \right) - \mathrm{erf}\left(\frac{\hat{T}_j - \mu_i}{\sigma_i} \right) \right] \qquad (35)
$$

In order to evaluate the parameters for the Gaussian kernel we must also estimate the domains $[\hat{T}_j, \hat{T}_{j+1})$ of each Gaussian function. If the Euclidean distance is used in order to decide the activation region for a new incoming data sample as in Equation (4), we can estimate the boundary $\hat{T}_j$ between two activation regions j and $j + 1$ as:

$$
\hat{T}_j = \frac{\hat{\mu}_j + \hat{\mu}_{j+1}}{2} \qquad (36)
$$

for $j = 1, \ldots, L - 1$.

In the case when the Euclidean distance is replaced with the Mahalanobis distance (8), the boundary condition can be found by solving the equation:

$$
\left(\frac{\hat{T}_j - \hat{\mu}_j}{\hat{\sigma}_j} \right)^2 = \left(\frac{\hat{T}_j - \hat{\mu}_{j+1}}{\hat{\sigma}_{j+1}} \right)^2 \qquad (37)
$$

for $j = 1, \ldots, L - 1$. The first and the last boundaries are defined as $T_0 = -\infty$ and $T_L = \infty$. The $2L - 2$ parameters (Gaussian centers and boundaries) for the case described by Equation (36) and $3L - 2$ parameters (including the shape parameters) for Equation (37) have to be evaluated. In order to do this, analytical methods can be employed by evaluating the centers of the Gaussian functions and the boundaries, iteratively.

The relationship which gives the optimal boundary between two classes, each of them modeled by a Gaussian *pdf*, can be derived as:

$$
\frac{(T_1 - \mu_1)^2}{2\sigma_1^2} - \frac{(T_1 - \mu_2)^2}{2\sigma_2^2} = \ln \frac{\sigma_1 \varepsilon_2}{\sigma_2 \varepsilon_1} \qquad (38)
$$

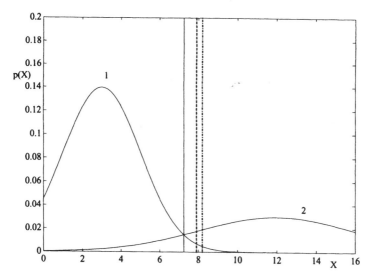

Figure 1. The decision boundary between two Gaussian density probability functions ('–' denotes the optimal boundary, '- -' the boundary found by using marginal median LVQ and '··' the boundary found using classical LVQ).

Two Gaussian *pdf* functions are shown in Figure 1: $p_1(X)$ with $\mu_1 = 3$, $\sigma_1 = 2$, $\varepsilon_1 = 0.7$ and $p_2(X)$ with $\mu_2 = 12$, $\sigma_2 = 4$, $\varepsilon_2 = 0.3$. The optimal boundary of Equation (38) is compared with the boundary obtained by means of MMLVQ and with the boundary given by classical LVQ. From this figure it is clear that the bias $|T_1 - \hat{T}_1|$ provided by MMLVQ is smaller than that of the classical LVQ.

The convergence is the property of a neural network to achieve a stable state after a finite number of iterations in the learning stage. The convergence can be defined individually for a weight or globally, expressing the state of the network by a cost function. Here we analyze the capability of different MRBF weights to achieve a stable state.

Let us consider the following distributions:

$$f(X) = \frac{1}{2}N(5, \sigma) + \frac{1}{2}N(10, \sigma) \tag{39}$$

$$f(X) = \frac{1}{3}N(3, \sigma) + \frac{1}{3}N(5, \sigma) + \frac{1}{3}N(10, \sigma) \tag{40}$$

Let us assume $\sigma = 2$ in the model of Equation (39). We use MRBF to estimate the parameters of the distribution $N(5, 2)$. We find the expectation for the median by replacing Equation (29) in Equation (26) and by computing the integral numerically. In Figure 2a, we compare the expected bias for the marginal median LVQ against the expected bias of the mean. In Figure 2b, a comparison between the expected bias of the MAD estimator (14) and that of the classical estimator for scale, derived from Equation (7), is provided. The expectation for scale parameter using the MAD estimator is obtained after replacing Equation (29) in Equation (33). It is clear from these plots that median and MAD algorithms provide better parameter estimation when estimating overlapping Gaussian functions, than the arithmetic mean and sample deviation.

We estimate the center and the scale parameter for the distribution $N(5, \sigma)$ using both classical and robust type learning for the distributions given in Equations (39) and (40). The class which corresponds to $N(5, \sigma)$ is bounded in the case of Equation (40) and unbounded to the left in the case of Equation (39). Thus in the case of Equation (39), the data samples used for learning are drawn from a "medium-tailed" distribution and in the case of Equation (40) from a "short-tailed" one. The stationary state of the bias from the estimation $E[\hat{\mu}] - \mu$ is depicted in Figure 3a for the distribution (39) and in Figure 3b for the distribution of Equation (40), both with respect to the scale parameter σ. The comparison results for estimating the stationary state of the bias for the scale parameter $E[\hat{\sigma}] - \sigma$ are given in Figure 3c and in Figure 3d. From these plots it is evident that if a certain overlap occur among different Gaussian functions, the respective amount of data samples consist of outliers while median and MAD estimators give less bias than mean and classical sample deviation estimators.

If the Gaussian functions are far away one from each other with respect to the variance, the amount of outliers decreases and both algorithms provide similar results. However, if isolated Gaussian functions are truncated, e.g., due to the decision (4) or (8), then robust estimators are more accurate than those based on classical statistics.

We consider four artificially generated distributions, each consisting of two dimensional clusters.

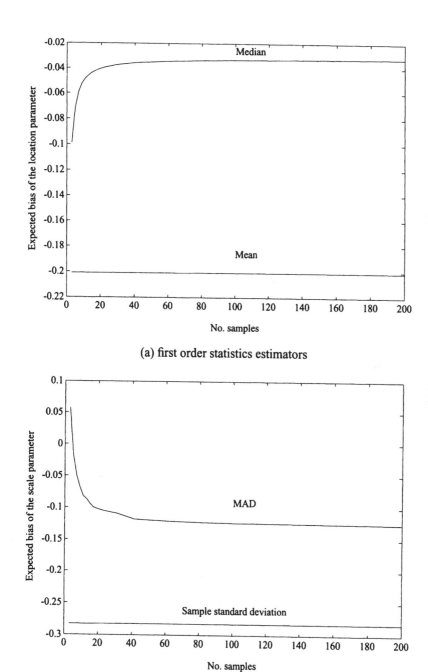

(a) first order statistics estimators

(b) second order statistics estimators

Figure 2. The parameter bias versus the number of data samples in the 1-D case.

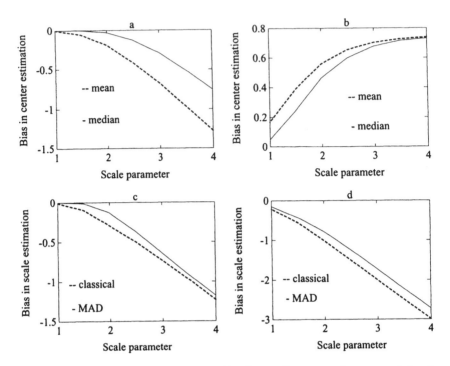

Figure 3. Theoretical analysis of the bias for median type estimators and classical statistics estimators in evaluating the RBF parameters: (a) center for $N(5, \sigma)$ in the distribution of Equation (39) ; (b) center for $N(5, \sigma)$ in Equation (40) ; (c) scale parameter for $N(5, \sigma)$ in Equation (39) ; (d) scale parameter for $N(5, \sigma)$ in Equation (40).

A 2-D Gaussian distribution is denoted by $N(\mu_1, \mu_2; \sigma_1, \sigma_2; r)$, where r is the correlation factor. The Gaussian clusters are grouped in two classes in order to form more complex distributions:

Distribution I:

$$P_1^I(X) = N(2, 1; 3, 1; 0) + N(8, 7; 3, 1; 0)$$
$$P_2^I(X) = N(8, 2; 1, 3; 0) + N(2, 6; 1, 3; 0) \qquad (41)$$

Distribution II:

$$P_1^{II}(X) = N(6, 0; 4, 1; 0) + N(0, 6; 1, 4; 0)$$
$$P_2^{II}(X) = N(6, 6; 2, 2; 0) \qquad (42)$$

Two more distributions are obtained from the first two by adding uniformly distributed data samples:

Distribution III:

$$P_1^{III}(X) = \epsilon\, P_k^I + (1 - \epsilon)\, U([-5, 15], [-5, 15]) \qquad (43)$$

Distribution IV:

$$P_1^{IV}(X) = \epsilon\, P_k^{II} + (1 - \epsilon)\, U([-5, 15], [-5, 15]) \qquad (44)$$

where $k \in \{1, 2\}$ and $\epsilon = 0.9$. We denote by $U([-5, 15], [-5, 15])$ a uniform distribution having the domain $[-5, 15] \times [-5, 15]$.

For MRBF, we consider a running window of W=401 samples in Equation (13) and topologies of 2-4-2 and 2-3-2 respectively. Both Euclidean and Mahalanobis distances were considered in order to decide which neuron will be updated for a new data sample. Equal numbers of data samples were used in the learning stage for each of the training algorithms. We have tested the ability of classification for both networks after the learning stage was concluded. The miss-classification error compares the given true output $F_k(X)$ with the network output $Y_k(X)$:

$$\{X \in \mathbb{R}^N \mid \exists k \, |F_k(X) - Y_k(X)| > 0.5\} \qquad (45)$$

and is represented as a fraction of the total number of samples. This factor evaluates the accuracy of the Bayesian decision rule implemented by each of the networks. The second comparison criteria is the approximation of the *pdf* functions, when we implement the respective functions using the parameters estimated by the network.

The optimal network is obtained when the network weights are equal with the parameters of the Distributions I and II (see Equations (41) and (42)). The mean square error (MSE) calculated between the ideal function and the estimated one is defined as:

$$MSE = \frac{1}{M} \sum_{k=1}^{M} \int_{\mathcal{D}} (p_k(X) - \hat{p}_k(X))^2 \, dX \qquad (46)$$

where the domain is $\mathcal{D} = (-\infty, \infty) \times (-\infty, \infty)$ and $\hat{p}_k(X)$ is the hyper surface modeled by the k-th output unit.

Data samples from the first two distributions are presented in Figures 4 and 5. The same figures display also the boundaries found by means of

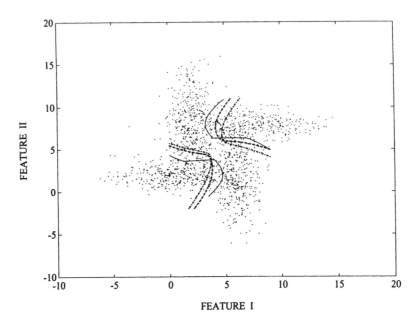

Figure 4. Samples from the distribution I and the boundaries between the classes marked with: '-' for optimal classifier, '- -' for MRBF and '--' for RBF.

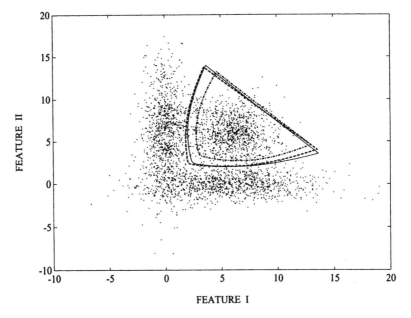

Figure 5. Samples from the distribution II and the boundaries between the classes marked with: '-' for optimal classifier, '- -' for MRBF and '--' for RBF.

Table 1. Comparison between the classical estimation for RBF and the MRBF algorithm.

| Distribution | Method | Distance Measures | | | |
| | | Euclidean | | Mahalanobis | |
		Error (%)	MSE	Error (%)	MSE
I	RBF	21.26	13.69	17.17	6.90
	MRBF	17.58	8.65	13.75	2.75
	Optim	12.13	0.00	12.13	0.00
II	RBF	3.89	3.69	2.95	1.24
	MRBF	2.90	1.20	2.61	0.82
	Optim	2.52	0.00	2.52	0.00
III	RBF	26.63	34.22	35.05	48.59
	MRBF	21.11	10.11	18.82	5.74
	Optim	15.78	0.00	15.78	0.00
IV	RBF	15.28	32.36	22.21	39.61
	MRBF	8.78	5.50	7.24	2.49
	Optim	7.18	0.00	7.18	0.00

neural networks as well as the optimal boundaries. From these figures it is evident that MRBF approximates better the boundaries between classes than classical statistical estimators for the RBF. The improvement is clear for MRBF in all cases considered in Table 1. However, when the mixture of bivariate normal distributions is contaminated with uniform noise (e.g. in distributions III and IV), the difference is very large because the robust type learning is insensitive at extreme observations. By using the Mahalanobis distance (8) instead of the Euclidean one, we obtain better results for both algorithms, except in the case when we use classical estimators for the uniform contaminated model, Equations (43) and (44). We can see from Table 1 that the MRBF algorithm with the Mahalanobis distance gives the best results.

In Figure 6, we evaluate the global convergence of the algorithms in the case of distribution I. The learning curves represent the estimation of the *pdf* functions given by MSE (46), with respect to the number of samples drawn. From this plot it is clear that the MRBF network results to a smaller MSE when compared with classical RBF network. The improvement produced by using the Mahalanobis distance instead of the Euclidean distance is also clear from this plot.

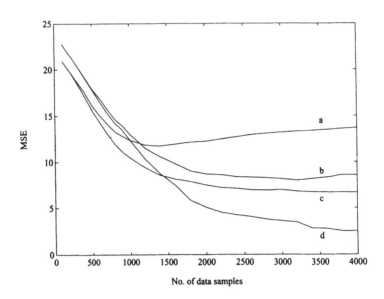

Figure 6. The learning curves in the case when the samples are drawn from the distribution I. We have marked with a the RBF and with b the MRBF when using Euclidean distance and with c, d the RBF and the MRBF when using Mahalanobis distance, respectively.

4   Experimental Results

We have tested the robust statistics based training algorithms as described in Section 2, when modeling a synthetic object. We consider the modeling of a 3-D shape consisting of six spheres of equal radius with the centers located at (40,50,50), (60,50,50), (50,40,50), (50,60,50), (50,50, 40), (50,50,60). The resulting shape is displayed in Figure 7a. The coordinates of the voxels composing the shape are considered as inputs in the neural network. The modeling results when using RBF, Alpha-Trimmed Mean RBF and MRBF network are displayed in Figures 7b, 7c, and 7d, respectively. The algorithm employed for the RBF network has been described in Section 2.1, that for the MRBF network in Section 2.2 and for Alpha-Trimmed Mean RBF in Section 2.3. After training, the shape is reconstructed from the parameters embedded in the neural network. When calculating the spread of the ellipsoids by trimming as in Equation (22) we use a factor in order to compensate for data loss [42], [43]. We distort the shape of the artificial object by adding noise. The noise is uniformly distributed in the volume $[0, 100] \times [0, 100] \times [0, 100]$ and

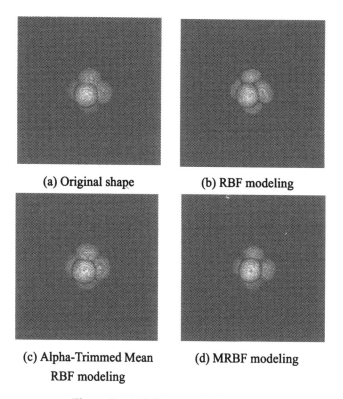

(a) Original shape   (b) RBF modeling

(c) Alpha-Trimmed Mean   (d) MRBF modeling
RBF modeling

Figure 7. Modeling a synthetic shape.

has probability of occurrence 0.2 % in the entire volume. In the locations where the noisy samples are added, the pixel values are switched from the grey level of the object to that of the background and vice versa. The noisy image is displayed in Figure 8a. The objects reconstructed based on the classical training algorithm for RBF, Alpha-Trimmed Mean RBF and MRBF algorithm are displayed in Figures 8b, 8c, and 8d, respectively. Two measures are considered for numerical comparison. The first error criterion measures the average bias in center location:

$$E = \frac{1}{G} \sum_{k=1}^{G} \|\mu_k - \hat{\mu}_k\|^2 \tag{47}$$

where $G = 6$ represents the number of spheres and μ_k, $\hat{\mu}_k$ are the original and the estimated position of their centers respectively. A second measure is the volume error and it is calculated as the absolute difference between the volume of the original shape (Figure 7a) and the vol-

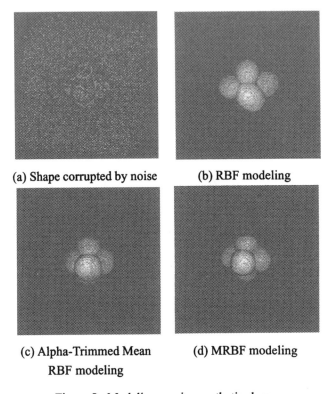

(a) Shape corrupted by noise   (b) RBF modeling

(c) Alpha-Trimmed Mean   (d) MRBF modeling
   RBF modeling

Figure 8. Modeling a noisy synthetic shape.

ume representing the reconstructed object based on the estimated parameters, normalized at the size of the original object. The average of the results when applying several times RBF, MRBF and Alpha-Trimmed Mean RBF are provided in Table 2. We can observe from this Table as well as from Figures 7 and 8 that Alpha-Trimmed Mean RBF provides a better result than that of RBF when estimating the original shape from Figure 7a, and better modeling capabilities than MRBF when estimating the parameters from the noisy shape. These results show the capability of robust learning algorithms in training RBF networks when modeling a composite shape as well as its robustness to noise corruption.

5   Conclusions

Robust statistics has been employed in a variety of applications and is known for providing good estimates in the case when data is corrupted by

Table 2. Modeling a synthetic 3-D shape when using LVQ-based RBF, MRBF and Alpha-Trimmed Mean RBF algorithms.

Algorithm	Noise-free Model		Noisy Model	
	Center Bias Estimation	Modeling Error (%)	Center Bias Estimation	Modeling Error (%)
RBF	2.02	11.59	5.38	59.03
MRBF	3.64	27.03	4.30	32.32
α-Trimmed Mean RBF	1.40	5.99	2.93	20.37

noise. Due to its efficiency and speed, in this study we chose a two-stage learning algorithm for training RBF networks. In the first stage the center and the scale parameter of the Gaussian functions are estimated using an approach similar to the learning vector quantization. A general model of training algorithms based on robust statistics is introduced. We present in detail Median RBF and Alpha-Trimmed Mean RBF algorithms. In these algorithms both first and second order statistics are estimated using robust statistics. Algorithms relying on robust statistics are not sensitive to outliers and they are known to provide lesser bias when data is corrupted by noise. Better estimates are obtained for the basis centers and their spread in the case when using robust statistics for estimating the hidden unit parameters, compared with classical training algorithms. We have computed the bias when estimating a mixture of overlapping Gaussians and found that it is smaller for the MRBF network when compared to the RBF network using the classical LVQ algorithm. The Alpha-Trimmed Mean RBF algorithm provides a parameter which regulates the number of data samples to be excluded from estimation. This parameter is calculated from the data distribution and is a function of its tail length. The backpropagation algorithm is used in the second stage for estimating the output weights. Modeling a 3-D shape has been considered for comparing the proposed algorithms. MRBF and Alpha-Trimmed Mean RBF networks proved to be efficient in a variety of artificial or real applications. They have better data modeling and probability estimation capabilities. When the amount of noisy data is big, or the data corresponds to overlapping Gaussian distributions, the difference with respect to the classical approach is very big.

References

[1] Hartman, E.J., Keeler, J.D., and Kowalski, J.M. (1990), "Layered neural networks with Gaussian hidden units as universal approximations," *Neural Computation*, vol. 2, pp. 210-215.

[2] Park, J. and Sandberg, J.W. (1991), "Universal approximation using radial basis functions network," *Neural Computation*, vol. 3, pp. 246-257.

[3] Poggio, T. and Girosi, F. (1990), "Networks for approximation and learning," *Proc. of IEEE*, vol. 78, no. 9, pp. 1481-1497.

[4] Casdagli, M. (1989), "Nonlinear prediction of chaotic time series," *Physica D*, vol. 35, pp. 335-356.

[5] Chng, E.S., Chen, S., and Mulgrew, B. (1996), "Gradient radial basis function networks for nonlinear and nonstationary time series prediction," *IEEE Trans. on Neural Networks*, vol. 7, no. 1, pp. 190-194.

[6] Moody, J. (1990), "Fast learning in networks of locally-tuned processing units," *Neural Networks*, vol. 3, pp. 437-443.

[7] Platt, J. (1991), "A resource-allocating network for functional interpolation," *Neural Computation*, vol. 3, pp. 213-225.

[8] Whitehead, B.A. and Chaote, T.D. (1996), "Cooperative-competitive genetic evolution of radial basis function centers and width for time series prediction," *IEEE Trans. on Neural Networks*, vol. 7, no. 4, pp. 869-880.

[9] Borş, A.G. and Gabbouj, M. (1994), "Minimal topology for a radial basis function neural network for pattern classification," *Digital Signal Processing: a Review Journal*, vol. 4, pp. 173-188.

[10] Haykin, S. (1994), *Neural Networks: a Comprehensive Foundation*, Upper Saddle River, NJ: Prentice Hall.

[11] Tou, J.T. and Gonzalez, R.C. (1974), *Pattern Recognition Principles*, Reading, Massachusetts: Addison-Wesley.

[12] Niranjan, M., Robinson, A.J., and Fallside, F. (1989), "Pattern recognition with potential functions in the context of neural networks," *Proc. of the Scandinavian Conf. on Pattern Recognition*, Oulu, Finland, pp. 96-103.

[13] Cha, I. and Kassam, S.A. (1996), "RBFN restoration of nonlinearly degraded images," *IEEE Trans. on Image Processing*, vol. 5, no. 6, pp. 964-975.

[14] Kohonen, T.K. (1989), *Self-Organization and Associative Memory*, Berlin: Springer-Verlag.

[15] Specht, D.F. (1990), "Probabilistic neural networks and the polynomial adaline as complementary techniques for classification," *IEEE Trans. on Neural Networks*, vol. 1, no. 1, pp. 111-121.

[16] Broomhead, D.S. and Lowe, D. (1988), "Multivariable functional interpolation and adaptive networks," *Complex Systems*, vol. 2, pp. 321-355.

[17] Niranjan, M. and Fallside, F. (1990), "Neural networks and radial basis functions in classifying static speech patterns," *Computer Speech and Language*, vol. 4, pp. 275-289.

[18] Sanner, R.M. and Slotine, J.-J.E. (1992), "Gaussian networks for direct adaptive control," *IEEE Trans on Neural Networks*, vol. 3, no. 6, pp. 837-863.

[19] Chen, S., Cowan, C.F.N., and Grant, P.M. (1991), "Orthogonal least squares learning algorithm for radial basis function networks," *IEEE Trans. on Neural Networks*, vol. 2, no. 2, pp. 302-309.

[20] Musavi, M.T., Ahmed, W., Chan, K.H., Faris, K.B., and Hummels, D.M. (1992), "On the training of radial basis function classifiers," *Neural Networks*, vol. 5, pp. 595-603.

[21] Lee, S. and Kil, R.M. (1991), "A Gaussian potential function network with hierarchically self-organizing learning," *Neural Networks*, vol. 4, pp. 207-224.

[22] Howell, J. and Buxton, H. (1995), "Invariance in radial basis function neural networks in human face classification," *Proc. of Int. Workshop on Automatic Face- and Gesture-Recognition*, Zurich, Switzerland, pp. 221-226.

[23] Wei, G.-Q. and Hirzinger, G. (1997), "Parametric shape-from-shading by radial basis functions," *IEEE Trans. on Pattern Analysis and Machine Intelligence*, vol. 19, no. 4, pp. 353-365.

[24] Matej, S. and Lewitt, R.M. (1996), "Practical considerations for 3-D image reconstruction using spherically symmetric volume elements," *IEEE Trans. on Medical Imaging*, vol. 15, no. 1, pp. 68-78.

[25] Carr, J.C., Fright, W.R., and Beatson, R.K. (1997), "Surface interpolation with radial basis functions for medical imaging," *IEEE Trans. on Medical Imaging*, vol. 16, no. 1, pp. 96-107.

[26] Widrow, B. and Stearns, S.D. (1985), *Adaptive Signal Processing*, Englewood Cliffs, NJ: Prentice Hall.

[27] Chen, S., Gibson, G.J., Cowan, C.F.N., and Grant, P.M. (1991), "Reconstruction of binary signals using an adaptive radial-basis-function equalizer," *Signal Processing*, vol. 22, pp. 77-93.

[28] Chen, S. and Mulgrew, B. (1992), "Overcoming co-channel interference using an adaptive radial basis function equaliser," *Signal Processing*, vol. 28, pp. 91-107.

[29] Yair, E., Zeger, K., and Gersho, A. (1992), "Competitive learning and soft competition for vector quantizer design," *IEEE Trans. on Signal Processing*, vol. 40, no. 2, pp. 294-309.

[30] Seber, G. (1984), *Multivariate Observations*, John Wiley.

[31] Campbell, N.A. (1980), "Robust procedures in multivariate analysis. I: Robust covariance estimation," *Appl. Statist.*, vol. 29, no. 3, pp. 231-237.

[32] Hardie, R.C. and Arce, G.R. (1991), "Ranking in R^p and its use in multivariate image estimation," *IEEE Trans. on Circuits and Systems for Video Technology*, vol. 1, no. 2, pp. 197-209.

[33] Pitas, I. and Venetsanopoulos, A.N. (1990), *Nonlinear Digital Filters: Principles and Applications*, Kluwer Academic.

[34] Pitas, I., Kotropoulos, C., Nikolaidis, N., Yang, R., and Gabbouj, M. (1996), "Order statistics learning vector quantizer," *IEEE Trans. on Image Processing*, vol. 5, no. 6, pp. 1048-1053.

[35] Hogg, R.V. (1974), "Adaptive robust procedures: a partial review and some suggestions for future applications and theory," *J. Am. Stat. Assoc.*, vol. 69, no. 348, pp. 909-923.

[36] Prescott, P. (1978), "Selection of trimming proportions for robust adaptive trimmed means," *J. Am. Stat. Assoc.*, vol. 73, no. 361, pp. 133-140.

[37] Titterington, D.M. (1978), "Estimation of correlation coefficients by ellipsoidal trimming," *Appl. Stat.*, vol. 27, no. 3, pp. 227-234.

[38] Papoulis, A. (1984), *Probability, Random Variables and Stochastic Processes*, McGraw-Hill.

[39] Borş, A.G. and Pitas, I. (1998), "Optical flow estimation and moving object segmentation based on median radial basis function network," *IEEE Trans. on Image Processing*, vol. 7, no. 5, pp. 693-702.

[40] Giakoumis, I. and Pitas, I. (1998), "Digital restoration of painting cracks," *Proc. IEEE Int. Symposium on Circuits and Systems (ISCAS'98)*, Monterey, California, USA.

[41] Chatzis, V., Borş, A.G., and Pitas, I. (1999), "Multimodal decision-level fusion for person authentication," *IEEE Trans. on Systems, Man, and Cybernetics, Part A: Systems and Humans*, vol. 29, no. 6, pp. 674-680.

[42] Borş, A.G. and Pitas, I. (1999), "Object classification in 3-D images using alpha-trimmed mean radial basis function network," *IEEE Trans. on Image Processing*, vol. 8, no. 12, pp. 1744-1756.

[43] Borş, A.G. and Pitas, I. (1998), "Object segmentation in 3-D images based on alpha-trimmed mean radial basis function network," *Proc. European Conference on Signal Processing (EUSIPCO'98)*, vol. II, pp. 1093-1096, Rhodes, Greece.

Chapter 7

An Introduction to Kernel Methods

C. Campbell

Kernel methods give a systematic and principled approach to training learning machines and the good generalization performance achieved can be readily justified using statistical learning theory or Bayesian arguments. We describe how to use kernel methods for classification, regression and novelty detection and in each case we find that training can be reduced to optimization of a convex cost function. We describe algorithmic approaches for training these systems including model selection strategies and techniques for handling unlabeled data. Finally we present some recent applications. The emphasis will be on using RBF kernels which generate RBF networks but the approach is general since other types of learning machines (e.g., feed-forward neural networks or polynomial classifiers) can be readily generated with different choices of kernel.

1 Introduction

Radial Basis Function (RBF) networks have been widely studied because they exhibit good generalization and universal approximation through use of RBF nodes in the hidden layer. In this Chapter we will outline a new approach to designing RBF networks based on *kernel methods*. These techniques have a number of advantages. As we shall see, the approach is systematic and properly motivated theoretically. The learning machine is also explicitly constructed using the most informative patterns in the data. Because the dependence on the data is clear it is much easier to explain and interpret the model and data cleaning [16] could be implemented to improve performance. The learning process involves optimization of a cost function which is provably convex. This contrasts with neural network approaches where the exist of false local minima in the error function can complicate the learning process. For kernel methods there are comparatively few parameters required for tuning the system. Indeed, recently proposed model selection schemes could lead to the elimination of these parameters altogether. Unlike neural network approaches the architecture is determined by the algorithm and not found by experimentation. It is also possible to give confidence estimates on the classification accuracy on new test examples. Finally these learning machines typically exhibit good generalization and perform well in practice.

In this introduction to the subject, we will focus on Support Vector Machines (SVMs) which are the most well known learning systems based on kernel methods. The emphasis will be on classification, regression and novelty detection and we will not cover other interesting topics, for example, kernel methods for unsupervised learning [43], [52]. We will begin by introducing SVMs for binary classification and the idea of kernel substitution. The kernel representation of data amounts to a nonlinear projection of data into a high-dimensional space where it is easier to separate the two classes of data. We then develop this approach to handle noisy datasets, multiclass classification, regression and novelty detection. We also consider strategies for finding the kernel parameter and techniques for handling unlabeled data. In Section 3, we then describe algorithms for training these systems and in Section 4, we describe some current applications. In the conclusion, we will briefly discuss other types of learning machines based on kernel methods.

2   Kernel Methods for Classification, Regression, and Novelty Detection

2.1   Binary Classification

From the perspective of statistical learning theory the motivation for considering binary classifier SVMs comes from theoretical bounds on the generalization error [58], [59], [10]. For ease of explanation we give the theorem in the Appendix 1 (Theorem 1) and simply note here that it has two important features. Firstly, the error bound is minimized by maximizing the *margin*, γ, i.e., the minimal distance between the hyperplane separating the two classes and the closest datapoints to the hyperplane

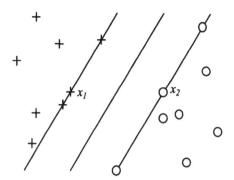

Figure 1. The *margin* is the perpendicular distance between the separating hyperplane and a hyperplane through the closest points (these are *support vectors*).
The region between the hyperplanes on each side is called the *margin band*. x_1
and x_2 are examples of support vectors of opposite sign.

(Figure 1). Secondly, the upper bound on the generalization error do not
depend on the dimension of the space.

The learning task. Let us consider a binary classification task with datapoints x_i $(i = 1, \ldots, m)$ having corresponding labels $y_i = \pm 1$ and let
the decision function be:

$$f(\mathbf{x}) = \text{sign}\,(\mathbf{w} \cdot \mathbf{x} + b) \tag{1}$$

If the dataset is separable then the data will be correctly classified if
$y_i(\mathbf{w} \cdot \mathbf{x}_i + b) > 0\ \forall i$. Clearly this relation is invariant under a positive
rescaling of the argument inside the *sign*-function, hence we can define a
canonical hyperplane such that $\mathbf{w} \cdot \mathbf{x} + b = 1$ for the closest points on one
side and $\mathbf{w} \cdot \mathbf{x} + b = -1$ for the closest on the other. For the separating
hyperplane $\mathbf{w} \cdot \mathbf{x} + b = 0$ the normal vector is clearly $\mathbf{w}/\,||\mathbf{w}||$. Hence the
margin is given by the projection of $x_1 - x_2$ onto this vector where x_1
and x_2 are closest points on opposite sides of the separating hyperplane
(see Figure 1). Since $\mathbf{w} \cdot \mathbf{x}_1 + b = 1$ and $\mathbf{w} \cdot \mathbf{x}_2 + b = -1$ this means the
margin is $\gamma = 1/\,||\mathbf{w}||$. To maximize the margin, the task is therefore:

$$\min \left[\frac{1}{2} ||\mathbf{w}||^2 \right] \tag{2}$$

subject to the constraints:

$$y_i\,(\mathbf{w} \cdot \mathbf{x}_i + b) \geq 1 \qquad \forall i \tag{3}$$

and the learning task reduces to minimization of the primal objective function:

$$L = \frac{1}{2}(\mathbf{w} \cdot \mathbf{w}) - \sum_{i=1}^{m} \alpha_i \left(y_i(\mathbf{w} \cdot \mathbf{x}_i + b) - 1\right) \tag{4}$$

where α_i are Lagrange multipliers (hence $\alpha_i \geq 0$). Taking the derivatives with respect to b and $\mathbf{w}$ gives:

$$\sum_{i=1}^{m} \alpha_i y_i = 0 \tag{5}$$

$$\mathbf{w} = \sum_{i=1}^{m} \alpha_i y_i \mathbf{x}_i \tag{6}$$

and resubstituting these expressions back in the primal gives the Wolfe dual:

$$W(\alpha) = \sum_{i=1}^{m} \alpha_i - \frac{1}{2} \sum_{i,j=1}^{m} \alpha_i \alpha_j y_i y_j \left(\mathbf{x}_i \cdot \mathbf{x}_j\right) \tag{7}$$

which must be maximized with respect to the α_i subject to the constraint:

$$\alpha_i \geq 0 \qquad \sum_{i=1}^{m} \alpha_i y_i = 0 \tag{8}$$

Kernel substitution. This constrained quadratic programming (QP) problem will give an optimal separating hyperplane with a maximal margin if the data is separable. However, we have still not exploited the second observation from theorem 1: the error bound does not depend on the dimension of the space. This feature enables us to give an alternative kernel representation of the data which is equivalent to a mapping into a high dimensional space where the two classes of data are more readily separable. This space is called *feature space* and must be a pre-Hilbert or inner product space. For the dual objective function in (7) we notice that the datapoints, $\mathbf{x}_i$, only appear inside an inner product. Thus the mapping is achieved through a replacement of the inner product:

$$\mathbf{x}_i \cdot \mathbf{x}_j \rightarrow \phi(\mathbf{x}_i) \cdot \phi(\mathbf{x}_j) \tag{9}$$

The functional form of the mapping $\phi(\mathbf{x}_i)$ does not need to be known since it is implicitly defined by the choice of *kernel*:

$$K(\mathbf{x}_i, \mathbf{x}_j) = \phi(\mathbf{x}_i) \cdot \phi(\mathbf{x}_j) \tag{10}$$

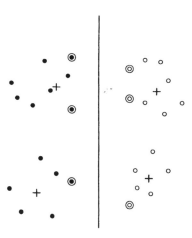

Figure 2. A classical RBF network finds the centers of RBF nodes by k-means clustering (marked by crosses). In contrast an SVM with RBF kernels uses RBF nodes centered on the support vectors (circled), i.e., the datapoints closest to the separating hyperplane (the vertical line illustrated).

which is the inner product in the higher dimensional Hilbert space. With a suitable choice of kernel the data can become separable in feature space despite being non-separable in the original input space. Thus, for example, whereas data for n-parity is non-separable by a hyperplane in input space it can be separated in the feature space defined by RBF kernels:

$$K(\mathbf{x}_i, \mathbf{x}_j) = e^{-\|\mathbf{x}_i - \mathbf{x}_j\|^2 / 2\sigma^2} \tag{11}$$

Other choices of kernel are possible, e.g.:

$$K(\mathbf{x}_i, \mathbf{x}_j) = (\mathbf{x}_i \cdot \mathbf{x}_j + 1)^d \qquad\qquad K(\mathbf{x}_i, \mathbf{x}_j) = \tanh(\beta \mathbf{x}_i \cdot \mathbf{x}_j + b) \tag{12}$$

which would define polynomial and feedforward neural network classifiers. Each choice of kernel will define a different type of feature space and the resulting classifiers will perform differently on test data, though good generalization should be assured from Theorem 1. For an SVM with RBF kernels the resulting architecture is an RBF network. However, the method for determining the number of nodes and their centers is quite different from standard RBF networks with the number of nodes equal to the number of support vectors and the centers of the RBF nodes identified with the support vectors themselves (Figure 2).

Feasible kernels implicitly describing this mapping must satisfy *Mer-*

cer's conditions described in more detail in Appendix 2. The class of mathematical objects which can be used as kernels is very general and includes, for example, scores produced by dynamic alignment algorithms [18], [63] and a wide range of functions.

For the given choice of kernel the learning task therefore involves maximization of the objective function:

$$W(\alpha) = \sum_{i=1}^{m} \alpha_i - \frac{1}{2} \sum_{i,j=1}^{m} \alpha_i \alpha_j y_i y_j K(\mathbf{x}_i, \mathbf{x}_j) \tag{13}$$

subject to the constraints of Equation (8). The associated *Karush-Kuhn-Tucker* (KKT) conditions are:

$$
\begin{aligned}
y_i (\mathbf{w} \cdot \mathbf{x}_i + b) - 1 &\geq 0 & \forall i \\
\alpha_i &\geq 0 & \forall i \\
\alpha_i (y_i(\mathbf{w} \cdot \mathbf{x}_i + b) - 1) &= 0 & \forall i
\end{aligned} \tag{14}
$$

which are always satisfied when a solution is found. Test examples are evaluated using a decision function given by the sign of:

$$f(\mathbf{z}) = \sum_{i=1}^{m} y_i \alpha_i K(\mathbf{x}_i, \mathbf{z}) + b \tag{15}$$

Since the bias, b, does not feature in the above dual formulation it is found from the primal constraints:

$$
\begin{aligned}
b = -\frac{1}{2} \Bigg[& \max_{\{i|y_i=-1\}} \left(\sum_{j \in \{SV\}}^{m} y_j \alpha_j K(\mathbf{x}_i, \mathbf{x}_j) \right) \\
& + \min_{\{i|y_i=+1\}} \left(\sum_{j \in \{SV\}}^{m} y_j \alpha_j K(\mathbf{x}_i, \mathbf{x}_j) \right) \Bigg]
\end{aligned} \tag{16}
$$

using the optimal values of α_j. When the maximal margin hyperplane is found in feature space, only those points which lie closest to the hyperplane have $\alpha_i > 0$ and these points are the *support vectors* (all other points have $\alpha_i = 0$). This means that the representation of the hypothesis is given solely by those points which are closest to the hyperplane and *they are the most informative patterns in the data.* Patterns which are

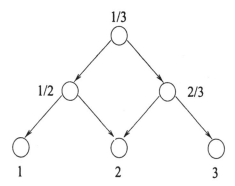

Figure 3. A multi-class classification problem can be reduced to a series of binary classification tasks using a tree structure with a binary decision at each node.

not support vectors do not influence the position and orientation of the separating hyperplane and so do not contribute to the hypothesis (Figure 1).

We have motivated SVMs using statistical learning theory but they can also be understood from a Bayesian perspective [51], [25], [26]. Bayesian [53] and statistical learning theory can also be used to define confidence measures for classification. From the latter we find that the confidence of a classification is directly related to the magnitude of $f(\mathbf{z})$ on a test example [46].

2.2   Multiclass Classification

Many real-life datasets involve multiclass classification and various schemes have been proposed to handle this [28]. One approach is to generalize the binary classifier to an $n-$class classifier with weights and biases $(\mathbf{w}_k, b_k), k = 1, \dots, n$ for each class and a decision function [64]:

$$f(\mathbf{z}) = \arg \max_{1 \leq k \leq n} (\mathbf{w}_k \cdot \mathbf{z} + b_k) \tag{17}$$

However, this type of classifier has a similar level of performance to the simpler scheme of n binary classifiers each of which performs one-against-all classification. Binary classifiers can also be incorporated into a directed acyclic graph (Figure 3) so that multiclass classification is decomposed to binary classification at each node in the tree [34].

2.3   Allowing for Training Errors: Soft Margin Techniques

Most real life datasets contain noise and an SVM can fit to this noise leading to poor generalization. The effect of outliers and noise can be reduced by introducing a *soft margin* [8] and two schemes are currently used. In the first (L_1 error norm) the learning task is the same as in Equations (13,8) except for the introduction of the box constraint:

$$0 \leq \alpha_i \leq C \tag{18}$$

while in the second (L_2 error norm) the learning task is as in Equations (13,8) except for addition of a small positive constant to the leading diagonal of the kernel matrix [8], [48]:

$$K(\mathbf{x}_i, \mathbf{x}_i) \leftarrow K(\mathbf{x}_i, \mathbf{x}_i) + \lambda \tag{19}$$

C and λ control the trade-off between training error and generalization ability and are chosen by means of a validation set. The effect of these soft margins is illustrated in Figure 4 for the ionosphere dataset from the UCI Repository [57].

The justification for these approaches comes from statistical learning theory (cf. Theorems 2 and 3 in Appendix 1). Thus for the L_1 error norm (and prior to introducing kernels) condition (3) is relaxed by introducing a positive slack variable ξ_i:

$$y_i (\mathbf{w} \cdot \mathbf{x}_i + b) \geq 1 - \xi_i \tag{20}$$

and the task is now to minimize the sum of errors $\sum_{i=1}^{m} \xi_i$ in addition to $||\mathbf{w}||^2$:

$$\min \left[\frac{1}{2}\mathbf{w} \cdot \mathbf{w} + C \sum_{i=1}^{m} \xi_i \right] \tag{21}$$

This is readily formulated as a primal objective function:

$$
\begin{aligned}
L(\mathbf{w}, b, \alpha, \xi) \ = \ & \frac{1}{2}\mathbf{w} \cdot \mathbf{w} + C \sum_{i=1}^{m} \xi_i \\
& - \sum_{i=1}^{m} \alpha_i \left[y_i (\mathbf{w} \cdot \mathbf{x}_i + b) - 1 + \xi_i \right] - \sum_{i=1}^{m} r_i \xi_i
\end{aligned} \tag{22}
$$

with Lagrange multipliers $\alpha_i \geq 0$ and $r_i \geq 0$. The derivatives with respect to $\mathbf{w}$, b and ξ give:

$$\frac{\partial L}{\partial \mathbf{w}} = \mathbf{w} - \sum_{i=1}^{m} \alpha_i y_i \mathbf{x}_i = 0 \qquad (23)$$

$$\frac{\partial L}{\partial b} = \sum_{i=1}^{m} \alpha_i y_i = 0 \qquad (24)$$

$$\frac{\partial L}{\partial \xi_i} = C - \alpha_i - r_i = 0 \qquad (25)$$

Resubstituting these back in the primal objective function we obtain the same dual objective function as before, Equation (13). However, $r_i > 0$ and $C - \alpha_i - r_i = 0$, hence $\alpha_i \leq C$ and the constraint $0 \leq \alpha_i$ is replaced by $0 \leq \alpha_i \leq C$. Patterns with values $0 < \alpha_i < C$ will be referred to later as *non-bound* and those with $\alpha_i = 0$ or $\alpha_i = C$ will be said to be *at bound*. For an L_1 error norm we find the bias in the decision function of Equation (15) by using the final KKT condition in Equation (14). Thus if i is a *non-bound* pattern it follows that $b = y_i - \sum_j \alpha_j y_j K(\mathbf{x}_i, \mathbf{x}_j)$ assuming $y_i = \pm 1$.

The optimal value of C must be found by experimentation using a validation set (Figure 4) and it cannot be readily related to the characteristics of the dataset or model. In an alternative approach [44], a soft margin parameter, $\nu = 1/mC$, can be interpreted as an upper bound on the fraction of training errors and a lower bound on the fraction of patterns which are support vectors.

For the L_2 error norm the primal objective function is:

$$L(\mathbf{w}, b, \alpha, \xi) = \frac{1}{2}\mathbf{w} \cdot \mathbf{w} + C \sum_{i=1}^{m} \xi_i^2$$
$$- \sum_{i=1}^{m} \alpha_i \left[y_i (\mathbf{w} \cdot \mathbf{x}_i + b) - 1 + \xi_i \right] - \sum_{i=1}^{m} r_i \xi_i \qquad (26)$$

with $\alpha_i \geq 0$ and $r_i \geq 0$. After obtaining the derivatives with respect to $\mathbf{w}$, b and ξ, substituting for $\mathbf{w}$ and ξ in the primal objective function and noting that the dual objective function is maximal when $r_i = 0$, we

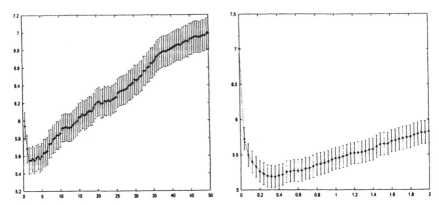

Figure 4. *Left:* generalization error as a percentage (y-axis) versus C (x-axis) and *right:* generalization error as a percentage (y-axis) versus λ (x-axis) for soft margin classifiers based on L_1 and L_2 error norms respectively. The UCI ionosphere dataset was used with RBF kernels ($\sigma = 1.5$) and 100 samplings of the data.

obtain the following dual objective function after kernel substitution:

$$W(\alpha) = \sum_{i=1}^{m} \alpha_i - \frac{1}{2} \sum_{i,j=1}^{m} y_i y_j \alpha_i \alpha_j K(\mathbf{x}_i, \mathbf{x}_j) - \frac{1}{4C} \sum_{i=1}^{m} \alpha_i^2 \qquad (27)$$

With $\lambda = 1/2C$ this gives the same dual objective function as before (Equation (13)) but with the substitution of Equation (19). For many real-life datasets there is an imbalance between the amount of data in different classes, or the significance of the data in the two classes can be quite different. For example, for the detection of tumors on MRI scans it may be best to allow a higher number of false positives if this improved the true positive detection rate. The relative balance between the detection rate for different classes can be easily shifted [61] by introducing asymmetric soft margin parameters. Thus for binary classification with an L_1 error norm $0 \leq \alpha_i \leq C_+$ ($y_i = +1$), and $0 \leq \alpha_i \leq C_-$ ($y_i = -1$), while $K(\mathbf{x}_i, \mathbf{x}_i) \leftarrow K(\mathbf{x}_i, \mathbf{x}_i) + \lambda_+$ (if $y_i = +1$) and $K(\mathbf{x}_i, \mathbf{x}_i) \leftarrow K(\mathbf{x}_i, \mathbf{x}_i) + \lambda_-$ (if $y_i = -1$) for the L_2 error norm.

2.4   Novelty Detection

For many real-world problems the task is not to classify but to detect novel or abnormal instances. For the above example involving classification of tumors it could be the case that the classification system does not correctly detect a tumor with a rare shape which is distinct from all members of the training set. On the other hand, a novelty detector would still potentially highlight the object as abnormal. Novelty detection has potential applications in many problem domains such as condition monitoring or medical diagnosis. Novelty detection can be viewed as modeling the *support* of a data distribution (rather than having to find a real-valued function for estimating the density of the data itself). Thus, at its simplest level, the objective is to create a binary-valued function which is positive in those regions of input space where the data predominantly lies and negative elsewhere.

One approach [54] is to find a hypersphere with a minimal radius R and centre a which contains most of the data: novel test points lie outside the boundary of this hypersphere. The technique we now outline was originally suggested by Vapnik [58], [5], interpreted as a novelty detector by Tax and Duin [54] and used by the latter authors for real life applications [55]. The effect of outliers is reduced by using slack variables ξ_i to allow for datapoints outside the sphere and the task is to minimize the volume of the sphere and number of datapoints outside, i.e.,

$$\min \left[R^2 + \frac{1}{m\nu} \sum_i \xi_i \right]$$

subject to the constraints:

$$(\mathbf{x}_i - \mathbf{a})^T (\mathbf{x}_i - \mathbf{a}) \leq R^2 + \xi_i$$

and $\xi_i \geq 0$, and where ν controls the tradeoff between the two terms. The primal objective function is then:

$$L(R, \mathbf{a}, \alpha_i, \xi_i) = R^2 + \frac{1}{m\nu} \sum_{i=1}^{m} \xi_i$$

$$- \sum_{i=1}^{m} \alpha_i \left(R^2 + \xi_i - (\mathbf{x}_i \cdot \mathbf{x}_i - 2\mathbf{a} \cdot \mathbf{x}_i + \mathbf{a} \cdot \mathbf{a}) \right) - \sum_{i=1}^{m} \gamma_i \xi_i \quad (28)$$

with $\alpha_i \geq 0$ and $\gamma_i \geq 0$. After kernel substitution the dual formulation amounts to maximization of:

$$W(\alpha) = \sum_{i=1}^{m} \alpha_i K(\mathbf{x}_i, \mathbf{x}_i) - \sum_{i,j=1}^{m} \alpha_i \alpha_j K(\mathbf{x}_i, \mathbf{x}_j) \quad (29)$$

with respect to α_i and subject to $\sum_{i=1}^{m} \alpha_i = 1$ and $0 \leq \alpha_i \leq 1/m\nu$. If $m\nu > 1$ then *at bound* examples will occur with $\alpha_i = 1/m\nu$ and these correspond to outliers in the training process. Having completed the training process a test point z is declared novel if:

$$K(\mathbf{z}, \mathbf{z}) - 2 \sum_{i=1}^{m} \alpha_i K(\mathbf{z}, \mathbf{x}_i) + \sum_{i,j=1}^{m} \alpha_i \alpha_j K(\mathbf{x}_i, \mathbf{x}_j) - R^2 \geq 0 \qquad (30)$$

where R^2 is first computed by finding an example which is *non-bound* and setting this inequality to an equality.

An alternative approach has been developed by Schölkopf *et al.* [41]. Suppose we restrict our attention to RBF kernels: in this case the data lie in a region on the surface of a hypersphere in feature space since $\phi(\mathbf{x}) \cdot \phi(\mathbf{x}) = K(\mathbf{x}, \mathbf{x}) = 1$ from (11). The objective is therefore to separate off this region from the surface region containing no data. This is achieved by constructing a hyperplane which is maximally distant from the origin with all datapoints lying on the opposite side from the origin and such that $\mathbf{w} \cdot \mathbf{x}_i + b \geq 0$. This construction can be extended to allow for outliers by introducing a slack variable ξ_i giving rise to the following criterion:

$$\min \left[\frac{1}{2} \|\mathbf{w}\|^2 + \frac{1}{m\nu} \sum_{i=1}^{m} \xi_i + b \right] \qquad (31)$$

subject to:

$$\mathbf{w} \cdot \mathbf{x}_i + b \geq -\xi_i \qquad (32)$$

with $\xi_i \geq 0$. The primal objective function is therefore:

$$L(\mathbf{w}, \xi, b, \alpha, \beta) = \frac{1}{2} \|\mathbf{w}\|^2 + \frac{1}{m\nu} \sum_{i=1}^{m} \xi_i + b$$
$$- \sum_{i=1}^{m} \alpha_i (\mathbf{w} \cdot \mathbf{x}_i + b + \xi_i) - \sum_{i=1}^{m} \beta_i \xi_i \qquad (33)$$

and the derivatives:

$$\frac{\partial L}{\partial \mathbf{w}} = \mathbf{w} - \sum_{i=1}^{m} \alpha_i \mathbf{x}_i = 0 \qquad (34)$$

$$\frac{\partial L}{\partial \xi} = -\alpha_i - \beta_i + \frac{1}{m\nu} = 0 \qquad (35)$$

$$\frac{\partial L}{\partial b} = 1 - \sum_{i=1}^{m} \alpha_i = 0 \qquad (36)$$

Since $\alpha_i, \beta_i \geq 0$ the derivative $\partial L / \partial \xi = 0$ implies $0 \leq \alpha_i \leq 1/m\nu$. After kernel substitution the dual formulation involves minimization of:

$$W(\alpha) = \frac{1}{2} \sum_{i,k=1}^{m} \alpha_i \alpha_j K(\mathbf{x}_i, \mathbf{x}_j) \tag{37}$$

subject to:

$$0 \leq \alpha_i \leq \frac{1}{m\nu} \qquad \sum_{i=1}^{m} \alpha_i = 1 \tag{38}$$

To determine the bias we find an example, k say, which is non-bound (α_i and β_i are nonzero and $0 < \alpha_i < 1/m\nu$) and determine b from:

$$b = - \sum_{j=1}^{m} \alpha_j K(\mathbf{x}_j, \mathbf{x}_k) \tag{39}$$

The support of the distribution is then modeled by the decision function:

$$f(\mathbf{z}) = \text{sign} \left(\sum_{j=1}^{m} \alpha_j K(\mathbf{x}_j, \mathbf{z}) + b \right) \tag{40}$$

In the above models, the parameter ν has a neat interpretation as an upper bound on the fraction of outliers and a lower bound of the fraction of patterns which are support vectors [41]. Schölkopf *et al.* [41] provide good experimental evidence in favor of this approach including the highlighting of abnormal digits in the USPS handwritten character dataset. The method also works well for other types of kernel. This and the earlier scheme for novelty detection can also be used with an L_2 error norm in which case the constraint $0 \leq \alpha_i \leq 1/m\nu$ is removed and an addition to the kernel diagonal (19) used instead.

2.5 Regression

For real-valued outputs the learning task can also be theoretically motivated from statistical learning theory. Theorem 4 in Appendix 1 gives a bound on the generalization error to within a margin tolerance θ. We can visualize this as a band or tube of size $\pm(\theta - \gamma)$ around the hypothesis function $f(\mathbf{x})$ and any points outside this tube can be viewed as training errors (Figure 5).

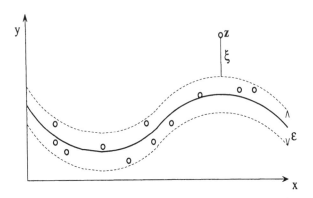

Figure 5. The ϵ-insensitive band around a nonlinear regression function. The variables ξ measure the cost of training errors corresponding to points outside the band, e.g., z.

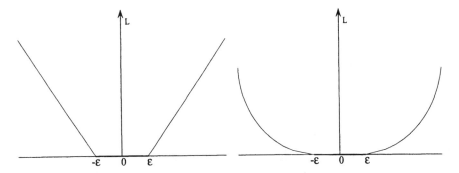

Figure 6. Left figure: a linear ϵ-insensitive loss function versus $y_i - \mathbf{w} \cdot \mathbf{x}_i - b$. Right figure: a quadratic ϵ-insensitive loss function.

Thus, instead of Equation (3) we now use constraints $y_i - \mathbf{w} \cdot \mathbf{x}_i - b \leq \epsilon$ and $\mathbf{w} \cdot \mathbf{x}_i + b - y_i \leq \epsilon$ to allow for a deviation ϵ between the eventual targets y_i and the function $f(\mathbf{x}) = \mathbf{w} \cdot \mathbf{x} + b$, modeling the data. As before, we would also minimize $||\mathbf{w}||^2$ to increase flatness or penalize over-complexity. To account for training errors we introduce slack variables $\xi_i, \hat{\xi}_i$ for the two types of training error and an ϵ-*insensitive loss function* (Figure 6). These slack variables are zero for points inside the tube and progressively increase for points outside the tube according to the loss function used. This general approach is called ϵ-SV regression [58] and is the most common approach to SV regression, though not the only one [9], [59]. For a *linear ϵ-insensitive loss function* the task is therefore to minimize:

$$\min \left[||\mathbf{w}||^2 + C \sum_{i=1}^{m} \left(\xi_i + \widehat{\xi}_i \right) \right] \tag{41}$$

subject to

$$
\begin{aligned}
y_i - \mathbf{w} \cdot \mathbf{x}_i - b &\le \epsilon + \xi_i \\
(\mathbf{w} \cdot \mathbf{x}_i + b) - y_i &\le \epsilon + \widehat{\xi}_i
\end{aligned}
\tag{42}
$$

where the slack variables are both positive $\xi_i, \widehat{\xi}_i \ge 0$. After kernel substitution the dual objective function is:

$$
\begin{aligned}
W(\alpha, \widehat{\alpha}) = &\sum_{i=1}^{m} y_i(\alpha_i - \widehat{\alpha}_i) - \epsilon \sum_{i=1}^{m}(\alpha_i + \widehat{\alpha}_i) \\
&- \frac{1}{2} \sum_{i,j=1}^{m} (\alpha_i - \widehat{\alpha}_i)(\alpha_j - \widehat{\alpha}_j) K(x_i, x_j)
\end{aligned}
\tag{43}
$$

which is maximized subject to

$$\sum_{i=1}^{m} \widehat{\alpha}_i = \sum_{i=1}^{m} \alpha_i \tag{44}$$

and:

$$0 \le \alpha_i \le C \qquad 0 \le \widehat{\alpha}_i \le C \tag{45}$$

Similarly a *quadratic ϵ-insensitive loss function* gives rise to:

$$\min \left[||\mathbf{w}||^2 + C \sum_{i=1}^{m} \left(\xi_i^2 + \widehat{\xi}_i^2 \right) \right] \tag{46}$$

subject to (42), giving a dual objective function:

$$
\begin{aligned}
W(\alpha, \widehat{\alpha}) = &\sum_{i=1}^{m} y_i(\alpha_i - \widehat{\alpha}_i) - \epsilon \sum_{i=1}^{m}(\alpha_i + \widehat{\alpha}_i) \\
&- \frac{1}{2} \sum_{i,j=1}^{m} (\alpha_i - \widehat{\alpha}_i)(\alpha_j - \widehat{\alpha}_j) \left(K(\mathbf{x}_i, \mathbf{x}_j) + \delta_{ij}/C \right)
\end{aligned}
\tag{47}
$$

which is maximized subject to (44). The decision function is then:

$$f(\mathbf{z}) = \sum_{i=1}^{m} (\alpha_i - \widehat{\alpha}_i) K(\mathbf{x}_i, \mathbf{z}) + b \tag{48}$$

We still have to compute the bias, b, and we do so by considering the KKT conditions for regression. For a linear loss function prior to kernel substitution these are:

$$\alpha_i \left(\epsilon + \xi_i - y_i + \mathbf{w} \cdot \mathbf{x}_i + b \right) = 0$$
$$\hat{\alpha}_i \left(\epsilon + \hat{\xi}_i + y_i - \mathbf{w} \cdot \mathbf{x}_i - b \right) = 0 \qquad (49)$$

where $\mathbf{w} = \sum_{j=1}^{m} y_j(\alpha_j - \hat{\alpha}_j)\mathbf{x}_j$, and:

$$(C - \alpha_i)\,\xi_i = 0$$
$$(C - \hat{\alpha}_i)\,\hat{\xi}_i = 0 \qquad (50)$$

From the latter conditions we see that only when $\alpha_i = C$ or $\hat{\alpha}_i = C$ are the slack variables non-zero: these examples correspond to points outside the ϵ-insensitive tube. Hence from Equation (49) we can find the bias from a non-bound example with $0 < \alpha_i < C$ using $b = y_i - \mathbf{w} \cdot \mathbf{x}_i - \epsilon$ and similarly for $0 < \hat{\alpha}_i < C$ we can obtain it from $b = y_i - \mathbf{w} \cdot \mathbf{x}_i + \epsilon$. Though the bias can be obtained from one such example it is best to compute it using an average over all points on the margin.

From the KKT conditions we also deduce that $\alpha_i \hat{\alpha}_i = 0$ since α_i and $\hat{\alpha}_i$ cannot be simultaneously non-zero because we would have non-zero slack variables on both sides of the band. Thus, given that α_i is zero if $\hat{\alpha}_i > 0$ and *vice versa*, we can use a more convenient formulation for the actual optimization task, e.g., maximize:

$$W(\gamma) = -\epsilon \sum_{i=1}^{m} |\gamma_i| + \sum_{i=1}^{m} y_i \gamma_i - \frac{1}{2} \sum_{i,j=1}^{m} \gamma_i \gamma_j K(\mathbf{x}_i, \mathbf{x}_j) \qquad (51)$$

subject to $\sum_{i=1}^{m} \gamma_i = 0$ for a linear ϵ-insensitive loss function.

Apart from the formulations given here it is possible to define other loss functions giving rise to different dual objective functions. In addition, rather than specifying ϵ *a priori* it is possible to specify an upper bound ν ($0 \leq \nu \leq 1$) on the fraction of points lying outside the band and then find ϵ by optimizing over the primal objective function:

$$\frac{1}{2}||\mathbf{w}||^2 + C \left(\nu m \epsilon + \sum_{i=1}^{m} |y_i - f(\mathbf{x}_i)| \right) \qquad (52)$$

with ϵ acting as an additional parameter to minimize over [38].

2.6   Enhanced Learning Strategies

Determining the kernel parameters. During the training process the kernel parameter (e.g., σ in Equation (11)) needs to be specified. If it is too small, for example, then generalization performance will suffer from overfitting (Figure 7). The kernel parameter is best found using cross-validation if sufficient data is available. However, recent model selection strategies can give a reasonable estimate for the kernel parameter based on theoretical arguments without use of validation data. As a first attempt, for the hard margin case, the generalization error bound (which we denote here as E) can be approximated by $E \simeq R^2/m\gamma^2$ [47] where R is the radius of the smallest ball containing the training data. Let α_i^0 be the values of the Lagrange multipliers at the optimum of $W(\alpha)$. From $\gamma = 1/\|\mathbf{w}\|$ we can deduce that $\gamma^2 = 1/\sum_{i\in\{SV\}} \alpha_i^0$ since if i is a support vector then $y_i(\sum_{j\in SV} \alpha_j^0 y_j(\mathbf{x}_i \cdot \mathbf{x}_j) + b) = 1$, thus:

$$
\begin{aligned}
\mathbf{w} \cdot \mathbf{w} &= \sum_{i,j\in\{SV\}} \alpha_i^0 \alpha_j^0 y_i y_j (\mathbf{x}_i \cdot \mathbf{x}_j) \qquad (53) \\
&= \sum_{i\in\{SV\}} \alpha_i^0 (1 - y_i b) \\
&= \sum_{i\in\{SV\}} \alpha_i^0
\end{aligned}
$$

since $\sum_{i\in\{SV\}} \alpha_i^0 y_i = 0$.

After kernel substitution, RBF kernels give $R \simeq 1$ since the data lie on the surface of a hypersphere. Hence, an estimate for σ could be found by sequentially training SVMs on a dataset at successively larger values of σ, evaluating E from the α_i^0 for each case and choosing that value of σ for which E is minimized. This method [9] will give a reasonable estimate if the data is spread evenly over the surface of the hypersphere but it is poor if the data lie in a flat ellipsoid, for example, since the radius R would be influenced by the largest deviations.

More refined estimates therefore take into account the distribution of the data. One approach [7] to finding the error bound is to notionally rescale data in kernel space to compensate for uneven distributions. This rescaling is achieved using the eigenvalues and eigenvectors of the matrix $K(\mathbf{x}_i, \mathbf{x}_j)$. A more complex strategy along these lines has also been

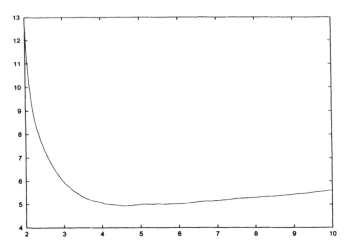

Figure 7. Generalization error as a percentage (y-axis) versus σ (x-axis) from an experiment using artificial data from the mirror symmetry problem and a SVM with an RBF kernel (the curve has been smoothed using 100,000 generated datapoints, allowing repeats). After first overfitting the data the generalization error passes through a minimum as σ increases.

proposed by Schölkopf *et al.* [42] which leads to an algorithm which has performed well in practice for a small number of datasets. A very efficient bound has also been derived recently by Herbrich *et al.* [20].

The most economical way to use the training data is to use a *leave-one-out* cross-validation procedure. In this procedure, single elements from the data set are sequentially removed, the SVM is trained on the remaining $m - 1$ elements and then tested on the removed datapoint. Using the approximation that the set of support vectors does not change for removal of single patterns, it is possible to derive tight bounds on the generalization error. Two examples of these model selection rules are the *span-rule* of Chapelle and Vapnik [7] and a rule proposed by Jaakkola and Haussler [22]. Based on recent studies with a limited number of datasets, these model selection strategies appear to work well. However, a comparative study of these different techniques and their application to a wider range of real-life datasets needs to be undertaken to establish if they are fully practical approaches.

Handling unlabeled data. For some real-life datasets the datapoints are initially unlabeled. Since the labels of points corresponding to *non-*

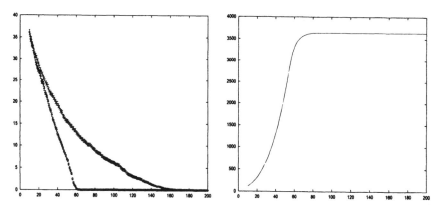

Figure 8. *Left figure*: generalization error (*y*-axis) as a percentage versus number of patterns (*x*-axis) for random selection (top curve) and selective sampling (bottom curve). *Right figure*: monitoring the value of the dual objective function provides a good stopping criterion for noisefree datasets. It this case the majority rule for random bit strings was used with 100 samplings of the data each split into 200 training and 200 test examples.

support vectors are not actually required for determining an optimal separating hyperplane these points do not need to be labeled. This issue is particularly important for practical situations in which labeling data is expensive or the dataset is large and unlabeled. Since SVMs construct the hypothesis using a subset of the data containing the most informative patterns they are good candidates for *active* or *selective sampling* techniques which would predominantly request the labels for those patterns which will become support vectors

During the process of active selection the information gained from an example depends both on the position (available information) and on its label (unavailable information before querying). Thus we must follow a heuristic strategy to maximize information gain at each step. Firstly we note that querying a point within the margin band (Figure 1) *always* guarantees a gain whatever the label of the point: we do not gain by querying a point outside the band unless the current hypothesis predicts the label incorrectly. The best points to query are indeed those points which are closest to the current hyperplane [6]. Intuitively this makes sense since these are most likely to be maximally ambiguous with respect to the current hypothesis and hence the best candidates for ensuring that the information received is maximized. Hence a good strategy [6] is to start by

requesting the labels for a small initial set of data and then successively
querying the labels of points closest to the current hyperplane. For noisefree datasets, plateauing of the dual objective function provides a good
stopping criterion (since learning non-support vectors would not change
the value of $W(\alpha)$ - see Figure 8(right)), whereas for noisy datasets emp-
tying of the margin band and a validation phase provide the best stopping
criterion [6]. Active selection works best if the hypothesis modeling the
data is *sparse* (i.e., there are comparatively few support vectors to be
found by the query learning strategy) in which case good generalization
is achieved despite requesting only a subset of labels in the dataset (Figure 8).

3   Algorithmic Approaches to Training VMs

For classification, regression or novelty detection we see that the learning task involves optimization of a quadratic cost function and thus techniques from quadratic programming are most applicable including quasi-
Newton, conjugate gradient and primal-dual interior point methods. Certain QP packages are readily applicable such as MINOS and LOQO.
These methods can be used to train an SVM rapidly but they have the disadvantage that the kernel matrix is stored in memory. For small datasets
this is practical and QP routines are the best choice, but for larger datasets
alternative techniques have to be used. These split into two categories:
techniques in which kernel components are evaluated and discarded during learning and *working set* methods in which an evolving subset of data
is used. For the first category the most obvious approach is to sequentially
update the α_i and this is the approach used by the Kernel Adatron (KA)
algorithm [15]. For binary classification (with no soft margin or bias) this
is a simple gradient ascent procedure on (13) in which $\alpha_i > 0$ initially
and the α_i are subsequently sequentially updated using:

$$\alpha_i \leftarrow \beta_i \theta(\beta_i) \quad \text{where } \beta_i = \alpha_i + \eta \left(1 - y_i \sum_{j=1}^{m} \alpha_j y_j K(\mathbf{x}_i, \mathbf{x}_j)\right) \quad (54)$$

and $\theta(\beta)$ is the Heaviside step function. The optimal learning rate η can
be readily evaluated: $\eta = 1/K(\mathbf{x}_i, \mathbf{x}_i)$ and a sufficient condition for convergence is $0 < \eta K(\mathbf{x}_i, \mathbf{x}_i) < 2$. With the given decision function of

Equation (15), this method is very easy to implement and can give a quick impression of the performance of SVMs on classification tasks. It is equivalent to Hildreth's method in optimization theory and can be generalized to the case of soft margins and inclusion of a bias [27]. However, it is not as fast as most QP routines, especially on small datasets.

3.1   Chunking and Decomposition

Rather than sequentially updating the α_i the alternative is to update the α_i in parallel but using only a subset or *chunk* of data at each stage. Thus a QP routine is used to optimize the objective function on an initial arbitrary subset of data. The support vectors found are retained and all other datapoints (with $\alpha_i = 0$) discarded. A new working set of data is then derived from these support vectors and additional datapoints which maximally violate the storage constraints. This *chunking* process is then iterated until the margin is maximized. Of course, this procedure may still fail because the dataset is too large or the hypothesis modeling the data is not sparse (most of the α_i are non-zero, say). In this case *decomposition* [31] methods provide a better approach: these algorithms only use a fixed size subset of data with the α_i for the remainder kept fixed.

3.2   Decomposition and Sequential Minimal Optimization

The limiting case of decomposition is the Sequential Minimal Optimization (SMO) algorithm of Platt [33] in which only two α_i are optimized at each iteration. The smallest set of parameters which can be optimized with each iteration is plainly two if the constraint $\sum_{i=1}^{m} \alpha_i y_i = 0$ is to hold. Remarkably, if only two parameters are optimized and the rest kept fixed then it is possible to derive an analytical solution which can be executed using few numerical operations. The algorithm therefore selects two Lagrange multipliers to optimize at every step and separate heuristics are used to find the two members of the pair. Due to its decomposition of the learning task and speed it is probably the method of choice for training SVMs and hence we will describe it in detail here for the case of binary classification.

The outer loop. The heuristic for the first member of the pair provides the outer loop of the SMO algorithm. This loop iterates through the entire training set to determining if an example violates the KKT conditions and, if it does, to find if it is a candidate for optimization. After an initial pass through the training set the outer loop does not subsequently iterate through the entire training set. Instead it iterates through those examples with Lagrange multipliers corresponding to non-bound examples (neither 0 nor C). Examples violating the KKT conditions are candidates for immediate optimization and update. The outer loop makes repeated passes over the non-bound examples until all of the non-bound examples obey the KKT conditions. The outer loop then iterates over the entire training set again. The outer loop keeps alternating between single passes over the entire training set and multiple passes over the non-bound subset until the entire training set obeys the KKT conditions at which point the algorithm terminates.

The inner loop. During the pass through the outer loop let us suppose the algorithm finds an example which violates the KKT conditions (with an associated Lagrange multiplier we shall denote α_1 for convenience). To find the second member of the pair, α_2, we proceed to the inner loop. SMO selects the latter example to maximize the step-length taken during the joint 2-variable optimization process outlined below. To achieve this SMO keeps a record of each value of $E_i = f(\mathbf{x}_i) - y_i$ (where $f(\mathbf{x}) = \mathbf{w} \cdot \mathbf{x} + b$) for every non-bound example in the training set and then approximates the step-length by the absolute value of the numerator in equation (56) below, i.e., $|E_1 - E_2|$. Since we want to maximize the step-length, this means we choose the minimum value of E_2 if E_1 is positive and the maximum value of E_2 if E_1 is negative. As we point out below, this step may not make an improvement. If so, SMO iterates through the non-bound examples searching for a second example that can make an improvement. If none of the non-bound examples gives an improvement, then SMO iterates through the entire training set until an example is found that makes an improvement. Both the iteration through the non-bound examples and the iteration through the entire training set are started at random locations to avoid an implicit bias towards examples at the beginning of the training set.

The update rules. Having described the outer and inner loops for SMO we now describe the rules used to update the chosen pair of Lagrange multipliers (α_1, α_2). The constraint $\sum_{i=1}^{N} \alpha_i y_i = 0$ gives:

$$\alpha_1 y_1 + \alpha_2 y_2 = - \sum_{i \neq 1,2} \alpha_i y_i \qquad (55)$$

Since $y_i = \pm 1$ we have two possibilities. Firstly $y_1 = y_2$ in which case $\alpha_1 + \alpha_2$ is equal to some constant: $\alpha_1 + \alpha_2 = \lambda$, say, or $y_1 \neq y_2$ in which case $\alpha_1 - \alpha_2 = \lambda$. The next step is to find the maximum of the dual objective function with only two Lagrange multipliers permitted to change. Usually this leads to a maximum along the direction of the linear equality constraint though this not always the case as we discuss shortly. We first determine the candidate value for second Lagrange multiplier α_2 and then the ends of the diagonal line segment in terms of α_2:

$$\alpha_2^{new} = \alpha_2^{old} - \frac{y_2 (E_1 - E_2)}{\eta}, \qquad (56)$$

where $E_i = f^{old}(\mathbf{x}_i) - y_i$ and

$$\eta = 2K(\mathbf{x}_1, \mathbf{x}_2) - K(\mathbf{x}_1, \mathbf{x}_1) - K(\mathbf{x}_2, \mathbf{x}_2). \qquad (57)$$

If noise is present and we use a L_1 soft margin then the next step is to determine the two ends of the diagonal line segment. Thus if $y_1 \neq y_2$ the following bounds apply:

$$L = \max(0, \alpha_2^{old} - \alpha_1^{old}), \quad H = \min(C, C + \alpha_2^{old} - \alpha_1^{old}), \qquad (58)$$

and if $y_1 = y_2$ then:

$$L = \max(0, \alpha_1^{old} + \alpha_2^{old} - C), \quad H = \min(C, \alpha_2^{old} + \alpha_1^{old}). \qquad (59)$$

The constrained maximum is then found by clipping the unconstrained maximum to the ends of the line segment:

$$\alpha_2^{new,clipped} = \begin{cases} H, & if \ \alpha_2^{new} \geq H; \\ \alpha_2^{new}, & if \ L < \alpha_2^{new} < H; \\ L, & if \ \alpha_2^{new} \leq L. \end{cases} \qquad (60)$$

Next the value of α_1 is determined from the clipped α_2:

$$\alpha_1^{new} = \alpha_1^{old} + y_1 y_2 (\alpha_2^{old} - \alpha_2^{new,clipped}). \tag{61}$$

This operation moves α_1 and α_2 to the end point with the highest value of $W(\alpha)$. Only when $W(\alpha)$ is the same at both ends will no improvement be made. After each step, the bias b is recomputed so that the KKT conditions are fulfilled for both examples. If the new α_1 is a non-bound variable then b_1 is determined from:

$$\begin{aligned} b_1 = {} & b_1^{old} - E_1 - y_1(\alpha_1^{new} - \alpha_1^{old})K(\mathbf{x}_1, \mathbf{x}_1) \\ & - y_2(\alpha_2^{new,clipped} - \alpha_2^{old})K(\mathbf{x}_1, \mathbf{x}_2). \end{aligned} \tag{62}$$

Similarly if the new α_2 is non-bound then b_2 is determined from:

$$\begin{aligned} b_2 = {} & b_2^{old} - E_2 - y_1(\alpha_1^{new} - \alpha_1^{old})K(\mathbf{x}_1, \mathbf{x}_2) \\ & - y_2(\alpha_2^{new,clipped} - \alpha_2^{old})K(\mathbf{x}_2, \mathbf{x}_2). \end{aligned} \tag{63}$$

If b_1 and b_2 are valid they should be equal. When both new Lagrange multipliers are at bound and if L is not equal to H, then all thresholds on the interval between b_1 and b_2 are consistent with the KKT conditions and we choose the threshold to be halfway in between b_1 and b_2.

The SMO algorithm has been refined to improve speed [24] and generalized to cover the above three tasks of classification [33], regression [49], and novelty detection [41].

4   Applications

SVMs have been successfully applied to a number of applications ranging from particle identification [2], face detection [32], and text categorization [23], [13], [11] to engine knock detection [37], bioinformatics [4], [65], and database marketing [3]. In this section, we discuss three successful application areas as illustrations: machine vision, handwritten character recognition and bioinformatics. This is a rapidly changing area so more contemporary accounts are best obtained from relevant websites (e.g., [17]).

Machine vision. SVMs are very suited to the binary or multiclass classification tasks which commonly arise in machine vision. As an example we consider a multiclass classification task involving face identification [14]. This experiment used the standard ORL dataset [30] consisting of 10 images per person from 40 different persons. Three methods were tried: a direct SVM classifier which learnt the original images directly (apart from some local rescaling), a classifier which used more extensive preprocessing involving rescaling, local sampling and local principal component analysis, and an invariant SVM classifier which learnt the original images plus a set of images which have been translated and zoomed. For the invariant SVM classifier the training set of 200 images (5 per person) was increased to 1400 translated and zoomed examples and an RBF kernel was used. On the test set these three methods gave generalization errors of 5.5%, 3.7% and 1.5% respectively. This was compared with a number of alternative techniques [14] with the best result among the latter being 2.7%. Face and gender detection have also been successfully achieved. 3D object recognition [36] is another successful area of application including 3D face recognition, pedestrian recognition, etc.

Handwritten digit recognition. The United States Postal Service (USPS) dataset consists of 9298 handwritten digits each consisting of a 16×16 vector with entries between -1 and 1. An RBF network and an SVM were compared on this dataset. The RBF network had spherical Gaussian RBF nodes with the same number of Gaussian basis functions as there were support vectors for the SVM. The centroids and variances for the Gaussians were found using classical k-means clustering. For the SVM Gaussian kernels were used and the system was trained with a soft margin (with $C = 10.0$). A set of one-against-all classifiers were used since this is a multi-class problem. With a training set of 7291, the number of errors on the test set of 2007 was:

Digit	0	1	2	3	4	5	6	7	8	9
Classical RBF	20	16	43	38	46	31	15	18	37	26
SVM	16	8	25	19	29	23	14	12	25	16

and the SVM therefore outperformed the RBF network on all digits. SVMs have also been applied to the much larger NIST dataset of handwritten characters consisting of 60,000 training and 10,000 test images each with 400 pixels. SVMs with polynomial kernels perform at a comparable level to the best alternative techniques [59] with an 0.8% error on the test set.

Bioinformatics. Large-scale DNA sequencing projects are producing large volumes of data and there is a considerable demand for sophisticated methods for analyzing biosequences. Bioinformatics presents a large number of important classification tasks such as prediction of protein secondary structure, classification of gene expression data, recognizing splice junctions, i.e., the boundaries between exons and introns, etc. SVMs have been found to be very effective on these tasks. For example, SVMs outperformed four standard machine learning classifiers when applied to the functional classification of genes using gene expression data from DNA microarray hybridization experiments [4]. Several different similarity metrics and kernels were used and the best performance was achieved using an RBF kernel (the dataset was very imbalanced so asymmetric soft margin parameters were used). A second successful application has been protein homology detection to determine the structural and functional properties of new protein sequences [21]. Determination of these properties is achieved by relating new sequences to proteins with known structural features. In this application the SVM outperformed a number of established systems for homology detection for relating the test sequence to the correct families. As a third application we also mention the detection of translation initiation sites [65] (the points on nucleotide sequences where regions encoding proteins start). SVMs performed very well on this task using a kernel function specifically designed to include prior biological information.

5   Conclusion

Kernel methods have many appealing features. We have seen that they can be applied to a wide range of classification, regression and novelty detection tasks but they can also be applied to other areas we have not covered such as operator inversion and unsupervised learning. They can be used to generate many possible learning machine architectures (RBF networks, feedforward neural networks) through an appropriate choice of kernel. In particular the approach is properly motivated theoretically and systematic in execution.

Our focus has been on SVMs but the concept of kernel substitution of the inner product is a powerful idea separate from margin maximization and it can be used to define many other types of learning machines which can exhibit superior generalization [19], [29] or which use few patterns to construct the hypothesis [56]. We have not been able to discuss these here but they also perform well and appear very promising. The excellent potential of this approach certainly suggests it will remain and develop as an important set of tools for machine learning.

Acknowledgements

The author would like to thank Nello Cristianini and Bernhard Schölkopf for comments on an earlier draft.

Appendices

Appendix 1: Generalization Bounds

The generalization bounds mentioned in Section 2 are derived within the framework of probably approximately correct or *pac* learning. The principal assumption governing this approach is that the training and test data are independently and identically (iid) generated from a fixed distribution denoted $\mathcal{D}$. The distribution over input-output mappings will be denoted $(\mathbf{x}, y) \in X \times \{-1, 1\}$ and we will further assume that X is an inner product space. With these assumptions *pac*-learnability can be described as follows. Consider a class of possible target concepts C and a learner L using a hypothesis space H to try and learn this concept class. The class C is *pac*-learnable by L if for any target concept $c \in C$, L will with probability $(1 - \delta)$ output a hypothesis $h \in H$ with a generalization error $err_{\mathcal{D}}(h) < \epsilon(m, H, \delta)$ given a sufficient number, m, of training examples and computation time. The *pac* bound $\epsilon(m, H, \delta)$ is derived using probabilistic arguments [1], [62] and bounds the tail of the distribution of the generalization error $err_{\mathcal{D}}(h)$.

For the case of a thresholding learner L with unit weight vector on an inner product space X and a margin $\gamma \in \Re^+$ the following theorem can be derived if the dataset is linearly separable:

Theorem 1 Suppose examples are drawn independently according to a distribution whose support is contained in a ball in $\Re^n$ centered at the origin, of radius R. If we succeed in correctly classifying m such examples by a canonical hyperplane, then with confidence $1 - \delta$ the generalization error will be bounded from above by [47]:

$$\epsilon(m, H, \delta) = \frac{2}{m} \left(\frac{64R^2}{\gamma^2} \log \left(\frac{\gamma em}{8R^2} \right) \log \left(\frac{32m}{\gamma^2} \right) + \log \left(\frac{4}{\delta} \right) \right) \quad (64)$$

provided $64R^2/\gamma^2 < m$. This result is not dependent on the dimensionality of the space and also states that the bound is reduced by maximizing the margin γ. Though this is our main result motivating maximization of the margin for SVMs it does not handle the case of non-separable data or the existence of noise. As pointed out in the main text these instances are handled by introducing an L_1 or L_2 soft margin. The following two bounds do not depend on the training data being linearly separable and cover these two cases [48]:

Theorem 2 Suppose examples are drawn independently according to a distribution whose support is contained in a ball in $\Re^n$ centered at the origin, of radius R. There is a constant c such that with confidence $1 - \delta$ the generalization error will be bounded from above by:

$$\epsilon(m, H, \delta) = \frac{c}{m} \left(\frac{R^2 + \|\xi\|_1^2 \log (1/\gamma)}{\gamma^2} \log^2(m) + \log \left(\frac{1}{\delta} \right) \right) \quad (65)$$

where ξ is the margin slack vector.

Theorem 3 Suppose examples are drawn independently according to a distribution whose support is contained in a ball in $\Re^n$ centered at the origin, of radius R. There is a constant c such that with confidence $1 - \delta$ the generalization error will be bounded from above by:

$$\epsilon(m, H, \delta) = \frac{c}{m} \left(\frac{R^2 + \|\xi\|_2^2}{\gamma^2} \log^2(m) + \log \left(\frac{1}{\delta} \right) \right) \quad (66)$$

where ξ is the margin slack vector.

For both these theorems we see that maximizing the margin alone does not necessarily reduce the bound and it is necessary to additionally reduce the norms of the slack variables.

Both these theorems can be adapted to the case of regression. However, in contrast to Theorems 1-3 above it is no longer appropriate to fix the norm of the weight vector since invariance under positive rescaling of the weight vector only holds for a thresholding decision function. For regression the relevant theorem for an L_2 norm on the slack variables is then:

Theorem 4 Suppose examples are drawn independently according to a distribution whose support is contained in a ball in $\Re^n$ centered at the origin, of radius R. Furthermore fix $\gamma \leq \theta$ where θ is a positive real number. There is a constant c such that with probability $1 - \delta$ over m random examples, the probability that a hypothesis with weight vector $\mathbf{w}$ has output more than θ away from its true value is bounded above by:

$$\epsilon(m, H, \delta) = \frac{c}{m} \left(\frac{\|\mathbf{w}\|_2^2 R^2 + \|\xi\|_2^2}{\gamma^2} \log^2(m) + \log\left(\frac{1}{\delta}\right) \right) \quad (67)$$

where $\xi = \xi(\mathbf{w}, \theta, \gamma)$ is the margin slack vector. This theorem motivates the loss functions used in Section 2.5 on regression.

Finally, we note that the above classification theorems have also been extended to estimation of the support of a distribution [41]. However, current bounds are not good indicators of the probability of occurrence of novel points outside a distribution and hence we do not quote them here for this reason.

Appendix 2: Kernel Substitution and Mercer's Theorem

In Section 2, we introduced the idea of kernel substitution, equivalent to introducing an implicit mapping of the data into a high-dimensional feature space. By this means, nonlinear datasets which are unlearnable by a linear learning machine in input space become learnable in feature space. In input space the hypothesis modeling the data is of the form:

$$f(\mathbf{x}) = \mathbf{w} \cdot \mathbf{x} + b \quad (68)$$

For binary classification, for example, we saw in Section 2.3 that the weight vector **w** can be written as:

$$\mathbf{w} = \sum_{i=1}^{m} \alpha_i y_i \mathbf{x}_i \tag{69}$$

If the dataset is separable, the separating hyperplane passes through the convex hull defined by the datapoints and hence it is apparent that **w** can be expressed as such an expansion in terms of the datapoints. With this expansion the decision function of Equation (68) can therefore be rewritten:

$$f(\mathbf{x}) = \sum_{i=1}^{m} \alpha_i y_i (\mathbf{x}_i \cdot \mathbf{x}_j) + b \tag{70}$$

For the learning task of Equations (8,13) and this decision function the datapoints only appear in the form of inner products, justifying kernel substitution and with the choice of kernel implicitly selecting a particular feature space:

$$K(\mathbf{x}_i, \mathbf{x}_j) = \phi(\mathbf{x}_i) \cdot \phi(\mathbf{x}_j) \tag{71}$$

This raises the issue of which types of kernel function are allowed. The requirements on the kernel function are defined by the two theorems below. First we observe that the kernel function is symmetric. In addition we also note from that for a real vector **v** we have

$$\mathbf{v}^T \mathbf{K} \mathbf{v} = \left\| \sum_{i=1}^{m} v_i \phi(\mathbf{x}_i) \right\|_2^2 \geq 0 \tag{72}$$

where the matrix **K** has components $K(\mathbf{x}_i, \mathbf{x}_j)$, $(i = 1, \ldots, m; j = 1, \ldots, m)$. This suggests the following theorem which can be proved:

Theorem 5 Let $K(\mathbf{x}, \mathbf{y})$ be a real symmetric function on a finite input space, then it is a kernel function if and only if the matrix **K** with components $K(\mathbf{x}_i, \mathbf{x}_j)$ is positive semi-definite.

More generally, for C a compact subset of $\Re^N$ we have:

Theorem 6 (Mercer's theorem) If $K(\mathbf{x}, \mathbf{y})$ is a continuous symmetric kernel of a positive integral operator T, i.e.,

$$(Tf)(\mathbf{y}) = \int_C K(\mathbf{x}, \mathbf{y}) f(\mathbf{x}) d\mathbf{x} \tag{73}$$

with:

$$\int_{C \times C} K(\mathbf{x}, \mathbf{y}) f(\mathbf{x}) f(\mathbf{y}) d\mathbf{x} d\mathbf{y} \geq 0 \qquad (74)$$

for all $f \in L_2(C)$ then it can be expanded in a uniformly convergent series in the eigenfunctions ψ_j and positive eigenvalues λ_j of T, thus:

$$K(\mathbf{x}, \mathbf{y}) = \sum_{j=1}^{n_e} \lambda_j \psi_j(\mathbf{x}) \psi_j(\mathbf{y}) \qquad (75)$$

where n_e is the number of positive eigenvalues.

This theorem holds for general compact spaces, and generalizes the requirement to infinite feature spaces. Equation (74) generalizes the semi-positivity condition for finite spaces given in Theorem 5. The expansion in Equation (75) is a generalization of the usual concept of an inner product in Hilbert space with each dimension rescaled by $\sqrt{\lambda_j}$.

References

[1] Anthony, M. and Barlett, P. (1999), *Learning in Neural Networks: Theoretical Foundations*, Cambridge University Press.

[2] Barabino, N., Pallavicini, M., Petrolini, A., Pontil, M., and Verri, A. (1999), "Support vector machines vs multi-layer perceptrons in particle identification," *Proceedings of the European Symposium on Artifical Neural Networks '99*, D-Facto Press, Belgium, pp. 257-262.

[3] Bennett, K.P., Wu, D., and Auslender, L. (1998), "On support vector decision trees for database marketing," Research Report No. 98-100, Rensselaer Polytechnic Institute, Troy, NY.

[4] Brown, M., Grundy, W., Lin, D., Cristianini, N., Sugnet, C., Ares Jr., M., and Haussler, D. (1999), "Support vector machine classification of microarray gene expression data," University of California, Santa Cruz, Technical Report UCSC-CRL-99-09.

[5] Burges, C. (1998), "A tutorial on support vector machines for pattern recognition," *Data Mining and Knowledge Discovery*, vol. 2, pp. 121-167.

[6] Campbell, C., Cristianini, N., and Smola, A. (2000), "Instance selection using support vector machines," submitted to *Machine Learning*.

[7] Chapelle, O. and Vapnik, V. (2000), "Model selection for support vector machines," in Solla, S.A., Leen, T.K., and Muller, K.-R. (Eds.), *Advances in Neural Information Processing Systems*, vol. 12, MIT Press. To appear.

[8] Cortes, C. and Vapnik, V. (1995), "Support vector networks," *Machine Learning*, vol. 20, pp. 273-297.

[9] Cristianini, N., Campbell, C., and Shawe-Taylor, J. (1999), "Dynamically adapting kernels in support vector machines," in Kearns, M., Solla, S.A., and Cohn, D. (Eds.), *Advances in Neural Information Processing Systems*, vol. 11, MIT Press, pp. 204-210.

[10] Cristainini, N. and Shawe-Taylor, J. (2000), *An Introduction to Support Vector Machines and other Kernel-Based Learning Methods*, Cambridge University Press. To appear January.

[11] Drucker, H., Wu, D., and Vapnik, V. (1999), "Support vector machines for spam categorization," *IEEE Trans. on Neural Networks*, vol. 10, pp. 1048-1054.

[12] Drucker, H., Burges, C., Kaufman, L., Smola, A., and Vapnik, V. (1997), "Support vector regression machines," in Mozer, M., Jordan, M., and Petsche, T. (Eds.), *Advances in Neural Information Processing Systems*, vol. 9, MIT Press, Cambridge, MA.

[13] Dumais, S., Platt, J., Heckerman, D., and Sahami, M. (1998), "Inductive learning algorithms and representations for text categorization," *7th International Conference on Information and Knowledge Management*.

[14] Fernandez, R. and Viennet, E. (1999), "Face identification using support vector machines," *Proceedings of the European Symposium on Artificial Neural Networks (ESANN99)*, D.-Facto Press, Brussels, pp. 195-200.

[15] Friess, T.-T., Cristianini, N., and Campbell, C. (1998), "The kernel adatron algorithm: a fast and simple learning procedure for support vector machines," *15th Intl. Conf. Machine Learning*, Morgan Kaufman Publishers, pp. 188-196.

[16] Guyon, I., Matic, N., and Vapnik, V. (1996), "Discovering informative patterns and data cleaning," in Fayyad, U.M., Piatetsky-Shapiro, G., Smyth, P., and Uthurusamy, R. (Eds.), *Advances in Knowledge Discovery and Data Mining*, MIT Press, pp. 181-203.

[17] Cf.: http://www.clopinet.com/isabelle/Projects/SVM/applist.html .

[18] Haussler, D. (1999), "Convolution kernels on discrete structures," UC Santa Cruz Technical Report UCS-CRL-99-10.

[19] Herbrich, R., Graepel, T., and Campbell, C. (1999), "Bayesian learning in reproducing kernel Hilbert spaces," submitted to *Machine Learning*.

[20] Herbrich, R., Graeppel, T., and Bollmann-Sdorra, P. (2000), "A PAC-Bayesian study of linear classifiers: why SVMs work," preprint under preparation, Computer Science Department, TU, Berlin.

[21] Jaakkola, T., Diekhans, M., and Haussler, D. (1999), "A discriminative framework for detecting remote protein homologies," MIT preprint.

[22] Jaakkola, T. and Haussler, D. (1999), "Probabilistic kernel regression models," *Proceedings of the 1999 Conference on AI and Statistics*.

[23] Joachims, T. (1998), "Text categorization with support vector machines: learning with many relevant features," *Proc. European Conference on Machine Learning* (ECML).

[24] Keerthi, S., Shevade, S., Bhattacharyya, C., and Murthy, K. (1999), "Improvements to Platt's SMO algorithm for SVM classifier design," Tech. Report, Dept. of CSA, Banglore, India.

[25] Kwok, J. (1999), "Moderating the outputs of support vector machine classifiers," *IEEE Transactions on Neural Networks*, vol. 10, pp. 1018-1031.

[26] Kwok, J. (1999), "Integrating the evidence framework and support vector machines," *Proceedings of the European Symposium on Artificial Neural Networks (ESANN99)*, D.-Facto Press, Brussels, pp. 177-182.

[27] Luenberger, D. (1984), *Linear and Nonlinear Programming*, Addison-Wesley.

[28] Mayoraz, E. and Alpaydin, E. (1999), "Support vector machines for multiclass classification," *Proceedings of the International Workshop on Artifical Neural Networks (IWANN99)*, IDIAP Technical Report 98-06.

[29] Mika, S., Ratsch, G., Weston, J., Schölkopf, B., and Muller, K.-R. (1999), "Fisher discriminant analysis with kernels," *Proceedings of IEEE Neural Networks for Signal Processing Workshop*.

[30] Olivetti Research Laboratory (1994), *ORL dataset*, http://www.orl. co.uk/facedatabase.html .

[31] Osuna, E. and Girosi, F. (1999) "Reducing the run-time complexity in support vector machines," in Schölkopf, B., Burges, C., and Smola, A. (Eds.), *Advances in Kernel Methods: Support Vector Learning*, MIT press, Cambridge, MA, pp. 271-284.

[32] Osuna, E., Freund, R., and Girosi, F. (1997) "Training support vector machines: an application to face detection," *Proceedings of CVPR'97*, Puerto Rico.

[33] Platt, J. (1999), "Fast training of SVMs using sequential minimal optimization," in Schölkopf, B., Burges, C., and Smola, A. (Eds.), *Advances in Kernel Methods: Support Vector Learning*, MIT press, Cambridge, MA, pp. 185-208.

[34] Platt, J., Cristianini, N., and Shawe-Taylor, J. (2000), "Large margin DAGS for multiclass classification," in Solla, S.A., Leen, T.K., and Muller, K.-R. (Eds.), *Advances in Neural Information Processing Systems*, 12 ed., MIT Press.

[35] Papageorgiou, C., Oren, M., and Poggio, T. (1998), "A general framework for object detection," *Proceedings of International Conference on Computer Vision*, pp. 555-562.

[36] Roobaert, D. (1999), "Improving the generalization of linear support vector machines: an application to 3D object recognition with cluttered background," *Proc. Workshop on Support Vector Machines at the 16th International Joint Conference on Artificial Intelligence*, July 31-August 6, Stockholm, Sweden, pp. 29-33.

[37] Rychetsky, M., Ortmann, S., and Glesner, M. (1999), "Support vector approaches for engine knock detection," *Proc. International Joint Conference on Neural Networks (IJCNN 99)*, July, Washington, U.S.A.

[38] Schölkopf, B., Bartlett, P., Smola, A., and Williamson, R. (1998), "Support vector regression with automatic accuracy control," in Niklasson, L., Bóden, M., and Ziemke, T. (Eds.), *Proceedings of the 8th International Conference on Artificial Neural Networks*, Perspectives in Neural Computing, Berlin, Springer Verlag.

[39] Schölkopf, B., Bartlett, P., Smola, A., and Williamson, R. (1999), "Shrinking the tube: a new support vector regression algorithm," in Kearns, M.S., Solla, S.A., and Cohn, D.A. (Eds.), *Advances in Neural Information Processing Systems*, 11, MIT Press, Cambridge, MA.

[40] Schölkopf, B., Burges, C., and Smola, A. (1998), *Advances in Kernel Methods: Support Vector Machines*, MIT Press, Cambridge, MA.

[41] Schölkopf, B., Platt, J.C., Shawe-Taylor, J., Smola, A.J., and Williamson, R.C. (1999), "Estimating the support of a high-dimensional distribution," Microsoft Research Corporation Technical Report MSR-TR-99-87.

[42] Schölkopf, B., Shawe-Taylor, J., Smola, A., and Williamson, R. (1999), "Kernel-dependent support vector error bounds," *Ninth International Conference on Artificial Neural Networks*, IEE Conference Publications No. 470, pp. 304-309.

[43] Schölkopf, B., Smola, A., and Muller, K.-R. (1999), "Kernel principal component analysis," in Schölkopf, B., Burges, C., and Smola, A. (Eds.), *Advances in Kernel Methods: Support Vector Learning*, MIT Press, Cambridge, MA, pp. 327-352.

[44] Schölkopf, B., Smola, A., Williamson, R.C., and Bartlett, P.L. (1999), "New support vector algorithms," *Neural Computation*.

[45] Schölkopf, B., Sung, K., Burges, C., Girosi, F., Niyogi, P., Poggio, T., and Vapnik, V. (1997), "Comparing support vector machines with Gaussian kernels to radial basis function classifiers," *IEEE Transactions on Signal Processing*, vol. 45, pp. 2758-2765.

[46] Shawe-Taylor, J. (1997), "Confidence estimates of classification accuracy on new examples," in Ben-David, S. (Ed.), EuroCOLT97, *Lecture Notes in Artificial Intelligence*, vol. 1208, pp. 260-271.

[47] Shawe-Taylor, J., Bartlett, P.L., Williamson, R.C., and Anthony, M. (1998), "Structural risk minimization over data-dependent hierarchies," *IEEE Transactions on Information Theory*, vol. 44, pp. 1926-1940.

[48] Shawe-Taylor, J. and Cristianini, N. (1999), "Margin distribution and soft margin," in Smola, A., Barlett, P., Schölkopf, B., and Schuurmans, C. (Eds.), *Advances in Large Margin Classifiers*, Chapter 2, MIT Press.

[49] Smola, A. and Schölkopf, B. (1998), "A tutorial on support vector regression," Tech. Report, NeuroColt2 TR 1998-03.

[50] Smola, A. and Schölkopf, B. (1997), "From regularization operators to support vector kernels," in Mozer, M., Jordan, M., and Petsche, T. (Eds), *Advances in Neural Information Processing Systems*, 9, MIT Press, Cambridge, MA.

[51] Smola, A., Schölkopf, B., and Müller, K.-R. (1998), "The connection between regularization operators and support vector kernels," *Neural Networks*, vol. 11, pp. 637-649.

[52] Smola, A., Williamson, R.C., Mika, S., and Schölkopf, B. (1999), "Regularized principal manifolds," *Computational Learning Theory: 4th European Conference*, volume 1572 of *Lecture Notes in Artificial Intelligence*, Springer, pp. 214-229.

[53] Sollich, P. (2000), "Probabilistic methods for support vector machines," in Solla, S., Leen, T., and Muller, K.-R. (Eds.), *Advances in Neural Information Processing Systems*, 12, MIT Press, Cambridge, MA. (To appear.)

[54] Tax, D. and Duin, R. (1999), "Data domain description by support vectors," in Verleysen, M. (Ed.), *Proceedings of ESANN99*, D. Facto Press, Brussels, pp. 251-256.

[55] Tax, D., Ypma, A., and Duin, R. (1999), "Support vector data description applied to machine vibration analysis," in Boasson, M., Kaandorp, J., Tonino, J., Vosselman, M. (Eds.), *Proc. 5th Annual Conference of the Advanced School for Computing and Imaging*, Heijen, NL, June 15-17, pp. 398-405.

[56] Tipping, M. (2000), "The relevance vector machine," in Solla, S., Leen, T., and Muller, K.-R. (Eds.), *Advances in Neural Information Processing Systems*, MIT Press, Cambridge, MA. (To appear.)

[57] http://www.ics.uci.edu/~mlearn/MLRepository.html .

[58] Vapnik, V. (1995), *The Nature of Statistical Learning Theory*, Springer, N.Y.

[59] Vapnik, V. (1998), *Statistical Learning Theory*, Wiley.

[60] Vapnik, V. and Chapelle, O. (1999), "Bounds on error expectation for support vector machines," submitted to *Neural Computation*.

[61] Veropoulos, K, Campbell, C., and Cristianini, N. (1999), "Controlling the sensitivity of support vector machines," *Proceedings of the International Joint Conference on Artificial Intelligence (IJCAI)*, Stockholm, Sweden.

[62] Vidyasagar, M. (1997), *A Theory of Learning and Generalisation*, Springer-Verlag, Berlin.

[63] Watkins, C. (1999), "Dynamic alignment kernels," Technical Report, UL Royal Holloway, CSD-TR-98-11.

[64] Weston, J. and Watkins, C. (1999), "Multi-class support vector machines," in Verleysen, M. (Ed.), *Proceedings of ESANN99*, D. Facto Press, Brussels, pp. 219-224.

[65] Zien, A., Rätsch, G., Mika, S., Schölkopf, B., Lemmen, C., Smola, A., Lengauer, T., and Müller, K.-R. (1999), "Engineering support vector machine kernels that recognize translation initiation sites," presented at the German Conference on Bioinformatics.

Chapter 8

Unsupervised Learning Using Radial Kernels

C. Fyfe, D. MacDonald, P.L. Lai, R. Rosipal, and D. Charles

In this chapter, we use radial kernels in unsupervised learning methods; we show that we may use efficient linear operations after the nonlinear kernel transformation and still have the net effect of performing an equivalent nonlinear operation on the input data. We first review the use of radial kernels for Kernel Principal Component Analysis (KPCA) and demonstrate its use on toy data. One of the disadvantages of unsupervised kernel methods is that they treat all data points as equally important and we investigate methods of obviating this in the context of a high-dimensional astronomical data set. We then apply kernel methods to Factor Analysis and Exploratory Projection Pursuit and illustrate their power on the well-known Iris data set. Finally, we derive a kernel implementation of Canonical Correlation Analysis and illustrate it on real and artificial data.

1 Introduction

In this chapter, we use radial kernels to learn mappings in an unsupervised manner. The use of radial kernels has been derived from the work of Vapnik [21], Burges [2], etc., in the field of Support Vectors Machines. Support Vector Machines for regression, for example, perform a nonlinear mapping of the data set into some high dimensional feature space in which we may then perform linear operations. Since the original mapping was nonlinear, any linear operation in this feature space corresponds to a nonlinear operation in data space.

We first review recent work on Kernel Principal Component Analysis (KPCA) [12]-[20] which has been the most frequently reported linear operation involving unsupervised learning in feature space. We then extend the method to perform other Kernel-based operations: Kernel Principal Factor Analysis, Kernel Exploratory Projection Pursuit and Kernel Canonical Correlation Analysis. For each operation, we derive the appropriate rules and give exemplar simulation results. Since this book is on Radial Basis Functions, we will report results only using radial kernels, however the theory is quite general and many interesting results may be had using non-radial kernels.

2 Kernel PCA

This section is based very much on the analysis in [16] and [17]. A very good Matlab simulation of Kernel PCA can be found at http://svm.first.gmd.de. In the next section, we show that sample Principal Component Analysis (PCA) may be performed on the samples of a data set in a particular way which will be useful in the performance of PCA in the nonlinear feature space.

2.1 The Linear Kernel

PCA finds the eigenvectors and corresponding eigenvalues of the covariance matrix of a data set. Let $\chi = \{x_1, ..., x_M\}$ be iid (independent, identically distributed) samples drawn from a data source. If each x_i is n-dimensional, $\exists$ at most n eigenvalues/eigenvectors. Let C be the covariance matrix of the data set; then C is $n \times n$. Then the eigenvectors, e_i, are n dimensional vectors which are found by solving

$$Ce = \lambda e \tag{1}$$

where λ is the eigenvalue corresponding to e. We will assume the eigenvalues and eigenvectors are arranged in non-decreasing order of eigenvalues and each eigenvector is of length 1. We will use the sample covariance matrix as though it was the true covariance matrix and so

$$C \approx \frac{1}{M} \sum_{j=1}^{M} x_j x_j^T \tag{2}$$

Now each eigenvector lies in the span of χ; i.e., the set $\chi = \{x_1, ..., x_M\}$ forms a basis set (normally overcomplete since $M > n$) for the eigenvectors. So each e_i can be expressed as

$$e_i = \sum_j \alpha_i^j x_j \tag{3}$$

If we wish to find the principal components of a new data point x we project it on the eigenvectors previously found: the first principal component is $(x.e_1)$, the second is $(x.e_2)$, etc. These are the coordinates of x in the eigenvector basis. There are only n eigenvectors (at most) and so there can only be n coordinates in the new system: we have merely rotated the data set.

Now consider projecting one of the data points from χ on the eigenvector e_1; then

$$x_k.e_1 = x_k. \sum_j \alpha_1^j x_j = \alpha_1. \sum_j x_k x_j \tag{4}$$

Now let K be the matrix of dot products. Then $K_{ij} = x_i x_j$.

Multiplying both sides of (1) by x_k we get

$$x_k C e_1 = \lambda e_1.x_k \tag{5}$$

and using the expansion for e_1, and the definition of the sample covariance matrix, C, gives

$$\frac{1}{M}K^2\alpha_1 = \lambda_1 K\alpha_1 \tag{6}$$

Now it may be shown [17] that all interesting solutions of this equation are also solutions of

$$K\alpha_1 = M\lambda_1\alpha_1 \tag{7}$$

whose solution is that α_1 is the principal eigenvector of K.

2.2   Nonlinear Kernels

Now we preprocess the data using $\Phi : \chi \to F$. So F is now the space spanned by $\Phi(x_1), ..., \Phi(x_M)$. The above arguments all hold and the eigenvectors of the dot product matrix $K_{ij} = (\Phi(x_i).\Phi(x_j))$. But now the *Kernel Trick*: provided we can calculate K we don't need the individual terms $\Phi(x_i)$.

In this chapter, we will exclusively use Gaussian kernels so that

$$K_{ij} = (\Phi(\mathbf{x}_i).\Phi(\mathbf{x}_j)) = \exp(-(\mathbf{x}_i - \mathbf{y}_i)^2/(2\sigma^2)) \qquad (8)$$

This kernel has been shown [17] to satisfy the conditions of Mercer's theorem and so can be used as a kernel for some function $\Phi(.)$. One issue that we must address in feature space is that the eigenvectors should be of unit length. Let $\mathbf{v}_i$ be an eigenvector of C. Then $\mathbf{v}_i$ is a vector in the space F spanned by $\Phi(\mathbf{x}_1), ..., \Phi(\mathbf{x}_M)$ and so can be expressed in terms of this basis. This is an at most M-dimensional subspace of a possibly infinite dimensional space which gives computational tractability to the kernel algorithms. Then

$$\mathbf{v}_i = \sum_{j=1}^{M} \alpha_j^i \Phi(\mathbf{x}_j) \qquad (9)$$

for eigenvectors $\mathbf{v}_i$ corresponding to non-zero eigenvalues. Therefore

$$
\begin{aligned}
\mathbf{v}_i^T \mathbf{v}_i &= \sum_{j,k=1}^{M} \alpha_j^i \Phi(\mathbf{x}_j)^T \Phi(\mathbf{x}_k) \alpha_k^i \\
&= \sum_{j,k=1}^{M} \alpha_j^i K_{jk} \alpha_k^i \\
&= \alpha^i.(K\alpha^i) \\
&= \lambda_i \alpha^i.\alpha^i
\end{aligned}
$$

Now α^i are (by definition of the eigenvectors of K) of unit magnitude. Therefore since we require the eigenvectors to be normalized in feature space, F, i.e. $\mathbf{v}_i^T \mathbf{v}_i = 1$, we must normalize the eigenvectors of K, α^i, by dividing each by the square root of their corresponding eigenvalues.

Now we can simply perform a principal component projection of any new point $\mathbf{x}$ by finding its projection onto the principal components of the feature space, F. Thus

$$\mathbf{v}_i.\Phi(\mathbf{x}) = \sum_{j=1}^{M} \alpha_i^j \Phi(\mathbf{x}_j).\Phi(\mathbf{x}) = \sum_{j=1}^{M} \alpha_i^j K(\mathbf{x}_j, \mathbf{x}) \qquad (10)$$

And the above argument shows that any operation which can be defined in terms of dot products can be Kernelized. We will in subsequent sections use similar arguments with Factor Analysis, Exploratory Projection

Pursuit and Canonical Correlation Analysis; however first we give an illustrative example.

There are many examples of KPCA in the literature (e.g., [13], [14], [17]) and we will in this Chapter only give results using KPCA later when we wish to compare it with other Kernel methods.

2.3   The Curse of Kernel Dimensionality

One of the difficulties associated with unsupervised kernel methods in general is that the nonlinear mapping, $\Phi()$ maps the input data to a feature space of high, possibly infinite, dimensionality. Now one of the advantages kernel methods are said to have is that they are actually working in a space of dimensionality equal only to the number of data points. This is true but in practice the dimensionality may be even less than that if two or more data points coincide. Then we have a reduced rank K matrix. Perhaps more common is the situation when two or more points lie very close to one another (in feature space) and then we have an ill-conditioned K matrix whose lower eigenvectors are very susceptible to noise. It is our finding that kernel methods are typically plagued with problems of this type, a fact which should not be surprising given that we are estimating M eigenvectors from M points. Some methods for creating a reduced set of vectors have been suggested in the past. In addition to addressing this problem, such methods also alleviate the computational problems associated with large matrices. We now suggest further methods to find a reduced set and perform an empirical study of some of these methods.

The data set we will use consists of 65 colour spectra of 115 asteroids used by [10]. The data set is composed of a mixture of the 52-colour survey by [1], together with the 8-colour survey conducted by [22] providing a set of asteroid spectra spanning 0.3-2.5mm. Success is measured in terms of the accuracy of classification of asteroids into the correct data types.

We report results in Table 1 (Kernel Factor Analysis is discussed in the next section – the results are shown here for completeness). The table shows the effectiveness of performing a linear classification of the pro-

Table 1. The percentage accuracy of two kernel methods when different means of creating the data vectors used to determine the kernels.

Initialization method	Kernel method	Dataset	Accuracy
Random	Principal Component Analysis	Asteroid	63%
k-Means	Principal Component Analysis	Asteroid	68%
SOM	Principal Component Analysis	Asteroid	74%
MoG	Principal Component Analysis	Asteroid	67%
Random	Principal Factor Analysis	Asteroid	65%
k-Means	Principal Factor Analysis	Asteroid	70%
SOM	Principal Factor Analysis	Asteroid	75%
MoG	Principal Factor Analysis	Asteroid	68%

jections onto feature space of the data. The methods for choosing a reduced set of points (called initialization methods in the table) were:

Random We simply randomly select a subset of the data set to use as the points which we use to perform a Kernel PCA. Typically we use 100 out of the 116 points.

k-Means We select 50 centers selected using the k-means algorithm. These centers became 'virtual points' on which the KPCA algorithm was performed. Often we found that some centers coincided in which case one was removed (see discussion on ill-conditioned covariance matrices).

SOM We begin with a 10×10 grid of output neurons in a Self-Organizing Map [7] and train the network on this data set. Typically around half the nodes are not responding to a part of the data space and are discarded. The centers from the other half are used as a form of 'virtual data' on which to perform the KPCA.

MoG We assume the data was formed from a Mixtures of Gaussian causes (we actually used diagonal covariance matrices for the Gaussian covariance matrices) and optimized the parameters of the model using the EM Algorithm. Typically we found that the data set was best explained by 20-30 Gaussians whose means were used as 'virtual data' on which the KPCA was performed. The centers were found using the EM algorithm.

We see from Table 1 that the SOM provided the best points (in terms of accuracy of the clustering) on which KPCA was performed. Perhaps the most interesting result is the difference between the SOM and the k-Means algorithm; this may best be explained by the fact that the centers in the k-Means algorithm are totally competitive and tend to move to the regions of greatest mass. In the SOM, the topology preservation causes some neurons to map to regions of lower probability density, something which in other guises is a drawback when the mapping has neurons whose centers are in areas of low mass. This study is part of a larger study over different data sets, however these results seem to be typical.

3   Kernel Principal Factor Analysis

A standard method of finding independent sources in a data set is the statistical technique of Factor Analysis (FA). PCA and FA are closely related statistical techniques both of which achieve an efficient compression of the data but in a different manner. They can both be described as methods to explain the data set in a smaller number of dimensions but FA is based on assumptions about the nature of the underlying data whereas PCA is model free.

We can also view PCA as an attempt to find a transformation from the data set to a compressed code, whereas in FA we try to find the linear transformation which takes us from a set of hidden factors to the data set. Since PCA is model free, we make no assumptions about the form of the data's covariance matrix. However FA begins with a specific model which is usually constrained by our prior knowledge or assumptions about the data set. The general FA model can be described by the following relationship:

$$\mathbf{x} = L\mathbf{f} + \mathbf{u} \tag{11}$$

where $\mathbf{x}$ is a vector representative of the data set, $\mathbf{f}$ is the vector of factors, L is the matrix of factor loadings and $\mathbf{u}$ is the vector of specific (unique) factors.

The usual assumptions built into the model are that:

- $E(\mathbf{f}) = 0$, $\text{Var}(\mathbf{f}) = I$, i.e., the factors are zero mean, of the same power and uncorrelated with each other;

- $E(\mathbf{u}) = 0$, $\mathrm{Cov}(\mathbf{u}_i, \mathbf{u}_j) = 0$, $\forall i, j$, i.e, the specific factors are also zero mean and uncorrelated with each other; and

- $\mathrm{Cov}(\mathbf{f}, \mathbf{u}) = 0$, i.e., the factors and specific factors are uncorrelated.

Let $C = E(\mathbf{x}\mathbf{x}^T)$ be the covariance matrix of $\mathbf{x}$ (again assuming zero mean data). Then $C = \Lambda\Lambda^T + \Phi$ where Φ is the covariance matrix of the specific factors, $\mathbf{u}$ and so Φ is a diagonal matrix, $diag\{\Phi_{11}, \Phi_{22}, ..., \Phi_{MM}\}$. Now whereas PCA attempts to explain C without a specific model, FA attempts to find parameters Λ and Φ which explain C and only if such models can be found will a Factor Analysis be successful.

Estimations of the Factor loading is usually done by means of one of two methods - Maximum Likelihood Estimation or Principal Factor Analysis [9]. Since Principal Factor Analysis is a method which may be performed using dot products, this is the method in which we shall be interested in this chapter.

3.1   Principal Factor Analysis

Expanding $C = E(\mathbf{x}\mathbf{x}^T)$, then

$$C_{ii} = \sum_j \lambda_{ij}^2 + \Phi_{ii}^2 = h_i^2 + \Phi_{ii}^2 \qquad (12)$$

i.e. the variance of the data set can be broken into two parts the first of which is known as the communality and is the variance of x_i which is shared via the factor loadings with the other variables. The second is the specific or unique variance associated with the ith input.

In Principal Factor Analysis (PFA), an initial estimate of the communalities is made. This is inserted into the main diagonal of the data covariance matrix and then a PCA is performed on the "reduced correlation matrix". A commonly used estimate of the communalities is the maximum of the square of the multiple correlation coefficient of the ith variable with every other variable.

We have previously [3] derived a neural network method of performing Principal Factor Analysis.

3.2   The Varimax Rotation

In PCA the orthogonal components are arranged in descending order of importance and a unique solution is always possible. The factor loadings in FA are not unique and there are likely to be substantial loadings on more than one factor that may be negative or positive. This often means that the results in standard FA are difficult to interpret. To overcome these problems it is possible to perform a rigid rotation of the axes of the factor space and so identify a more simplified structure in the data that is more easily interpretable. One well-known method of achieving this is the Varimax rotation [9]. This has as its rationale that factors should be formed with a few large loadings and as many near zero loadings as possible, normally achieved by an iterative maximization of a quadratic function of the factor loadings. It is worth noting that the Varimax rotation aims for a sparse response to the data and this has acknowledged as an efficient form coding. In the experiments presented here it can be seen that by using a Varimax rotation we can gain more straightforward, interpretable results than with PCA in kernel space.

3.3   Kernel Principal Factor Analysis

As before, let $\chi = x_1, ..., x_M$ be iid (independent, identically distributed) samples drawn from a data source. Let C be the covariance matrix of the data set and let us define $C^- = C - D$ where we will assume that D is a diagonal matrix of the form $D = \mu I$. We are thus stripping out the same amount of variance from each element in the diagonal of the covariance matrix of the data.

Then the eigenvectors of this reduced covariance matrix, e_i, are n dimensional vectors which are found by solving

$$C^- e_i = \lambda_i e_i \qquad (13)$$

where λ_i is the eigenvalue corresponding to e_i. We will assume the eigenvalues and eigenvectors are arranged in non-decreasing order of eigenvalues and each eigenvector is of length 1. We will use the sample covariance matrix as though it was the true covariance matrix and so

$$C^- \approx \frac{1}{M} \sum_{j=1}^{M} \mathbf{x}_j \mathbf{x}_j^T - \mu I \tag{14}$$

Then

$$C^- \mathbf{e}_i = \frac{1}{M} \sum_{j=1}^{M} \mathbf{x}_j \mathbf{x}_j^T \mathbf{e}_i - \mu I \mathbf{e}_i \tag{15}$$

$$\text{i.e., } \lambda_i \mathbf{e}_i = \frac{1}{M} \sum_{j=1}^{M} \mathbf{x}_j \mathbf{x}_j^T \mathbf{e}_i - \mu \mathbf{e}_i \tag{16}$$

$$\text{Thus, } \sum_{j=1}^{M} \mathbf{x}_j (\mathbf{x}_j^T \mathbf{e}_i) = M(\mu + \lambda_i) \mathbf{e}_i \tag{17}$$

Now repeating the argument of Section 2 gives us a solution, α_i which is a principal eigenvector of the K matrix with eigenvalue $\gamma_i = M(\lambda_i + \mu)$. Similarly, if we have a nonlinear mapping to a feature space, F, then $C^- \approx \frac{1}{M} \sum_{j=1}^{M} \Phi(\mathbf{x}_j) \Phi^T(\mathbf{x}_j) - \mu I$ and the above arguments continue to hold.

Note that the direction of each eigenvector is exactly the same as the KPCA solution but the corresponding eigenvalue is different.

Now the normalization of the eigenvectors in Feature space, $\mathbf{e}_i^T \mathbf{e}_i = 1$, forces us to normalize the eigenvectors of K, α_i, by dividing each by the square root of their corresponding eigenvalues, γ_i. But note now that these eigenvalues contain both a term from the eigenvalues of the covariance matrix and also μ. Thus the Varimax rotation may have a different solution when applied in the KPFA space compared with that found in the KPCA space.

However this assumption of noise in the feature space is less interesting than the assumption of noise in the data space which is then transformed by passing the noise through the nonlinearity into the feature space. Thus we now consider the situation in which the input data contains the noise and the nonlinear function, $\Phi()$ acts on both signal and noise. There seems to be no generic solution to this and so we must consider the effect of the noise through different functions.

- Consider the feature space of all monomials of degree 2 on two-dimensional data, i.e.,

$$\Phi(\mathbf{x}) = \Phi((x_1, x_2)) = (x_1^2, x_1 x_2, x_2^2) \tag{18}$$

Then if our model is such that $(x_1, x_2) = (x_1^- + \mu_1, x_2^- + \mu_2)$, then

$$\Phi(\mathbf{x}) = ((x_1^- + \mu_1)^2, (x_1^- + \mu_1)(x_2^- + \mu_2), (x_2^- + \mu_2)^2) \tag{19}$$

which, for zero mean noise, has expectation

$$\Phi(\mathbf{x}) = ((x_1^-)^2 + \mu^2, x_1^- x_2^-, (x_2^-)^2 + \mu^2) \tag{20}$$

So the noise in this space does not satisfy the conditions,

$$C^- \approx \frac{1}{M} \sum_{j=1}^{M} \Phi(\mathbf{x}_j) \Phi^T(\mathbf{x}_j) - \mu I$$

- Consider the space formed from the Gaussian function: now there is no known nonlinear function but we may consider the kernel matrix directly

$$
\begin{aligned}
K_{ij} &= \Phi(\mathbf{x}_i, \mathbf{x}_j) = \exp(-(\mathbf{x}_i - \mathbf{x}_j)^2/\sigma) \\
&= \exp(-(\mathbf{x}_i^- + \mu_i - \mathbf{x}_j^- - \mu_j)^2/\sigma)
\end{aligned}
$$

where we have used μ_i and μ_j as vectors of noise. Then while it is true that the expected value of this is given by

$$K_{ij} = exp(-(\mathbf{x}_i^- - \mathbf{x}_j^-)^2/\sigma) \tag{21}$$

this is true only of the expectation. Considering this on a data point by data point basis,

$$\exp(-(\mathbf{x}_i^- + \mu_i - \mathbf{x}_j^- - \mu_j)^2/\sigma) \neq exp(-(\mathbf{x}_i^- - \mathbf{x}_j^-)^2/\sigma) \tag{22}$$

other than the special case when $i = j$. Thus we have an interesting analogy to subtracting out a common term from the C covariance matrix: the K matrix is only absolutely correct along its main diagonal.

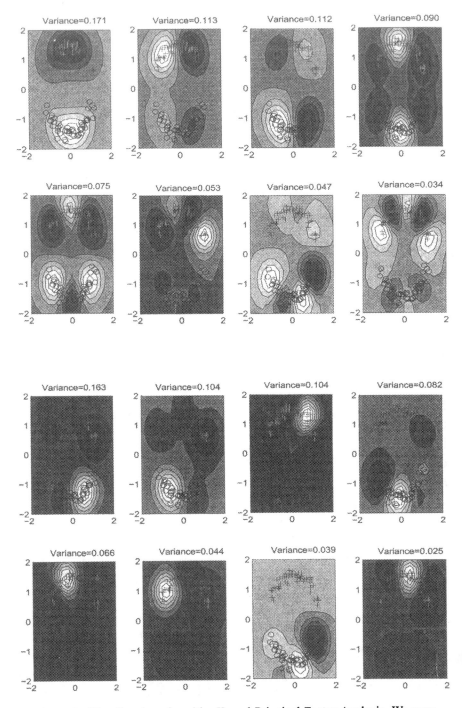

Figure 2. The directions found by Kernel Principal Factor Analysis. We may compare this with Figure 1.

3.4 Simulations

We first create artificial data in the form of two noisy arcs of a circle. The filters found by KPCA are shown in Figure 1 while those found by KPFA are shown in Figure 2; the FA results were achieved after a Varimax rotation. We see that the results from KPFA are more tightly defined (more local) than those from KPCA and that it concentrates on one of the two arcs at one time.

4   Kernel Exploratory Projection Pursuit

4.1   Exploratory Projection Pursuit

Exploratory Projection Pursuit attempts to project the data onto a low-dimensional subspace in order to look for structure in the projection. However not all projections reveal the data's structure equally well; so we define an index that measures how "interesting" a given projection is, and then represent the data in terms of the projections that are maximally interesting.

Friedman [5] notes that what constitutes an interesting direction is more difficult to define than what constitutes an uninteresting direction. The idea of "interestingness" is usually defined in relation to the oft-quoted observation of Diaconis and Freedman([4]) that most projections through most multi-dimensional data are almost Gaussian. This would suggest that if we wish to identify "interesting" features in data, we should look for those projections which are as non-Gaussian as possible.

Thus we require a method for moving a filter (a weight vector) so that it finds linear combinations of the data set which are as non-Gaussian as possible. Some possible measures of non-Gaussianity lie in the higher order statistics of the data: for example, the third moment measures skewness in a data set while the fourth measures the volume of the distribution found in the tails of the distribution. Since we are not interested in the mean or the variance of the distribution (one Gaussian is an uninteresting as any other Gaussian) we sphere (or whiten) the data to remove the first and second moments; we can envisage this as translating the data till its mean is over the origin and squeezing in or teasing out the data in each direction till it has equal spread in each direction. It is then with this sphered data that we look for interesting filters. We have previously given a neural implementation of Exploratory Projection Pursuit [6].

4.2   Kernel Exploratory Projection Pursuit

Smola et al. [19] have introduced the term Kernel Projection Pursuit: they argue that rather than finding the vector, v_1 which maximizes the variance of the projections in feature space

$$v_1 = \arg \max_{v \in V} \frac{1}{m} \sum_{i=1}^{m} (v.\Phi(x_i))^2 \qquad (23)$$

we may choose any other function of the projection to maximize. Thus we may choose

$$v_1 = \arg \max_{v \in V} \frac{1}{m} \sum_{i=1}^{m} q(v.\Phi(x_i)) \qquad (24)$$

where $q(.)$ may be a higher power or indeed we can use more general functions of all variable projections so that we have

$$v_1 = \arg \max_{v \in V} Q(\{v.\Phi(x_1), v.\Phi(x_2), ..., v.\Phi(x_m)\}) \qquad (25)$$

where $Q(.)$ may now be any function with a finite maximum. However, there is no necessity or capability when using that single operation to perform sphering of the data which the EPP method demands. Therefore we perform a two-stage operation just as we would if we were operating in data space.

The operation of KPCA gives us principal components in feature space. Since we are already centering these Kernels, all that is required for sphering is to divide each projection by the square root of its eigenvalue and we have a set of coordinates in feature space which is sphered. Now we may choose any method to search for higher order structure in feature space. We choose to use a neural method which we have already shown to perform EPP on sphered data in data space [6]. Let z_i be the projection of the data point x_i onto feature space after the sphering has been carried

out. Now **z** is fed forward through weights, W, to output neurons to give
a vector. Now the activation is passed back to the originating **z** values as
inhibition and then a non-linear function of the inputs is calculated:

$$y_i = \sum_j w_{ij} z_j$$
$$z_j \leftarrow z_j - w_{ij} y_i$$
$$s_i = tanh(y_i)$$

and then the new weights are calculated using simple Hebbian learning

$$\Delta w_{ij} = \beta z_j y_i$$

Note at this stage the operation of our algorithm is identical to that used
previously in data space. Because we are using the sphered projections
onto the eigenvectors, it is irrelevant as to whether these eigenvectors are
eigenvectors in the data space or eigenvectors in the (nonlinear) feature
space.

4.3   Simulations

We use the Iris data set to compare KPCA (Figure 3) and KEPP (Figure 4). Figure 3 shows the projection of the iris data set on the first two
principal component directions found by Kernel PCA. We can see that
one cluster has been clearly found but the other two clusters are very intertwined. In Figure 4 we see the projections of the same data set onto
the filters of the first two Exploratory Projection Pursuit directions. One
cluster has been split from the other two and in addition, the separation
between the second and third clusters is very much greater than with
KPCA. It is worth noting that this result was found with great repeatabil-
ity which is rather unlike many EPP methods working in data space. We
require more investigation of this feature.

5   Canonical Correlation Analysis

Canonical Correlation Analysis is a statistical technique used when we
have two data sets which we believe have some underlying correlation.
Consider two sets of input data; x_1 and x_2. Then in classical CCA, we

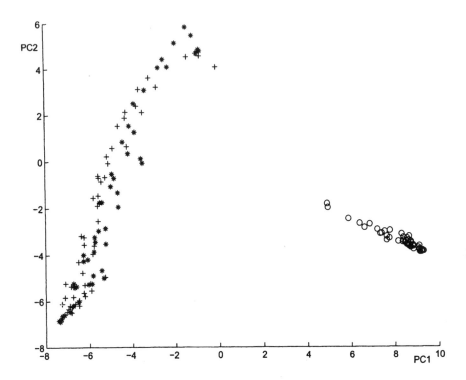

Figure 3. The projections on the first two kernel principal component directions of the iris data set; one cluster has clearly been identified but the other two are very intertwined.

attempt to find that linear combination of the variables which give us maximum correlation between the combinations. Let

$$\mathbf{y}_1 = \mathbf{w}_1\mathbf{x}_1 = \sum_j w_{1j}x_{1j}$$

$$\mathbf{y}_2 = \mathbf{w}_2\mathbf{x}_2 = \sum_j w_{2j}x_{2j}$$

where we have used $\mathbf{x}_{1j}$ as the jth element of $\mathbf{x}_1$.

Then we wish to find those values of $\mathbf{w}_1$ and $\mathbf{w}_2$ which maximize the correlation between $\mathbf{y}_1$ and $\mathbf{y}_2$. If the relation between $\mathbf{y}_1$ and $\mathbf{y}_2$ is believed to be causal, we may view the process as one of finding the best predictor of the set $\mathbf{x}_2$ by the set $\mathbf{x}_1$ and similarly of finding the best predictable criterion in the set $\mathbf{x}_2$ from the set $\mathbf{x}_1$ data set.

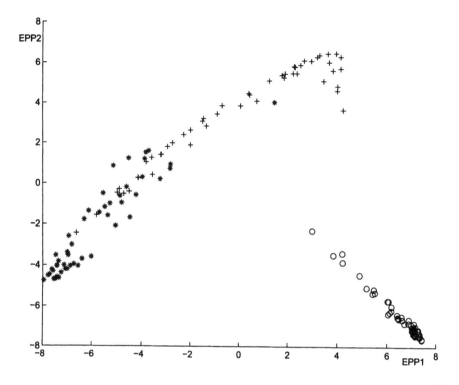

Figure 4. The projections of the first two kernel exploratory projection pursuit directions of the iris data set; one cluster has clearly been identified and the second and third clusters have been partially separated.

Then the standard statistical method (see [9]) lies in defining

$$\begin{aligned}
\Sigma_{11} &= E\{(\mathbf{x}_1 - \mu_1)(\mathbf{x}_1 - \mu_1)^T\} \\
\Sigma_{22} &= E\{(\mathbf{x}_2 - \mu_2)(\mathbf{x}_2 - \mu_2)^T\} \\
\Sigma_{12} &= E\{(\mathbf{x}_1 - \mu_1)(\mathbf{x}_2 - \mu_2)^T\} \\
\text{and } K &= \Sigma_{11}^{-\frac{1}{2}}\Sigma_{12}\Sigma_{22}^{-\frac{1}{2}}
\end{aligned} \tag{26}$$

where T denotes the transpose of a vector. We then perform a Singular Value Decomposition of K to get

$$K = (\alpha_1, \alpha_2, ..., \alpha_k)D(\beta_1, \beta_2, ..., \beta_k)^T \tag{27}$$

where α_i and β_i are the standardized eigenvectors of KK^T and K^TK respectively and D is the diagonal matrix of eigenvalues.

Then the first canonical correlation vectors (those which give greatest correlation) are given by

$$\mathbf{w}_1 = \Sigma_{11}^{-\frac{1}{2}}\alpha_1 \tag{28}$$

$$\mathbf{w}_2 = \Sigma_{22}^{-\frac{1}{2}}\beta_1 \tag{29}$$

with subsequent canonical correlation vectors defined in terms of the subsequent eigenvectors, α_i and β_i.

5.1 Kernel Canonical Correlation Analysis

Consider mapping the input data to a high dimensional (perhaps infinite dimensional) feature space, F. Now,

$$\Sigma_{11} = E\{(\Phi(\mathbf{x}_1) - \mu_1)(\Phi(\mathbf{x}_1) - \mu_1)^T\}$$
$$\Sigma_{22} = E\{(\Phi(\mathbf{x}_2) - \mu_2)(\Phi(\mathbf{x}_2) - \mu_2)^T\}$$
$$\Sigma_{12} = E\{(\Phi(\mathbf{x}_1) - \mu_1)(\Phi(\mathbf{x}_2) - \mu_2)^T\}$$

where now $\mu_i = E(\Phi(\mathbf{x}_i))$ for $i = 1, 2$. Let us assume for the moment that the data has been centered in feature space (we actually will use the same trick as [17] to centre the data later). Then we define

$$\Sigma_{11} = E\{\Phi(\mathbf{x}_1)\Phi(\mathbf{x}_1)^T\}$$
$$\Sigma_{22} = E\{\Phi(\mathbf{x}_2)\Phi(\mathbf{x}_2)^T\}$$
$$\Sigma_{12} = E\{\Phi(\mathbf{x}_1)\Phi(\mathbf{x}_2)^T\}$$

and we wish to find those values $\mathbf{w}_1$ and $\mathbf{w}_2$ which will maximize $\mathbf{w}_1^T\Sigma_{12}\mathbf{w}_2$ subject to the constraints $\mathbf{w}_1^T\Sigma_{11}\mathbf{w}_1 = 1$ and $\mathbf{w}_2^T\Sigma_{22}\mathbf{w}_2 = 1$.

In practice we will approximate Σ_{12} with $\frac{1}{n}\sum_i \Phi(\mathbf{x}_{1i})\Phi(\mathbf{x}_{2i})$, the sample average.

At this stage we can see the similarity with our nonlinear CCA: if we consider an instantaneous hill-climbing algorithm, we would derive precisely our NLCCA algorithm for the particular nonlinearity involved.

Now $\mathbf{w}_1$ and $\mathbf{w}_2$ exist in the feature space which is spanned by $\{\Phi(\mathbf{x}_{11}), \Phi(\mathbf{x}_{12}), ..., \Phi(\mathbf{x}_{1n}), \Phi(\mathbf{x}_{21}), ..., \Phi(\mathbf{x}_{2n})\}$ and therefore can be expressed as

$$\mathbf{w}_1 = \sum_{i=1}^{n} \alpha_{1i} \Phi(\mathbf{x}_{1i}) + \sum_{i=1}^{n} \alpha_{2i} \Phi(\mathbf{x}_{2i})$$

$$\mathbf{w}_2 = \sum_{i=1}^{n} \beta_{1i} \Phi(\mathbf{x}_{1i}) + \sum_{i=1}^{n} \beta_{2i} \Phi(\mathbf{x}_{2i})$$

With some abuse of the notation we will use $\mathbf{x}_i$ to be the ith instance from the set of data, i.e., from either the set of values of $\mathbf{x}_1$ or from those of $\mathbf{x}_2$ and write

$$\mathbf{w}_1 = \sum_{i=1}^{2n} \alpha_i \Phi(\mathbf{x}_i)$$

$$\mathbf{w}_2 = \sum_{i=1}^{2n} \beta_i \Phi(\mathbf{x}_i)$$

Therefore substituting this in the criteria we wish to optimize, we get

$$(\mathbf{w}_1^T \Sigma_{12} \mathbf{w}_2) = \frac{1}{n} \sum_{k,i} \alpha_k . \Phi^T(\mathbf{x}_k) \Phi(\mathbf{x}_{1i}) \sum_l \beta_l \Phi^T(\mathbf{x}_{2i}) \Phi(\mathbf{x}_l) \qquad (30)$$

where the sums over i are to find the sample means over the data set. Similarly with the constraints and so

$$\mathbf{w}_1^T \Sigma_{11} \mathbf{w}_1 = \frac{1}{n} \sum_{k,i} \alpha_k . \Phi^T(\mathbf{x}_k) \Phi(\mathbf{x}_{1i}) . \sum_l \alpha_l \Phi^T(\mathbf{x}_{1i}) \Phi(\mathbf{x}_l)$$

$$\mathbf{w}_2^T \Sigma_{22} \mathbf{w}_2 = \frac{1}{n} \sum_{k,i} \beta_k . \Phi^T(\mathbf{x}_k) \Phi(\mathbf{x}_{2i}) . \sum_l \beta_l \Phi^T(\mathbf{x}_{2i}) \Phi(\mathbf{x}_l)$$

Using $(K_1)_{ij} = \Phi^T(\mathbf{x}_i) \Phi(\mathbf{x}_{1j})$ and $(K_2)_{ij} = \Phi^T(\mathbf{x}_i) \Phi(\mathbf{x}_{2j})$ we then have that we require to maximize $\alpha^T K_1 K_2^T \beta$ subject to the constraints $\alpha^T K_1 K_1^T \alpha = 1$ and $\beta^T K_2 K_2^T \beta = 1$. Therefore if we define $\Sigma_{11} = K_1 K_1^T$, $\Sigma_{22} = K_2 K_2^T$ and $\Sigma_{12} = K_1 K_2^T$ we solve the problem in the usual way: by forming matrix $K = \Sigma_{11}^{-\frac{1}{2}} \Sigma_{12} \Sigma_{22}^{-\frac{1}{2}}$ and performing a singular value decomposition on it as before to get

$$K = (\gamma_1, \gamma_2, ..., \gamma_k) D(\theta_1, \theta_2, ..., \theta_k)^T \qquad (31)$$

where γ_i and θ_i are again the standardized eigenvectors of KK^T and K^TK respectively and D is the diagonal matrix of eigenvalues [1]

Then the first canonical correlation vectors in feature space are given by

$$\alpha_1 = \Sigma_{11}^{-\frac{1}{2}}\gamma_1 \qquad (32)$$

$$\beta_1 = \Sigma_{22}^{-\frac{1}{2}}\theta_1 \qquad (33)$$

with subsequent canonical correlation vectors defined in terms of the subsequent eigenvectors, γ_i and θ_i.

Now for any new values $\mathbf{x}_1$, we may calculate

$$\mathbf{w}_1.\Phi(\mathbf{x}_1) = \sum_i \alpha_i \Phi(\mathbf{x}_i)\Phi(\mathbf{x}_1) = \sum_i \alpha_i K_1(\mathbf{x}_i, \mathbf{x}_1) \qquad (34)$$

which then requires to be centered as before. We see that we are again performing a dot product in feature space (it is actually calculated in the subspace formed from projections of $\mathbf{x}_i$).

The optimal weight vectors are vectors in a feature space which we may never determine. We are simply going to calculate the appropriate matrices using the kernel trick - e.g. we may use Gaussian kernels so that

$$K_1(\mathbf{x}_{1i}, \mathbf{x}_{1j}) = exp(-(\mathbf{x}_{1i} - \mathbf{x}_{1j})^2) \qquad (35)$$

which gives us a means of calculating K_{11} without ever having had to calculate $\Phi(\mathbf{x}_{1i})$ or $\Phi(\mathbf{x}_{1j})$ explicitly.

5.2   Simulations

We have previously [8] tested a neural implementation of CCA on artificial data comprising a line and a circle. The best linear correlation of the data set was 0.623 while the nonlinear neural method was able to get a correlation of 0.865. We show in Figures 5 and 6 two simulations with noisy versions of the data: the first shows the contours of the first twelve directions of maximum correlation of the circle data; the second shows the contours of maximum correlation of the line data. We see first that we

---

[1]This optimization is applicable for all symmetric matrices (Theorem A.9.2, [9]).

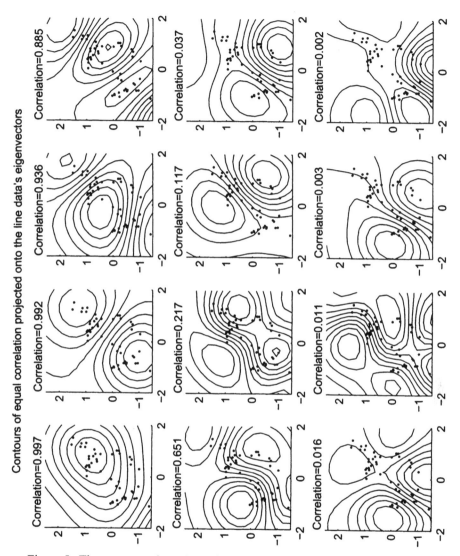

Figure 5. The contours of equal correlation when projected onto the first twelve cca directions of the first data set (the circle data)

have more than two non-zero correlation projections which is impossible with a linear method. We also see that we can achieve remarkably high correlations with this data set.

We have to be a little careful with these results since it is perfectly possible to create perfect correlations using radial kernels by simply setting the width of these kernels to ∞! Perhaps a better example is shown in Figure

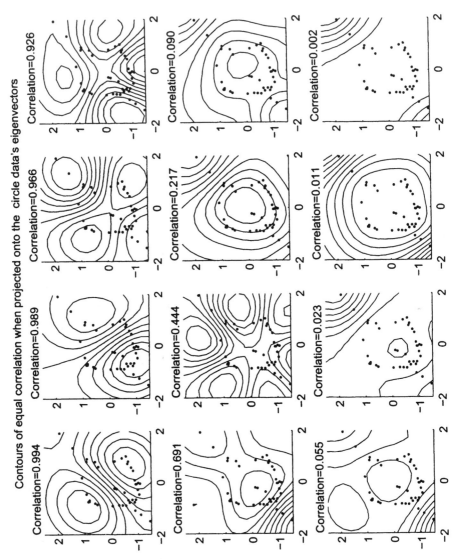

Figure 6. The contours of equal correlation when projected onto the first twelve cca directions of the second data set (the line data)

7 in which we show the results of this technique on a set of data discussed in ([9],p290); it comprises 88 students' marks on 5 module exams. The exam results can be partitioned into two data sets: two exams were given as close book exams (C) while the other three were opened book exams (O). The exams were on the subjects of Mechanics(C), Vectors(C), Algebra(O), Analysis(O), and Statistics(O). We thus split the five variables (exam marks) into two sets-the closed-book exams (x_{11}, x_{12}) and

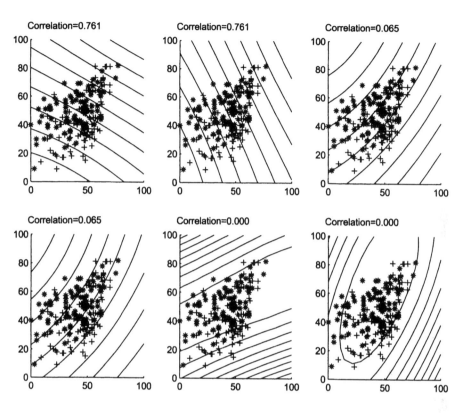

Figure 7. The kernel canonical correlation directions found using radial kernels. The contour lines are lines of equal correlation. Each pair of diagrams shows the equal correlation contours from the perspective of one of the data sets.

the opened-book exams (x_{21}, x_{22}, x_{23}). One possible quantity of interest here is how highly a student's ability on closed-book exams is correlated with his ability on open-book exams. Alternatively, one might try to use the open-book exam results to predict the closed-book results (or vice versa).

The results in Figure 7 are clearly very good but come with two caveats:

1. The method requires a dot product between members of the data set x_1 and x_2 and therefore the vectors must be of the same length. Therefore in the exam data, we must discard one set of exam marks.

2. The method requires a matrix inversion and the data sets may be such that one data point may be repeated (or almost) leading to a singularity

or badly conditioned matrices. One solution is to add noise to the data set; this is effective in the exam data set, is a nice solution if we were to consider biological information processors but need not always work. An alternative is to add μI, where I is the identity matrix to Σ_{11} and Σ_{22} - a method which was also used in [11]. This gives robust and reliable solutions.

6 Conclusion

We have reviewed the technique of Kernel Principal Component Analysis and extended the use of kernels to three other methods of unsupervised investigation of structure in data:

1. Principal Factor Analysis
2. Exploratory Projection Pursuit
3. Canonical Correlation Analysis

Each of these methods may be expressed in terms of a dot product. We have restricted our examples to simulations using Gaussian kernels but there are many other possible kernels (both radial and otherwise). It is an open research question as to which kernel is optimal in different situations.

References

[1] Bell, J.F., Owensby, P.D., Hawke, B.R., and Gaffey, M.J. (1988), "The 52 colour asteroid survey: final results and interpretation," *Lunalr Planet Sci. Conf, XiX*, p. 57.

[2] Burges, C.J.C. (1998), "A tutorial on support vector machines for pattern recognition," *Data Mining and Knowledge Discovery*, vol. 2, no. 2, pp. 1-43.

[3] Charle, D. and Fyfe, C. (1998), "Modelling multiple cause structure using rectification constraints," *Network: Computation in Neural Systems*.

[4] Diaconis, P. and Freedman D. (1984), "Asymptotics of graphical projections," *The Annals of Statistics*, vol. 12, no. 3, pp. 793-815.

[5] Friedman, J.H. (1987), "Exploratory projection pursuit," *Journal of the American Statistical Association*, vol. 82, no. 397, pp. 249-266, March.

[6] Fyfe, C. and Baddeley R. (1995), "Non-linear data structure extraction using simple Hebbian networks," *Biological Cybernetics*, vol. 72, no. 6, pp. 533-541.

[7] Kohonen T. (1995), *Self-Organising Maps*, Springer.

[8] Lai, P.L. and Fyfe, C. (1999), "A neural network implementation of canonical correlation analysis," *Neural Networks*, vol. 12, no. 10, pp. 1391-1397, Dec.

[9] Mardia, K.V., Kent J.T., and Bibby, J.M. (1979), *Multivariate Analysis*, Academic Press.

[10] Merenyi, E. (1994), "Self-organising ANNs for planetary surface composition research," *Journal of Geophysical Research*, vol. 99, no. E5, pp. 10847-10865.

[11] Mika, S., Ratsch, G., Weston, J., Scholkopf, B., and Müller, K.R. (1999), "Fisher discriminant analysis with kernels," *Proceedings of IEEE Neural Networks for Signal Processing Workshop*.

[12] Mika S., Scholkopf B., Smola, A., Muller K.R., Scholz M., and Ratsch G.(1999), "Kernel PCA and de-noising in feature spaces," *Advances in Neural Processing Systems, 11*.

[13] Romdhani, S., Gong, S., and Psarrou A. (1999), "A multi-view nonlinear active shape model using kernel PCA," *BMVC99*.

[14] Scholkopf, B., Mika, S., Burges C., Knirsch P., Muller K.R., Ratsch G., and Smola A.J., "Input space vs feature space in kernel-based methods," *IEEE Transactions on Neural Networks*, vol. 10, pp. 1000-1017.

[15] Scholkopf B., Mika S., Smola, A., Ratsch G., and Muller K.R. (1998), "Kernel PCA pattern reconstruction via approximate pre-images," in Niklasson, L., Boden, M., and Ziemke, R. (Eds.), *Proceedings of 8th International Conference on Artificial Neural Networks*, Springer Verlag, pp. 147-152.

[16] Scholkopf B., Smola, A., and Muller K.-R., (1996), "Nonlinear component analysis as a kernel eigenvalue problem," Technical Report 44, Max Planck Institut fur biologische Kybernetik, Dec.

[17] Scholkopf, B., Smola, A., and Muller, K.R. (1998), "Nonlinear component analysis as a kernel eigenvalue problem," *Neural Computation*, vol. 10, pp. 1299-1319.

[18] Scholkopf, B., Smola, A., and Muller, K.R. (1999), *Advances in Kernel Methods - Support Vector Learning*, chapter Kernel Principal Component Analysis, pp. 327-370, MIT Press.

[19] Smola, A.J., Mangasarian, O.L., and Scholkopf, B. (1999), "Sparse kernel feature analysis," Technical Report 99-04, University of Wiscosin Madison.

[20] Smola, A.J., Mika, S., Scholkopf, B., and Williamson, R.C. (2000), "Regularized principal maniforlds," *Machine Learning*, pp. 1-28. (Submitted.)

[21] Vapnik, V. (1995), *The nature of statistical learning theory*, Springer Verlag, New York.

[22] Zellner, B., Tholen, D.J., and Tedesco, E.F. (1985), "The eight colour asteroid survey: results from 589 minor planets," *Icarus*, pp. 355-416.

Chapter 9

RBF Learning in a Non-Stationary Environment: the Stability–Plasticity Dilemma

F.H. Hamker

This chapter focuses on learning with RBF networks in a non-stationary environment. A non-stationary environment demands a neural network to continuously learn. More difficult than following the change is the ability of learning new patterns without forgetting old prototype patterns, also termed as the stability-plasticity dilemma. A local representation and the ability to grow are important prerequisites to face the stability-plasticity dilemma, but not sufficient. Thus, in this contribution a growing RBF network is proposed that learns its number of nodes needed to solve the current task and dynamically adapts the learning rate of each node separately. As shown in several simulations, the RBF network possesses the major characteristics needed to cope with the stability-plasticity dilemma.

1   Introduction

Learning describes the mechanism by which a system obtains and adapts a coherence between the environment and the task. In the past, many learning methods have been proposed which also apply to RBF networks. Table 1 aims to bring some order into the terminology, especially from the viewpoint of the stability-plasticity dilemma. Classical RBF learning has dealt with a stationary environment. RBF kernels are placed into the weight space by several deterministic or batch learning procedures, e.g., based on an optimization of an optimal function. If not all of the training patterns are available all the time, the necessity arises for stochastic on-line learning, in which the parameters of the network are updated depending on the current sample only [12]. Generally, a stationary random

Table 1. Categorization of different learning tasks with regard to the stability-plasticity dilemma.

Environment	set of samples	each sample	
		adapt	adapt and preserve
stationary	incremental		
	batch or off-line	stochastic on-line	—
non-stationary	continuous		
	sequential	adaptive on-line	life long or sequential

process is assumed. Interesting real world applications for RBF networks turn up in a non-stationary environment where continuous learning is required. Especially in extension to adaptive on-line learning, where the network tracks changes over time, sequential learning with an RBF network seems to be advantageous, because of its local representation. Sequential learning addresses the ability of repeatedly training a network with new data, without destroying the old prototype patterns. This can be done either by one or by several training samples. Also life-long learning emphasizes learning throughout the entire lifetime without catastrophic interference. Like adaptive on-line learning, the network is faced with a continuous stream of pattern, but previously learned knowledge should be preserved, if it does not contradict to the current task. This demand immediately meets the stability-plasticity dilemma [20]. In some cases the term life-long learning is also used to address task independent learning.

1.1   Previous Approaches

Learning in artificial neural networks is inevitably connected with forgetting. Later input patterns tend to wash away prior knowledge [20]. While a gradual interference is unavoidable, the sudden and complete erasure of previously well learned pattern – a catastrophic interference – severely limits life-long learning. In distinction to networks with a global or distributed representation of knowledge, like a Multi-Layer-Perceptron, the local representation of Radial Basis Function (RBF) networks is well suited to cope with the problem of forgetting. Nevertheless, they have a fixed number of nodes which has to be determined by the designer. In growing RBF networks insertion is used to improve the mapping until a criterion is reached, e.g. a minimal overall error, a maximal number of nodes, or a low error on a validation data set.

There have been numerous attempts to insert new nodes in RBF networks during learning [11], [15], [27], [35], [36], [38], [40], [43]. The most common insertion or splitting criteria are (i) the insertion of a node at the location of the node with the largest error counter [15], [27], (ii) the insertion of a new node at the location of the node with the purest class counter [27], and (iii) the insertion of a node at the location of a new input vector, if it is not covered by the existing activation functions [2], [3], [35], [36], [38], [43]. The recently published M-RAN algorithm [41], [44] uses a combination of novelty in the input and output space and a threshold that is compared with the recent error. Although they used the term sequential learning, they have not addressed changing environments or the stability-plasticity dilemma. Most of the mentioned algorithms aim at an optimal design of the network as a result of an incremental learning process. Only a few focus on adaptive on-line learning [35] and continuous learning [42].

Nevertheless, all these algorithms disregard the stability-plasticity dilemma, if they are used in continuous learning tasks – unlike sometimes claimed, a growing network and a local representation is not sufficient. Why? What makes the difference in learning samples from a non-stationary environment compared to a stationary environment? First of all, possible discrete overlaps of decision areas in finite data sets turn into continuous overlaps, and non-separable areas may emerge, which can not be solved without error. Furthermore, the decision boundaries change over time. Learning in such an environment requires an incremental network that avoids a catastrophic allocation of new nodes. A growing RBF network, in which the insertion depends on the overall error on the current task, has to rely on a maximal number of nodes or on a minimal overall error. Neither of them can be determined with certainty in advance.

Other non-RBF approaches comprise ART-like networks [9], [10], [19], [30] which allow learning only if the pattern matches the stored prototype. While these networks are robust in unsupervised learning, error-driven learning can in case of overlapping decision regions result in a catastrophic allocation of new nodes, if in the course of the Inter-ART-Reset in ARTMAP no appropriate prototype is detected. Again also these networks have not been shown to cope with the hard problems of the stability-plasticity dilemma, such as continuous overlaps of different classes.

1.2   Proposed Approach

From the latter arguments it became clear that a better compromise is to dynamically learn how many nodes are needed for an appropriate solution without completely freezing the network and without prescribing a minimal error. Thus, referred to the stability-plasticity dilemma, the essential mechanisms for growing RBF networks are the insertion/deletion of nodes and the learning rate.

1.2.1   Insertion of Nodes

A general problem in learning is the bias-variance dilemma [18], where the bias is a measure in how far the average mapping function resembles the desired one and the variance describes the confidence of the mapping function concerning different input patterns. The conflict lies in minimizing the bias and avoiding a high variance, often termed as a good generalization.

In life-long learning tasks growing is an important feature to decrease the error of the task and to adapt to changing environments while preserving old prototype patterns. But for two reasons insertion has to be stopped: to prohibit a permanent increase in the number of nodes in overlapping decision areas, where the task can not be solved and to avoid overfitting. The approach preferred here, is to evaluate the previous insertion by the observation of the error. Because each insertion influences the local behaviour the observed error should also be a local measurement and not the average error on the task. Such an insertion-evaluation cycle allows a local optimization, but decreases the ability to allocate new nodes if previous insertions were not successful.

1.2.2 Adaptive Learning Parameters

As common procedure to minimize the bias in stochastic on-line learning the learning rate is slowly annealed to zero. In a changing environment, this approach turns into a conflict, as an annealed learning rate does not allow the weights to follow the changes fast enough. To overcome this problem in adaptive on-line learning different methods of adapting the scale factor of the learning parameter have been proposed. Thus the adjustment of the weight vector Δw depends on the old weight vector w and the current pattern x scaled by an adaptive factor $\eta(t)$ which is termed as learning of a learning rule [1].

$$\Delta w = \eta(t) \cdot f(w, x) \tag{1}$$

Theoretical considerations of finding the optimal learning rate often assume a global scale factor for all weight-adjustments that depends on the past errors (e.g., [32] and [39]). If the error is large, the learning rate takes on a large value. If the error decreases to zero, the learning rate decreases to zero. A different approach, almost independent on the chosen neural network, is derived by minimizing a misadjustment, i.e., a small bias and a small variance [25]. For practical purposes the bias and the variance is estimated from the statistics of the weights by time averages over a period T, which has to be chosen according to the typical time scale of changes. Still, this measure does not take into account the differences within the distribution in the input space. To address the stability-plasticity dilemma individual adaptive learning rates for each node are more suitable. One approach is to adapt the level of the learning rate according to the ratio between two local error counters with a different time constant, because this guarantees an asymptotic decrease in case of a local stationary distribution and an increase if the changing environment leads to new local errors.

1.2.3 Framework

The above proposals are implemented within the framework of the Cell Structures [4], [7], [14]-[16], because they already support the idea of local error counters. Cell Structures cluster the input space like typical RBF networks, but the nodes are organized within a graph in which the location of the centers and the connecting edges can be updated on-line. It was shown that a competitive Hebbian learning rule enables vector quantizisers to learn perfectly topology preserving mappings [34]. Utilizing this neighborhood relation leads to a cooperative training and performs a similarity regularization which can improve training performance as indicated by excellent results in incremental learning tasks [4], [5], [15], [24] and adaptive on-line learning [17].

The Cell Structures were designed to operate within different learning regimes such as self-organizing, error-driven (or supervised), and reinforcement learning. In their original formulation involving competitive Hebbian learning, all Cell Structures realize unsupervised learning. For supervised learning the output weights updated according to a stochastic gradient descent (least mean square rule, delta rule). They have also been used with reinforcement learning [6].

In extension to an exclusively unsupervised on-line adaptation of the input weights based on Self-Organizing Maps [29] and Neural Gas [33], but without a decay of learning parameters, an error-modulated learning [2] and a more sophisticated gradient-based learning [5] have been suggested. Both introduce an error dependency for the adaptation of centers similar to the one utilized in other RBF algorithms [28].

So far, the major drawback of the Cell Structures used in the context of life-long learning is their permanent increase in the number of nodes and in the drift of the centers to equal the input probability density in the unsupervised adaptation case and to equal the error probability density in the supervised adaptation case [21]. A predetermined number of nodes, a dependence on the overall error or on the quantization error are not appropriate, simply because appropriate figures for these criteria cannot be known in advance. Thus, the Cell Structures are only capable to follow an input probability density by using the utility-based removal [17] (high plasticity) or by freezing the amount of nodes and allowing only minor changes in the adaptation of the weights (high stability). This contribution extends the Cell Structures to learn how many nodes are needed for an appropriate solution and how to organize insertion and deletion of nodes in order to tackle the stability-plasticity dilemma.

2 The Algorithm

2.1 Structure

The extended Cell Structures, called Life-long Learning Cell Structures (LLCS), perform in their representation layer a vector quantization and consist of nodes or prototypes (Figure 1). The neighborhood relationship of the nodes is defined by an undirected graph G [34]. All edges that emanate from a node i determine its neighbors N_i. The age of each edge is continuously updated by a Hebbian adaptation rule. The total amount of nodes is denoted with n_N.

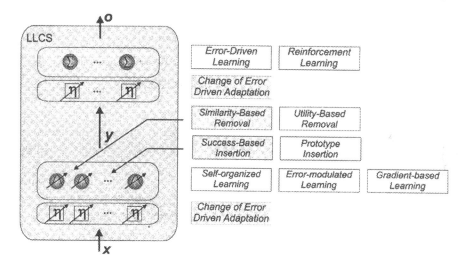

Figure 1. The representation layer composed of Gaussian activation functions performs an adjustable nonlinear transformation of the pattern x. The output layer assigns each activation distribution within the representation layer continuously to a class. By inserting new nodes in regions, which lead to high errors the overall performance is increased. The gray boxes indicate the extension of the Cell Structures for life-long learning in a non-stationary environment.

2.2 Variables of Each Node

Each node i has a few variables, that regulate learning and insertion of the nodes in the network (Figure 2):

w_i	n–dimensional weight vector in the input space
w_i^{out}	m–dimensional weight vector in the output space
σ_i	Width of the Gaussian. Extreme values of σ can be crucial to the performance. Good results are obtained by estimating the variance in the input-data of each best-matching node or by simply averaging the length of all emanating edges:

$$\sigma_i = \frac{1}{\|N_i\|} \sum_{j \in N_i} \|w_i - w_j\| \qquad (2)$$

To avoid abrupt changes, σ_i can be implemented by a moving average.

τ_{Si}	Short-term error counter. The estimate of the average short-term error is adapted according to the time-constant T_S.
τ_{Li}	Long-term error counter. Similar to the short-term error counter, the variable estimates the average error, but considers a larger time-constant T_L.
τ_{Ii}	Inherited error. This variable serves as a memory for the error at the moment of insertion. It is updated at each insertion, but only for the affected nodes. The inherited error of a new node receives the average long-term error τ_L of those two nodes, between which the new one is inserted. Each of both nodes memorize their present long-term error.
$\tau_{\vartheta i}$	Insertion threshold. An insertion is only allowed, if the long-term error exceeds this local threshold. It is increased, if a previous insertion was not successful. An exponential decrease according to the time-constant T_ϑ depends on a relevant change in the input probability distribution.
Y_i	Age of the node. It is decreased for the best-matching node according to the time-constant T_Y.

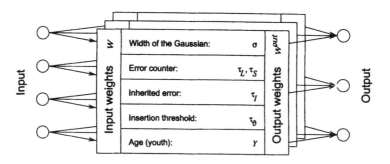

Figure 2. An RBF node of the Life-long Learning Cell Structures. Besides the width of the Gaussian each node has error and age counters. In contrast to the inherited error, which remains fixed until the node is selected for insertion, the error counters are defined as moving averages according to their individual time constant.

2.3   Adaptation of the Representation Layer

Only the unit and its neighbors that best match the input pattern are allowed to learn. To locate the best matching unit b, calculate for all nodes i the Euclidian distance d_i of the input pattern $x \in \mathbb{R}^n$ to the weight vector $w_i \in \mathbb{R}^n$.

$$d_b = \min_{i \in G}(d_i); \qquad d_i = \|x - w_i\| \quad \forall\, i \in G \tag{3}$$

There are many reasons why the learning rate should be adaptive. If the learning rate is held constant: a learning rate chosen too high will corrupt previously learned knowledge and disturb the stability of the output weights, a learning rate chosen too low does not allow the learner to follow a changing environment. Because Cell Structures provide a local processing strategy, a uniform learning rate does not make sense. Each node should hold its individual adaptive learning rate η^i. The weight change is performed by moving the prototype b and its neighbors $c \in N_b$ into the direction of the last training pattern.

$$\triangle w_b = \eta_b^i \cdot (x - w_b); \quad \triangle w_c = \eta_c^i \cdot (x - w_c) \qquad \forall\, c \in N_b \tag{4}$$

To estimate the appropriate learning rate two error counters with different time-constants detect relevant changes in the input probability density, expressed by the quality measure for learning B^L of the best-matching node b and its neighbors $c \in N_b$.

$$B^L_{(b/c)} = \frac{\tau_{S(b/c)} + 1}{\tau_{L(b/c)} + 1} \qquad \forall\, c \in N_b \qquad (5)$$

Learning of a node depends on its location within the BY-diagram (Figure 3). The learning rate η^i allows an adaptation of the weights if either the nodes are new or temporal changes of the error occur. It is determined for the best node b and its neighbors c by the base learning rate of the winner η_b and the learning rate of the neighbors η_n, modulated by a localized network based input adaptation term $\alpha^i_{(b/c)}$, which consists of quality measure for learning B^L, the age Y and a predefined input adaptation threshold ϑ^i_L

$$\eta^i_{(b/c)} = \begin{cases} 0 & \text{if} & \alpha^i_{(b/c)} < 0 \\ \eta_{(b/n)} & \text{if} & \alpha^i_{(b/c)} > 1 \\ \alpha^i_{(b/c)} \cdot \eta_{(b/n)} & \text{else} \end{cases} \qquad (6)$$

$$\text{with} \quad \alpha^i_{(b/c)} = \frac{B^L_{(b/c)}}{1 + \vartheta^i_L} + Y_{(b/c)} - 1$$

Within the adaptive phase the network approximates the input probability density and does not account for the local distribution of the error (unsupervised rule). To approximate the error probability density the learning rate must be extended by a gradient-based or error-modulated learning rule [7].

A newly inserted node always starts on the right side within the BY-diagram (Figure 3). The value of the quality measure for learning B^L depends on the nodes, which initiated this insertion, because their counters are used for the initialization. In case of a changing environment, the short term error can increase faster than the long term error which leads to a higher value of B^L. In the opposite case (insertion decreases the error) learning is reduced. If insertion takes place in regions of the input space where decision regions overlap, the quality measure for learning reaches $B^L \approx 1$ and learning is reduced with increasing age (decreasing Y) of the node. The gradient of this cooling process is exponential and dependent on the time-constant T_Y and on the proportion of the time-constants T_S, T_L. A stationary input probability density always forces the nodes to reach the state $Y \approx 0$; $B^L \approx 1$. Besides, suboptimal states are prevented by a further insertion until the local error is not lowered any more.

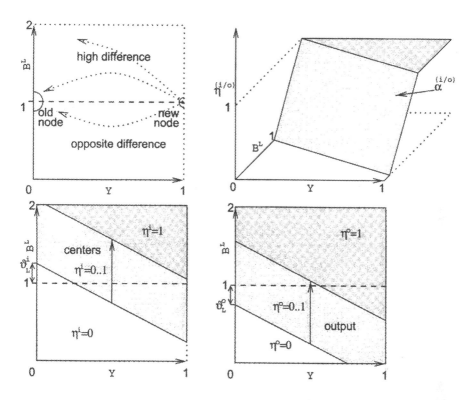

Figure 3. The figure shows the learning rate η in dependence of the quality measure for learning B^L, the age Y and the input/output adaptation threshold $\vartheta_L^{i/o}$. Top left: BY-Diagram to illustrate typical states of the nodes. Top right: Illustration of Equation (6). Bottom left: Learning of the centers and the influence of the user defined input adaptation threshold ϑ_L^i. Bottom right: Learning of the output weights and the influence of the user defined output adaptation threshold ϑ_L^o.

2.4 Adaptation of the Output Layer

In case of the example of error-driven learning discussed here, determine the squared error of the output $o \in \mathbb{R}^m$ and the target $\zeta \in \mathbb{R}^m$ when the input x is presented.

$$E_{task}(x) = \underset{error}{E_{squared}}(x) = \|\zeta - o\| \tag{7}$$

Similar as in the representation layer the local output learning rates η^o are determined by the quality measure B^L, the age Y, the output adaptation rate η_o and the output adaptation threshold ϑ_L^o.

$$\eta_i^o = \begin{cases} 0 & \text{if} & \alpha_i^o < 0 \\ \eta_o & \text{if} & \alpha_i^o > 1 \\ \alpha_i^o \cdot \eta_o & \text{else} \end{cases} \tag{8}$$

$$\text{with} \quad \alpha_i^o = \frac{B_i^L}{1 + \vartheta_L^o} + Y_i - 1 \quad \forall\, i \in G$$

Finally, the weights of the nodes j of the output layer are adapted.

$$\triangle w_{ji} = \eta_i^o \left(\zeta_j - o_j \right) y_i \qquad \forall\, j \in \{1 \dots m\},\ \forall\, i \in G \tag{9}$$

But only those, which show a sufficient high activation y_i in the representation layer, calculated with a Gaussian function.

$$y_i = e^{-\frac{\|x - w_i\|^2}{\sigma_i^2}} \qquad\qquad \forall i \in G \tag{10}$$

2.5 Insertion and Deletion of Nodes in the Representation Layer

According to the concept of the local error based insertion criterion the nodes in the representation layer compete to determine the node with the highest similarity to the pattern. By maintaining a local error counter for each node in the representation layer, new nodes are inserted next to input patterns which lead to high errors. This substance of the Cell Structures, the error-driven insertion, has its origin in the GCS. It ensures that the resources are spread over a period of presented patterns, which leads to a better exploitation of the overall resources. Additional criteria, e.g. a prototype-insertion [2], can be used simultaneously to speed up on-line learning.

How does the network learn whether a further insertion of nodes is useful to solve the task? After a number of learning steps, the average error of a node is compared to the error at the moment of the last insertion (Figure 4). If this error is greater or equal, the insertion was not successful and a local insertion threshold attached to each node is increased. If the threshold reaches the average error, a further insertion at that location is not allowed. To permit exploration in the future, the threshold has to be

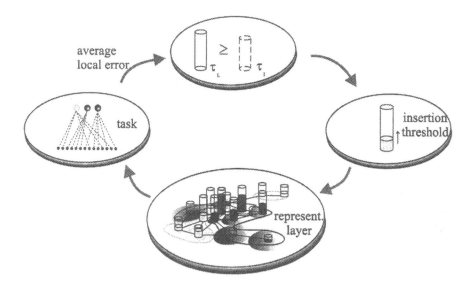

Figure 4. Insertion-evaluation cycle. By the comparison of the current local error with the previous error the last insertion is evaluated.

decreased by the change of the error. The chance of insertion is investigated after each $T_{ins} = \lambda \cdot n_N$ steps by determining the quality measure for insertion B^I considering the insertion tolerance ϑ_{ins}.

$$B_i^I = \tau_{Li} - \tau_{\vartheta i} \cdot (1 + \vartheta_{ins}) \qquad \forall\, i \in G \qquad (11)$$

But not only the distance between the long-term error τ_L and the insertion threshold τ_ϑ is decisive. An insertion is only allowed, if a node q is found with a maximal but positive insertion criterion K_{ins}, which also considers the age Y of the node. In this case a new node is inserted between q and f, which is determined among the neighbors of q.

$$0 < K_{ins,q} = \max_{i \in G} (K_{ins,i}); \quad K_{ins,i} = B_i^I - Y_i \quad \forall\, i \in G$$
$$B_f^I = \max_{c \in N_q} (B_c^I); \qquad (12)$$

This criterion is only error based, which supports the acquisition of nodes in regions with high errors independent of the input probability density. Insertion means the edge between q and f is deleted and a new node r is inserted, and connected with q and f. The weights w_r, w_r^{out} as well as the counters τ_{Sr}, τ_{Lr}, and $\tau_{\vartheta r}$ are determined by the arithmetical average of the corresponding weights and error counters of q and f.

The last insertion is evaluated by comparing the long-term error τ_L of q, f and r with the inherited error τ_I lowered by an insertion tolerance ϑ_{ins}.

$$\tau_{Li} \geq \tau_{Ii} - (1 - \vartheta_{ins}) \qquad \forall\, i \in \{q, f, r\} \tag{13}$$

If τ_L exceeds this memory term, the last insertion was not successful, and the insertion threshold has to be adapted.

$$\tau_{\vartheta i} := \tau_{\vartheta i} + \eta_\vartheta \cdot (\tau_{Li} - \tau_{\vartheta i} \cdot (1 - \vartheta_{ins}))$$
$$\forall\, i \in \{k | \tau_{Lk} > \tau_{Ik} \cdot (1 - \vartheta_{ins}); q, f, r\} \tag{14}$$

Finally, by the assignment of the present long-term error to the inherited error τ_I of q, f and r, the memory is updated.

$$\tau_{Ii} = \tau_{Li} \qquad \forall\, i \in \{q, r, f\} \tag{15}$$

If f and q do not exist, no insertion evaluation takes place.

Looking back at the previous discussion on the insertion of nodes, an incremental neural network can not know in advance whether a further insertion reveals a subtle distribution or turns out as a waste of resources. This is closely related to the bias-variance dilemma. An insertion improves the network performance on the current data, but might result in a loss of generalization. The proposed strategy to evaluate an insertion locally is a suitable criterion for simultaneously minimizing both bias and variance. In the Life-long-Learning Cell Structures the learning rate of the insertion threshold η_ϑ determines this generalization property. The larger the learning rate of the insertion threshold η_ϑ the larger the effect of a wrong insertion and the fewer insertions are possible until the insertion threshold reaches the long-term error. This criterion detects the decision boundaries between distinctly separated classes but avoids a too low bias in areas with much overlap. The insertion tolerance ϑ_{ins} determines how much the algorithm tolerates a fluctuation of the long-term error without initiating an insertion. It should therefore not be used to address the bias-variance dilemma.

Another criterion acts after an insertion and removes similar nodes. The larger ϑ_{del} the earlier similar nodes are deleted. A node d is only deleted, if it has a minimal age ϑ_{delY}, a sufficient stabilization ϑ_{delBL}, a minimal number of edges and if its criterion K is lower than the deletion threshold ϑ_{del}.

$$\vartheta_{del} > K_{del,d} = \min_{i \in G} (K_{del,i}) \wedge$$
$$\|N_d\| \geq 2 \wedge Y_d < \vartheta_{delY} \wedge B_d^L < \vartheta_{delBL} \tag{16}$$

with

$$K_{del,i} = \frac{\overline{\Delta w_i}}{\overline{l}} \cdot \overline{\Delta w_i^{out}} \qquad \forall i \in G \tag{17}$$

the local similarity of the input weights:

$$\overline{\Delta w_i} = \frac{1}{\|N_i\|} \sum_{j \in N_i} \|w_i - w_j\| \tag{18}$$

the average similarity of the input weights:

$$\overline{l} = \frac{1}{n_N} \sum_{j=1}^{n_N} \overline{\Delta w_j} \tag{19}$$

and the local similarity of the output weights:

$$\overline{\Delta w_i^{out}} = \frac{1}{\|N_i\|} \sum_{j \in N_i} \|w_i^{out} - w_j^{out}\| \tag{20}$$

2.6   Adaptation of the Counters and Edges of the Nodes in the Representation Layer

The long-term error counter τ_{Lb} and the short-term error counter τ_{Sb} for the winner b are updated as a moving average.

$$\tau_{(L/S)b} := e^{-\frac{1}{T_{(L/S)}}} \cdot \tau_{(L/S)b} + \left(1 - e^{-\frac{1}{T_{(L/S)}}}\right) \cdot E_{task}(x) \tag{21}$$

The age Y_b of the best-matching node b is simply decreased.

$$Y_b := e^{-\frac{1}{T_Y}} \cdot Y_b \tag{22}$$

A prerequisite for the flexibility of insertion in changing environments is the decrease of the insertion threshold $\tau_{\vartheta b}$, if the distribution of the error changes.

$$\tau_{\vartheta b} := (1 - \Lambda(\alpha_b)) \cdot e^{-\frac{1}{T_\vartheta}} \cdot \tau_{\vartheta b} \tag{23}$$

with

$$\alpha_b = \frac{1 + |B_b^L - 1|}{1 + \vartheta_L^i} - 1; \qquad \Lambda(x) = \begin{cases} 0 & if & x < 0 \\ 1 & if & x > 1 \\ x & else \end{cases} \qquad (24)$$

The edges of the graph are continuously updated. According to the Hebbian learning rule the age of all edges emanating from b are increased by one and the age of the edge between b and the second best s is set to zero. The second best node is defined as:

$$d_s = \min_{i \in G, i \neq b} (d_i); \qquad d_i = \|x - w_i\| \quad \forall i \in G \qquad (25)$$

If no edge between b and s exists, a new one is created. All edges older than ϑ_{age} and all nodes without an edge are removed.

2.7   Parameter Discussion

The algorithm expects the specification of several parameters. The major parameters that concern the insertion and deletion, i.e. the size of the network, are the learning rate of the insertion threshold η_ϑ and the deletion threshold ϑ_{del}. The sensitivity to temporal changes of the environment is adjusted by the relation of the time constants of the short-term error and the long-term error T_S/T_L. The insertion threshold ϑ_{ins} defines the sensitivity to changes of the long-term error regarding an insertion of nodes. Other parameters can be regarded as constants of the algorithm. This insensitivity to parameter settings is a general feature of the Cell Structures as indicated by a benchmark [24].

3   Illustration with Artificial Data Sets

To illustrate the function of the RBF learning in a non-stationary environment, the behavior of the network on a two-dimensional data set is observed (Figure 5). It is shown that even critical overlaps do not lead to a permanent insertion, while the network is not frozen.

In the first 20000 steps the input contains an awful overlap in the circular area which causes a high error. Thus, initially the internal states of the

Class			Environment (Frequency)					
			1	2	3	4	5	6
A	1	Rectangle	1	1	0	1	1	0
B	1	Line	1	1	1	0	0	1
C	2	Ellipse	0	1	1	1	1	0
D	3	Circular area	1	0	0	0	1	1
E	2	Circular area	1	1	1	0	0	1

Figure 5. Changing environment composed of five areas $(A - E)$ and three classes. The environment changes from 1-6 each 20000 steps. Simulation parameters: $\eta_b = 0.1$, $\eta_n = 0.01$, $\eta_o = 0.15$, $\eta_\vartheta = 0.5$, $T_S = 20$, $T_L = T_Y = T_\vartheta = 100$, $\lambda = 10$, $\vartheta_{age} = 50$, $\vartheta_L^i = 0.05$, $\vartheta_L^o = -0.05$, $\vartheta_{ins} = 0.1$, $\vartheta_{del} = 0.05$, $\vartheta_{delY} = 0.01$, $\vartheta_{delBL} = 0.01$.

nodes responsible for the overlapping area show a high long-term error. From left to right, two plots in Figure 6 show the states in each environment, the first after each 500 steps and the second after each 20000. As the learning parameter of the input weights expresses, the network is extremely plastic. Nevertheless after 20000 steps, the algorithm has learned by increasing its insertion threshold, that a further insertion does not improve the squared error and stabilizes, as can be seen from the learning parameters and the number of nodes.

Now the environment changes, new errors occur and the algorithm tries to minimize them by changing its weights and inserting new nodes. Although the environment gets much easier, there is still an unsolvable overlap between the ellipse and the line that would cause a further insertion of nodes. By increasing the insertion threshold of the relevant nodes, the algorithm learns to stop insertion in the overlapping area. At least after 40000 steps it has adopted to the environment such that no further learning is needed.

If the probability changes to zero in some regions, like in the environment from 40000 to 60000 steps, those remaining nodes, often called "dead nodes," play a major role for the stability-plasticity dilemma (Figure 7). They are in no way "dead nodes," instead they preserve the knowledge of previous situations for future decisions. If the old prototype patterns were removed, the knowledge would be lost and the same, already learned situations will again cause errors. Further insertions at the crossing of the line with the ellipse result in a better approximation. However, the number of nodes again stabilizes after 50000 steps.

In the environment from 60000 to 80000 steps, most of the nodes remain at their positions. The repeated appearance of area A does not raise the error – the knowledge was completely preserved. Since the environment shows no overlaps the error decreases to zero.

In the environment from 80000 to 100000 steps, the patterns from the circular area change from class two to class three (Figure 8). This change of the environment illustrates impressively the localized definition of the stability and plasticity. The network at 80500 steps remains completely stable aside from nodes covering area A. Only here, the network tries to cope with the new situation, inserts new nodes and increases their leaning rate. It turns out, that the new nodes all cover the same class and most of them were again deleted. Once more the network stabilizes.

Even serious changes in the environment from 100000 to 120000 are tolerated. The inversion of the occurrence of patterns in area A, B, and C does not affect the position of the centers. The overlap of area D and E raises the error and the network inserts new nodes but stabilizes again.

Summarizing, the algorithm is able to cope with all changing environments, like overlaps, never seen inputs and temporarily not appearing patterns.

4   Evaluation Using Real Data Sets

4.1   Performance Measures

Relevant issues for the application of the LLCS deal with non-stationary input probability distributions. Nevertheless, it was shown that the network automatically stops the insertion of further nodes on real benchmark data with a stationary probability distribution and achieves a performance which is as good as those of the Cell Structures selected by cross-validation [23], [24]. For the further evaluation of learning in changing environments a data set with strongly overlapping decision areas was de-

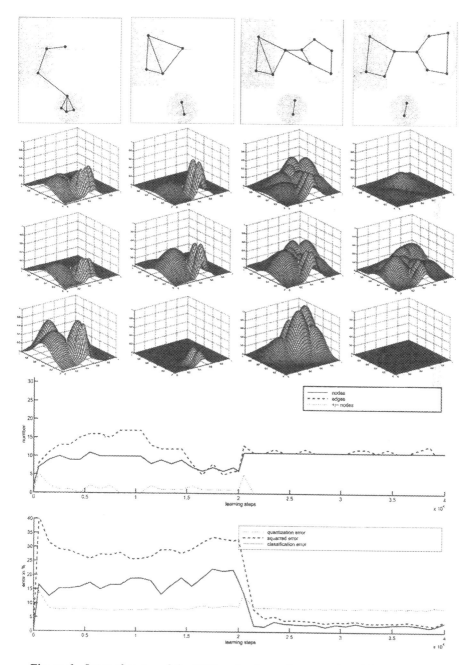

Figure 6. Internal states of the RBF nodes in environment 1 and 2. From the top to the bottom, the input weights w_i, the long-term error τ_{Li}, the insertion threshold $\tau_{\vartheta i}$, the adaptation term of the input learning rate α_i^i are presented.

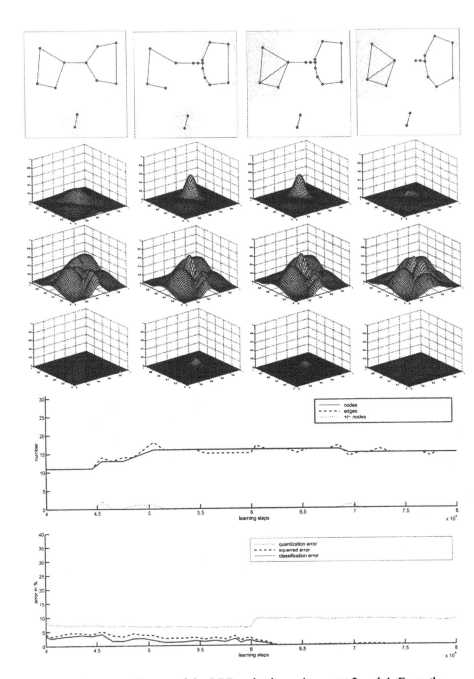

Figure 7. Internal states of the RBF nodes in environment 3 and 4. From the top to the bottom, the input weights w_i, the long-term error τ_{Li}, the insertion threshold $\tau_{\vartheta i}$, the adaptation term of the input learning rate α_i^i are presented.

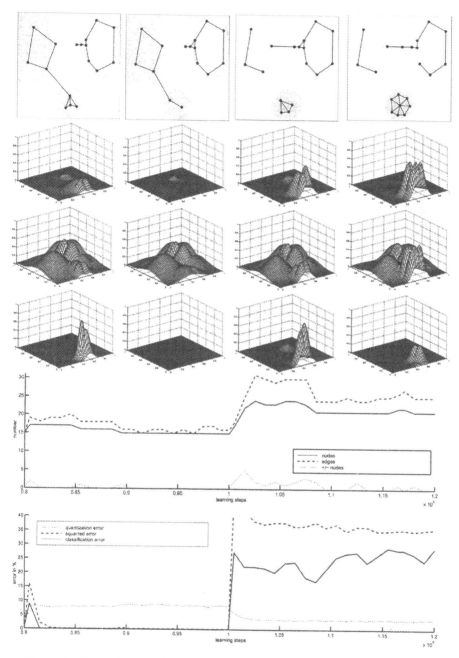

Figure 8. Internal states of the RBF nodes in environment 5 and 6. From the top to the bottom, the input weights w_i, the long-term error τ_{Li}, the insertion threshold $\tau_{\vartheta i}$, the adaptation term of the input learning rate α_i^i are presented.

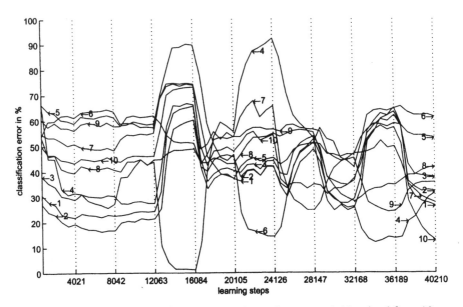

Figure 9. Average classification error of the environments 1-10 gained from 10
different runs by changing the environment after each 4021 steps. Parameters:
$\eta_\vartheta = 0.1$, $\vartheta_{del} = 0.2$, $\eta_b = 0.8$, $\eta_n = 0.01$, $\eta_o = 0.01$, $T_S = 100$, $T_L = T_Y = T_\vartheta = 200$, $\lambda = 100$, $\vartheta_{age} = 60$, $\vartheta_{ins} = 0.4$, $\vartheta_L^i = 0.1$, $\vartheta_L^o = -0.05$,
$\vartheta_{delY} = 0.01$, $\vartheta_{delB^L} = 0.01$.

signed. It consists of 10 environments with 29 features and four classes.
Each environment was build from four images which contain four different materials (classes), like journals, cardboard, newspaper and others,
recorded under different lightning conditions. The patterns are gained
from color-histograms of tiles sized 32x32 pixels. For details about the
data and the feature extraction see [22]. One after another the data from
an environment is only once presented (on-line learning). But even the
data from the environment is clumped into 402 blocks with 10 samples belonging to the same class, which makes learning more difficult
and more realistic to natural environments, which are structured in space
and/or time. The output of the network on all data sets are recorded in
parallel (Figure 9). This means the impact of training a particular data
set on the performance on any other data set can be analyzed. According
to the correspondence between different data sets learning in one environment is of advantage to some environments while others suffer from
strong overlaps.

Looking at Figure 9, we wonder if the network is stable or not. This raises the question how to measure the stability and plasticity of a neural net.

Plasticity means a neural network is capable to learn new patterns. A high plasticity reveals that the network is not frozen after different data sets have been presented. Thus, we have to focus not on the overall error, but on the difference of the performance between the network trained within an environment and a network that has seen different environments before. For a quantitative evaluation, two bounds were defined. The upper bound was gained by training the network only once in an environment. The lower bound was achieved by training the network in the same environment as long as the tested network was trained in different environments. Thus, the number of nodes is similar. Each bound is an average of 10 runs. The error can not fall below the lower bound. Achieving the upper bound is a good performance, an error lower than the upper bound is even better.

Stability is the crucial aspect of the stability-plasticity dilemma. The illustration on artificial data has impressively demonstrated the capability to preserve the prototypes while confronted with new patterns elsewhere from the input space. Nevertheless, if the environment changes, the new situation can be inconsistent with the former situation and the network has to adapt itself. This means it looses some previous knowledge in order to respond accurately. For a quantitative analysis of stability criteria like measuring the amount of forgetting [31], [37] and the amount of time to re-learn the patterns [26] are used. The latter offers only little insight into the stability characteristic, because it depends too much on the algorithms learning strategy. On the first sight the amount of forgetting seems to be a useful criterion, but forgetting is a necessary condition of plasticity in overlapping decision areas. An appropriate measure has to define which data has to be preserved and which should be adapted according to the plasticity condition. Prototypes in overlapping decision areas are expected to adapt to the new environment without affecting others, and unseen or new patterns should enlarge the knowledge. Thus, we have to estimate the amount of samples from the previous environment that is similar or new to the data from the current environment. We expect this amount of samples to be classified correctly while training with patterns from the current environment.

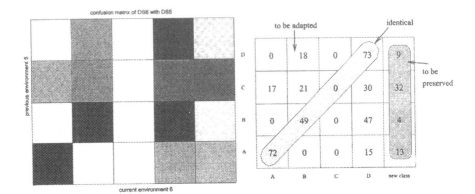

Figure 10. Left: Extract from the confusion matrix of two environments with $\gamma = 0.5$. The cut shows environment 6 and 5. A black rectangle indicates a large value. Right: Evaluation of the confusion matrix. The values on the main diagonal mark the correspondence of the environments. Even if the data from environment 5 was not presented for training, the samples of the main diagonal could be classified correctly while training in environment 6. The patterns of other fields except from the class C_{new} collide with the current environment and are expected to be not preserved according to the plasticity demand. But the amount of pattern from class C_{new} could be expected to be preserved when the network is trained on data from environment 6, because, although there might be an overlap, the patterns are less similar. For the above example the stability boundary $\overline{S_{0.5}}$ results in $\overline{S_{\gamma}} = 100\% - \frac{194\% + 58\%}{4} = 37\%$.

The overlap of different data sets can be estimated by a confusion matrix, which indicates to what extent feature vectors are assigned to a wrong class. This concept is extended to estimate the confusion of data from different environments. In order to achieve a more precise criterion all patterns that result in an output activation lower than a threshold $\gamma \in \{0.1, 0.3, 0.5\}$, were declared as a not sufficiently learned patterns with a separate class (new), instead of being assigned to the class with the largest output activation. Using this definition for the class C_{new} we obtain the stability boundary $\overline{S_{\gamma}}$:

$$\overline{S_{\gamma}} = 100\% - (\#correspondence + \#new_{\gamma})\% \qquad (26)$$

Figure 10 illustrates this context with the data from environment five and six. For different values of the variable γ different bounds emerge. The more the classification error remains lower than these bounds the more stable is the network when the environment changes.

4.2   Analysis of the Data

Each environment contains of 4096 samples. Most environments show a strong overlap between their classes (Figure 11). From the first environment to the third only slow changes, whereas afterwards abrupt changes

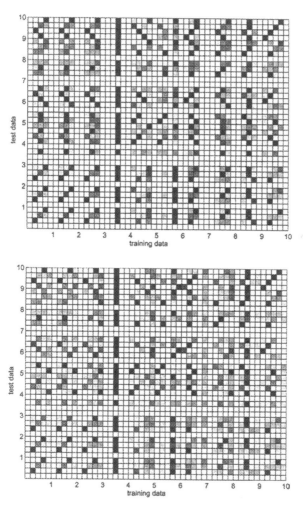

Figure 11. Confusion matrix of all data sets with $\gamma = 0.1$ (top) and $\gamma = 0.5$ (bottom) after the network was trained for three epochs on the data of an environment. See Figure 10 for the structure of the matrix. Environments with no overlap (high similarity) show a black diagonal within each 4x5 array. Activations at other areas indicate a complete overlap. A larger threshold γ results in a bigger class C_{new}.

occur. As can be seen from Figure 11, several environments do not contain all classes, especially environment four contains only patterns of one class that has a strong overlap to different classes in other environments. This is the reason of the large increase of error when data from environment four is presented (Figure 9). Especially the error of environment six increases strongly because both environments share no common class. Only the performance on environment nine can profit by the training with data of environment four, because both share similar patterns (Figure 11).

4.3   Analysis of Stability and Plasticity

The course of errors in Figure 12 demonstrates a good plasticity performance. After the environment changes the error decreases and in most cases it falls below the upper bound. Concerning stability, the change from environment 1 to environment 2 is remarkable. Here, the classification error is larger than the bound, but this is based on the short training time and the few number of nodes, which hinder a precise representation of the data. We have to keep in mind, that the bounds were estimated after the training of three epochs. The further course clearly indicates the preservation of old prototype patterns. Even networks with more conservative parameter sets show a convincing stability and plasticity performance, although these networks operate with less than half of the nodes as shown in [23].

5   Conclusion

Learning in changing environments is faced with the catastrophic interference, which mainly occurs in a distributed representation. But also localist or partly distributed representations suffer from interference, especially if the network does not have sufficient nodes. Thus, different strategies to insert new nodes in incremental neural networks were mentioned. A similarity based insertion as used in ART networks [8] and also in RBF networks [36], [44] has the advantage to increase the number of nodes without an instability concerning insertion, but at the expense of a low performance and a high number of nodes, because the optimal similarity is unknown, not equally distributed within the input space, and may change over time. A different strategy is to insert a new node according

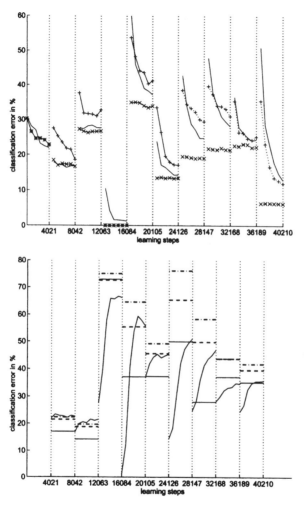

Figure 12. The course of the error in different environments are gained from the recordings of Figure 9. Top: Results of the plasticity analysis. The error of the network is shown when presented a never seen environment (–), compared to the upper bound (+) and the lower bound (x). Bottom: Results of the stability analysis. The figure shows the stability bounds estimated with $\gamma = 0.1$ ($- \cdot -$), $\gamma = 0.3$ ($- -$) and $\gamma = 0.5$ (—) compared to the error in the previously trained environment (–), e.g., environment 7 is trained and environment 6 is observed. The error of the first two environments exceeds the estimated bounds. This is due to the low number of nodes created so far. In most cases the error is about or below the lowest bound, which underlines the exceptional stability property of the LLCS. Only in some cases, mostly if the training on the previous data set does not decrease the error onto the level of the reference network, which determines the bound, the error exceeds the lowest bound. But even then the networks still preserve some knowledge.

to an error based criterion. A global error based insertion criterion is not useful for life-long learning, because the error is not known in advance and changes over time. Thus, a promising strategy is a local error based insertion criterion as used by GCS [14] or also in ARTMAP [9] triggered by the Inter-ART-Reset. But this raises the question how to suppress insertion in overlapping decision areas, where errors occur all the time. Furthermore, learning in changing environments has to address the question in which cases the weights of the network have to be adapted to learn new patterns and when the weights should not change to guarantee stability.

The evolved RBF network is based on the Cell Structures algorithm [4], [7], [14], [16] and extends it to locally adapt the stability and plasticity – for learning and for insertion. The essential innovation compared to the previous work is the new interpretation of the stability-plasticity dilemma by adapting the learning rate and the insertion capability of each node separately. This allows the network to self-stabilize in case of a stationary probability density of the input patterns and to switch locally to plasticity if relevant changes occur – a framework, useful as a general strategy of growing RBF networks.

The proposed algorithm is a favorable compromise to the stability-plasticity dilemma, which is characterized as:

- The stability and plasticity is defined locally in the network, i.e., for each center.

- The stability and plasticity concerns the adaptation of the centers, the learning of decision boundaries and the number of centers.

- The number of nodes are not predefined – instead an adequate number is learned by continuously adapting local insertion thresholds according to the performance of the network on the data.

- In case of a stable state, local plasticity only occurs due to relevant changes in the input probability density, i.e., changes in the error probability density.

Although still much has to be done, RBF networks embedded within a performance estimation to control the number of nodes and the learning parameters offer a serious approach for systems that act in changing environments.

Acknowledgments

The body of this work was done at the Department of Neuroinformatik, Technische Universität Ilmenau (Germany). I thank T. Vesper for his fruitful discussions and for implementing parts of the algorithm in his diploma thesis. As a foundation of this research, the combination of action and perception, a research orientation of Prof. H.-M. Gross is worth mentioning. I would also like to thank D. Surmeli for his helpful comments on a preliminary version of this chapter.

References

[1] Amari, S. (1967), "A theory of adaptive pattern classifiers," *IEEE Transactions on Electronic Computers*, vol. 16, pp. 299-307.

[2] Ahrns, I., Bruske, J., and Sommer, G. (1995), "On-line learning with dynamic cell structures," *Proceedings of the International Conference on Artificial Neural Networks*, pp. 141-146.

[3] Berthold, M.R. and Diamond, J. (1995), "Boosting the performance of RBF networks with dynamic decay adjustment," *Advances in Neural Information Processing Systems (NIPS 7)*, MIT Press, Cambridge, pp. 521-528.

[4] Bruske, J. and Sommer, G. (1995), "Dynamic cell structure learns perfectly topology preserving map," *Neural Computation*, vol. 7, pp. 845-865.

[5] Bruske, J., Hansen, M., Riehn, L., and Sommer, G. (1996), "Adaptive saccade control of a binocular head with dynamic cell structures," *Proceedings of the International Conference on Artificial Neural Networks*, pp. 215-220.

[6] Bruske, J., Ahrns, I., and Sommer, G. (1998), "An integrated architecture for learning of reative behaviors based on dynamic cell structures," *Robotics and Autonomous Systems*, vol. 22, pp. 87-102.

[7] Bruske, J. (1998), *Dynamische Zellstrukturen. Theorie und Anwendung eines KNN-Modells*, Ph.D. Thesis, Technische Fakultät der Christian Albrechts-Universität zu Kiel. (In German.)

[8] Carpenter, G.A. and Grossberg, S. (1987), "ART2: self-organisation of stable category recognition codes for analog input patterns," *Applied Optics*, vol. 26, pp. 4919-4930.

[9] Carpenter, G.A., Grossberg, S., and Reynolds, J.H. (1991), "ARTMAP: supervised real-time learning and classification of nonstationary data by a self-organizing-neural network," *Neural Networks*, vol. 4, pp. 543-564.

[10] Carpenter, G.A., Grossberg, S., Markuzon, N., Reynolds, J.H., and Rosen, D.B. (1992), Fuzzy ARTMAP: a neural network architecture for incremental supervised learning of analog multidimensional maps," *IEEE Transactions on Neural Networks*, vol. 3, pp. 698-713.

[11] Chen, Y.Q., Thomas, D.W., and Nixon, M.S. (1994), "Generating-shrinking algorithm for learning arbitrary classification," *Neural Networks*, vol. 7, pp. 1477-1489.

[12] Freeman, J.A.S. and Saad, D. (1997), "On-line learning in radial basis function networks," *Neural Computation*, vol. 9, pp. 1601-1622.

[13] French, R.M. (1999), "Catastrophic forgetting in connectionist networks," *Trends in Cognitive Sciences*, vol. 3, pp. 128-135.

[14] Fritzke, B. (1992), *Wachsende Zellstrukturen – ein selbstorganisierendes neuronales Netzwerkmodell*, Ph.D. Thesis, Technische Fakultät der Universität Erlangen-Nürnberg. (In German.)

[15] Fritzke, B. (1994), "Growing cell structures – a self-organizing network for unsupervised and supervised learning," *Neural Networks*, vol. 7, pp. 1441-1460.

[16] Fritzke, B. (1995), "A growing neural gas network learns topologies," *Advances in Neural Information Processing Systems (NIPS 7)*, MIT Press, Cambridge, pp. 625-632.

[17] Fritzke, B. (1997), "A self-organizing network that can follow non-stationary distributions," *Proceedings of the International Conference on Artificial Neural Networks*, Springer, pp. 613-618.

[18] Geman, S., Bienenstock, E. and Doursat, R. (1992), "Neural networks and the bias/variance dilemma," *Neural Computation*, vol. 4, pp. 1-58.

[19] Grossberg, S. (1976), "Adaptive pattern classification and universal recoding: I. Parallel development and coding of neural feature detectors," *Biological Cybernetics*, vol. 23, pp. 121-134.

[20] Grossberg, S. (1988), "Nonlinear neural networks: principles, mechanisms, and architectures," *Neural Networks*, vol. 1, pp. 17-61.

[21] Hamker, F.H. and Gross, H.-M. (1997), "Task-based representation in lifelong learning incremental neural networks," *VDI Fortschrittberichte*, Reihe 8, Nr. 663, Workshop SOAVE'97 (Ilmenau), pp. 99-108.

[22] Hamker, F., Debes, K., Pomierski, T., and Gross, H.-M. (1998), "Multisensorielles Integriertes Realzeit Inspektions-System MIRIS: Lösung der MIKADO-Sortieraufgabe," Schriftenreihe des FG Neuroinformatik der TU Ilmenau, Report 2/98. (In German.)

[23] Hamker, F. (1999), *Visuelle Aufmerksamkeit und lebenslanges Lernen im Wahrnehmungs-Handlungs-Zyklus*, Ph.D. Thesis, Technische Universität Ilmenau. (In German.)

[24] Heinke, D. and Hamker, F.H. (1998), "Comparing neural networks: a benchmark on growing neural gas, growing cell structures, and fuzzy ARTMAP," *IEEE Transactions on Neural Networks*, vol. 9, pp. 1279-1291.

[25] Heskes, T.M. and Kappen, B. (1993), "On-line learning processes in artificial neural networks," *Mathematical Foundations of Neural Networks*, Elsevier Science Publishers, Amsterdam, pp. 199-233.

[26] Hetherington, P. and Seidenberg, M. (1989), "Is there 'catastrophic interference' in connectionist networks?" *Proceedings of the 11th Annual Conference of the Cognitive Science Society*, LEA, Hillsdale, pp. 26-33.

[27] Karayiannis, N.B. and Mi, G.W. (1997), "Growing radial basis neu-
     ral networks: merging supervised and unsupervised learning with
     network growth techniques," *IEEE Transactions on Neural Net-
     works*, vol. 8, pp. 1492-1506.

[28] Karayiannis, N.B. (1999), "Reformulated radial basis neural net-
     works trained by gradient descent," *IEEE Transactions on Neural
     Networks*, vol. 10, pp. 657-671.

[29] Kohonen, T. (1982), "Self-organized formation of topologically
     correct feature maps," *Biological Cybernetics*, vol. 43, pp. 59-69.

[30] Lim, C.P. and Harrison, R.F. (1997), "An incremental adaptive net-
     work for on-line supervised learning and probability estimation,"
     Neural Networks, vol. 10, pp. 925-939.

[31] McCloskey, M. and Cohen, N. (1989), "Catastrophic interference in
     connectionist networks: The sequential learning problem," *The Psy-
     chology of Learning and Motivation*, Academic Press, New York,
     vol. 24, pp. 109-164.

[32] Murata, N., Müller, K.-R., Ziehe, A., and Amari, S. (1997), "Adap-
     tive on-line learning in changing environments," *Proceedings of the
     Conference on Neural Information Processing Systems (Nips 9)*,
     MIT Press, pp. 599-604.

[33] Martinetz, T.M. and Schulten, K.J. (1991), "A 'neural gas' network
     learns topologies," *Artificial Neural Networks*, volume I, Amster-
     dam: North Holland, pp. 397-402.

[34] Martinetz, T.M. and Schulten, K.J. (1994), "Topology representing
     networks," *Neural Networks*, vol. 7, pp. 507-522.

[35] Obradovic, D. (1996), "On-line training of recurrent neural net-
     works with continuous topology adaptation," *IEEE Transactions on
     Neural Networks*, vol. 7, pp. 222-228.

[36] Platt, J. (1991), "A resource-allocating network for function inter-
     polation," *Neural Computation*, vol. 3, pp. 213-225.

[37] Ratcliff, R. (1990), "Connectionist models of recognition memory: Constraints imposed by learning and forgetting functions," *Psychological Review*, vol. 97, pp. 285-308.

[38] Roy, A., Govil, S., and Miranda, R. (1997), "A neural-network learning theory and a polynomial time RBF algorithm," *IEEE Transactions on Neural Networks*, vol. 8, pp. 1301-1313.

[39] Sompolinsky, H., Barkai, N., and Seung, H.S. (1995), "On-line learning of dichotomies: algorithms and learning curves," *Neural Networks: the Statistical Mechanics Perspective*, World Scientific, Singapore, pp. 105-130.

[40] Shadafan, R.S. and Niranjan, M. (1994), "A dynamic neural network architecture by sequential partitioning of the input space," *Neural Computation*, vol. 6, pp. 1202-1223.

[41] Sundararajan, N., Saratchandran, P., and YingWei, L. (1999), *Radial basis function neural networks with sequential learning : MRAN and its applications*, Series: Progress in Neural Processing, vol. 11., World Scientific, Singapore.

[42] Tagscherer, M. (1998), "ICE – an incremental hybrid system for continuous learning," *Proceedings of the International Conference on Artificial Neural Networks*, pp. 597-602.

[43] Whitehead, B.A. and Choate, T.D. (1994), "Evolving space-filling curves to distribute radial basis functions over an input space," *IEEE Transactions on Neural Networks*, vol. 5, pp. 15-23.

[44] Yingwei, L., Sundararajan, N., and Saratchandran, P. (1998), "Performance evaluation of a sequential minimal Radial Basis Function (RBF) neural network learning algorithm," *IEEE Transactions on Neural Networks*, vol. 9, pp. 308-318.

Chapter 10

A New Learning Theory and Polynomial-Time Autonomous Learning Algorithms for Generating RBF Networks

A. Roy

Several new RBF network design and training algorithms have emerged from the field of Operations Research. This chapter will present these new learning methods, ones that can lead to the development of truly autonomous learning methods. Autonomous learning methods are crucial from a robotics and automation point of view. For autonomous robots of any type, ones that can learn on their own, it is absolutely necessary to have learning algorithms that can design and train neural networks on their own without any kind of human intervention. Polynomial time complexity is an essential property for developing autonomous learning algorithms. The new algorithms all have polynomial time complexity. The chapter will show how these methods decompose and simplify the learning problem and make it tractable.

This chapter will also summarize a new learning theory (a set of principles for brain-like learning) for the neural network field. The learning theory defines computational characteristics that are much more brain-like than that of classical connectionist learning. Robust and reliable learning algorithms would result if these learning principles are followed rigorously when developing neural network algorithms. This chapter will review some of the core ideas of classical connectionist learning and show the inadequacies of classical connectionist learning in this framework.

In addition, this chapter will summarize and discuss two algorithms for generating radial basis function (RBF) nets – one for function approximation, the other for classification. The design of these algorithms is based on the proposed set of learning principles. The net generated by these algorithms is not a typical RBF net, but a combination of "truncated" RBF and other types of hidden units. The algorithms use random clustering and linear programming (LP) models to design and train these "mixed" RBF nets. Polynomial time complexity of the algorithms have been proven.

1   Introduction

This chapter summarizes the ideas behind two polynomial-time RBF learning algorithms [37], [38]. These algorithms can both design and train RBF networks in polynomial-time complexity. Polynomial nature of learning algorithms is essential for developing autonomous learning algorithms, learning algorithms that do not require constant intervention by humans in order to learn. The basic principles used in the construction of these algorithms are also different from the ones used in connectionism and artificial neural network. Those principles are discussed first by presenting a new brain-like learning theory. The new learning principles are justified as being more brain-like than the ones used by connectionism.

The chapter is organized as follows. Section 2 reviews the basic connectionist framework as a starting point for discussion on connectionism and artificial neural networks. Section 3 presents the new learning theory and shows why some of the ideas of connectionism are not brain-like. In Section 4, the polynomial-time RBF algorithm for function approximation is presented. Section 5 presents the polynomial-time RBF algorithm for classification.

2   The Classical Connectionist Learning Framework

This section provides a brief overview of some of the basic ideas of connectionism. The next section presents a new learning theory and shows how its ideas differ from those of connectionism and why the connectionist ideas are not brain-like.

Connectionism is usually defined by the following elements [41]: (1) a set of processing units; (2) a state of activation for each unit; (3) an output function for each unit; (4) a pattern of connectivity among units; (5) an activation rule for combining the inputs impinging on a unit; (6) a learning rule whereby patterns of connectivity are modified by experience; and (7) an environment within which the system must operate. As is well-known, the following additional or related notions are implied here: (a) memoryless, instantaneous learning, (b) autonomous local learning by each processing unit or neuron, and (c) no controllers in the system, that is, there is no subsystem controlling other subsystems in this system ([5] and others).

In this massively parallel computing framework, each computing unit or element (a neuron or a cell in the brain) is envisioned to perform a very simple computation, such as $y_i = f(z_i)$, where z_i is assumed to be a real valued input to the ith neuron, y_i is either a binary or a real valued output of the ith neuron, and f a nonlinear function. The nonlinear function f, also called a node function, takes different forms in different models of the neuron; a typical choice for the node function is a step function or a sigmoid function. The neurons get their input signals from other neurons or from external sources. The output signal from a neuron may be sent to other neurons or to external objects.

Let $x_i = (x_{i1}, x_{i2}, \ldots, x_{in})$ be the vector of input signals to the ith neuron. Many neural network models assume that each input signal x_{ij} to the ith neuron is "weighted" by the strength w_{ij} of the ith neuron's connection to the jth source. The weighted inputs, $w_{ij} x_{ij}$, are then summed in these models to form the actual input z_i to the node function f at the ith neuron: $z_i = \Sigma w_{ij} x_{ij} + \theta_i$, where θ_i is a constant, called the threshold value.

2.1   Designing and Training Networks

A network of neurons is made to perform a certain task by designing and training an appropriate network through the process of learning. The design of a network generally involves determining: (a) the number of layers in the network, (b) the number of neurons in each layer, (c) the connectivity pattern between the layers and the neurons, (d) the node function to use at each neuron, and (e) the mode of operation of the network (e.g., feedback vs. feedforward). The training of a network usually involves determining the connection weights [w_{ij}] and the threshold values [θ_i] from a set of training examples. For some learning algorithms like back-propagation [40] and self-organizing maps [21], [22], the design of the network is provided by the user or some other external source. For other algorithms like Adaptive Resonance Theory [9]-[11], reduced coulomb energy [33], and radial basis function (RBF) networks [26], the design of the network is accomplished by the algorithm itself. However, other parameter values have to be externally supplied to these latter algorithms on a trial and error basis in order for them to perform the design task satisfactorily.

A network is trained to perform a certain task by adjusting the connection weights [w_{ij}] by means of a local learning rule or law. A local learning law is a means of gradually changing the connection weights [w_{ij}] by an amount Δw_{ij} after observing each training example. A learning law is generally based on the idea that a network is supposed to perform a certain task and that the weights have to be set such that the error in the performance of that task is minimized. A learning law is "local" because it is conceived that the individual neurons in a network are the ones making the changes to their connection weights or connection strengths, based on the error in their performance. Local learning laws are a direct descendent of the idea that the cells or neurons in a brain are autonomous learners. The idea of "autonomous learners" is derived, in turn, from the notion that there is no homunculus or "a little man" inside the brain that "guides and controls" the behavior of different cells in the brain [19]. This "no homunculus" argument says that there couldn't exist a distinct and separate physical entity in the brain that governs the behavior of other cells in the brain. In other words, as the argument goes, there are no "ghosts" in the brain. So any notion of "extracellular control" of synaptic modification (connection weight changes) is not acceptable to this framework.

So, under the connectionist theory of learning, the connection weight $w_{ij}(t)$, after observing the tth training example, is given by: $w_{ij}(t) = w_{ij}(t-1) + \Delta w_{ij}(t)$, where $\Delta w_{ij}(t)$ is the weight adjustment after the tth example is observed and the adjustment is determined by the local learning law being used. Much of the current research in artificial neural networks is on developing new or modifying old local learning laws (training algorithms). There are now hundreds of local learning laws (training algorithms), but the most well-known among them are back-propagation [40], ART [9]-[11], SOM [21], [22], and RBF networks [26] and their different variations.

3   A New Learning Theory –
an Outline of the Basic Ideas

This section outlines the basic ideas used in developing the RBF algorithms of this chapter and shows why some of the ideas used in connectionism and artificial neural networks are not brain-like at all.

3.1   Brain-Like Learning Need Not be Based on "Local Learning" Mechanisms

This section argues that the idea of "local learning" is not valid and it is refuted by recent evidence from neuroscience. The new learning theory therefore proposes that brain-like learning algorithms need not be based on local learning laws, but should freely explore other mechanisms.

3.1.1   Connectionisms Local Learning – What It Really Implies

Under the notion of "autonomous/independent learner" of connectionism, it is construed that individual neurons or cells in the brain "decide" on their own how to modify their synaptic strengths or connection weights, based on error signals and other performance-related information provided to them from other sources within the brain. In other words, the actual "adjustment decision" is not (or cannot be) conveyed to the neuron or cell from an outside source, although "any other" type of performance-related information can be supplied to it from outside. The "adjustment" of the input-output function of a neuron is strictly a "local decision" of the neuron. What all this means is that there is some restriction on the kind of information that can be supplied to a neuron or cell; in particular, the cells "operating properties" cannot be adjusted or influenced by means of signals coming from outside the cell. In other words, this implies that no other physical entity external to a neuron is allowed to "signal" it directly to adjust its synaptic strengths in a certain way, although other kinds of signals can be sent to it. All of the well-known local learning laws (learning or training algorithms) developed to date try to adhere to this notion.

3.1.2   The Contrary Evidence from Neuroscience about Local Learning

This notion, however, of "autonomous/independent learners" is not only problematic from a logical point of view, as discussed later, but is also not consistent with some recent findings in neuroscience; there is actually no neurobiological evidence to support this notion. There is now clear evidence from neuroscience for the "different pathways" by which "additional signals" could influence synaptic adjustments directly. There is a growing body of evidence that shows that the neuromodulator system of the brain controls synaptic adjustments within the brain ([8], [13], [14], [16], [17], [25], [35], [42], and others). The neurobiological evidence shows that there are many different neuromodulators and many different cellular pathways for them to affect cellular changes. Cellular mechanisms within the cell are used to convert those "extracellular" signals into long-lasting changes in cellular properties. Thus the connectionist notion of "autonomous/ independent learners" (local decision-making embodied in local learning rules of the neurons) is not consistent with these recent findings in neuroscience.

3.1.3   New Theory – Non-Local Means of Learning is Brain-Like

The evidence for external signals and external control inherent in neuromodulation clearly suggests that means other than "local learning" are being used in the brain to adjust and train networks. That evidence should allow the field of artificial neural networks to freely explore means other than local learning laws for adjusting and setting connection weights and other parameters in a network. Using such alternative "non-local" means of training, Roy *et al.* [36]-[39] have developed robust and reliable learning algorithms that have polynomial time computational complexity in both the design and training of networks. The exploration of other means of learning can resolve some of the major computational problems of the field.

3.2   New Theory –
Brain-Like Learning is Not Memoryless

Under connectionism and artificial neural networks, brain-like learning systems cannot record and store any training examples explicitly in its memory - in some kind of working memory of the learning system, that is - that can be readily accessed in the future, if needed, in order to learn. The learning mechanism can use any particular training example presented to it to adjust whatever network it is learning in, but must forget that example before examining others. That's how all connectionist and artificial neural network learning rules are designed to operate – they are designed to adjust a network from a single training instance. The learning rules are not designed to examine or use more than one training example at a time. This is the so-called "memoryless learning" of connectionism, where no storage of facts and information is allowed.

However, the main problem with this notion of memoryless learning is that it is completely inconsistent with the way humans learn; it completely violates very basic behavioral facts about human learning. Remembering relevant facts and examples is very much a part of the human learning process; as every person knows, it facilitates mental examination of facts and information that is the basis for all human learning. In order to examine facts and information and learn from it, humans need memory. There is extensive evidence in the experimental psychology literature on the use of memory in learning [43]. In many psychological experiments, memorization actually precedes the learning of rules.

There are other logical problems with the idea of memoryless learning. First, one cannot learn (generalize, that is) unless one knows what is there to learn (generalize). And one can know what is there to learn "only by" collecting and storing some information about the problem at hand. In other words, no system, biological or otherwise, can "prepare" itself to learn without having some information about what is there to learn (generalize). Second, there is no neural network learning system that can perform the following tasks without knowing anything about the problem and without having seen a single training example before the start of learning: (1) determine how many inputs and outputs there should be in the network, (2) determine what the network design should be (how many layers, how many nodes per layer, their connectivity pattern, their operating mechanism (feedback vs. feedforward), and so on), and (3) set the various learning parameters for the learning to take place. Again, there is no system, biological or otherwise, that can do that. So the notion of "memoryless learning" is a very serious misconception in these fields – it is not only inconsistent with the way humans learn, but is also illogical.

So the new learning theory argues that collection and storage of information prior to learning is definitely brain-like and brain-like learning systems should be allowed to store information about a problem prior to learning. In other words, it is perfectly valid for brain-like learning processes to use memory in learning.

3.3   New Theory – a Brain-Like Learning System Must Make an Explicit Attempt to Generalize

Learning of rules from examples involves generalization. Generalization implies the ability to derive a succinct description of a phenomenon, using a simple set of rules or statements, from a set of observations of the phenomenon. So, in this sense, the simpler the derived description of the phenomenon, the better is the generalization. For example, Einstein's $E = MC^2$ is a superbly succinct generalization of a natural phenomenon. And this is the essence of learning from examples. So any brain-like learning system must exhibit this property of the brain - the ability to generalize. That is, it must demonstrate that it makes an explicit attempt to generalize and learn. In order to generalize, the learning system must have the ability to design an appropriate network. Many connectionist and artificial neural network learning systems, however, depend on an external source to provide them with the network design [15], [20]-[22], [24], [40], [41]. Hence, they are inherently incapable of generalizing without external assistance. This implies again that some connectionist and artificial neural network learning systems are not brain-like. Under this new learning theory, a brain-like learning algorithm must make an explicit attempt to minimize the size of the network in order to generalize.

3.4 New Theory – There Should be Some Restriction on the Nature of Information That Can be Supplied to a Brain-Like Learning System

Humans, in general, are able to acquire a great deal of information about a learning problem from external sources. The information usually acquired includes examples or cases of the problem, cues about what features are important, relationship to other knowledge already acquired and so on. But, on the other hand, humans have no external control over the learning processes inside the brain. For example, one cannot supply the design of a network to the brain. Nor can one set the parameters of the "learning algorithm" inside the brain. Hence any brain-like learning system should also be restricted to accepting only the kind of information that is normally supplied externally to a human brain. Thus it should not obtain any information that pertains to the internal control of the learning algorithm, since humans cannot externally control the learning processes inside the brain. This restriction is quite severe. Perhaps none of the connectionist and artificial neural network learning systems can satisfy this requirement because they obtain quite a bit of algorithmic control information from external sources. Thus a requirement of this new learning theory is that a brain-like learning system should not receive any information that is not provided to the brain from its external environment.

4 Radial Basis Function (RBF) Nets for Function Approximation

RBF nets belong to the group of kernel function nets that utilize simple kernel functions that are distributed in different neighborhoods of the input space and whose responses are essentially local in nature. The architecture consists of one hidden and one output layer. This shallow architecture has great advantage in terms of computing speed compared to multiple hidden layer nets.

Each hidden node in a RBF net represents one of the kernel functions. An output node simply computes the weighted sum of the outputs of the hidden nodes. A kernel function is a local function and the range of its effect is determined by its center and width. Its output is high when the input is close to the center and it decreases rapidly to zero as the input's distance from the center increases. The Gaussian function is a popular kernel function and is used in these algorithms. The design and training of a RBF net consists of (1) determining how many kernal functions to use, (2) finding their centers and widths, and (3) finding the weights that connect them to the output node.

Mathematically, the overall response function of such a network with a single output node is given by

$$F(x) = \sum_{q=1}^{Q} h_q G_q(x), \tag{1}$$

$$G_q(x) = R(\|x - C_q\|/w_q^2) \tag{2}$$

Here, Q is the total number of hidden or RBF nodes, x is the input pattern vector, $G_q(x)$ is the response function of the qth kernel unit (RBF node), R is a radially symmetric function whose output is maximum at the center and decreases rapidly to zero as the input's distance from the center increases, C_q and w_q are the center and width of the qth unit, and h_q is the weight associated with the qth unit. Generally, a Gaussian function with unit normalization is chosen as the kernel function:

$$G_q(x) = \exp(-Z_q/w_q^2), \text{ and} \tag{3}$$

$$Z_q = \sum_{l=1}^{N} (C_{ql} - X_l)^2, \tag{4}$$

where an input is represented by the N-dimensional vector x, $x=(X_1,X_2,...,X_N)$ and the training set consists of n vectors of the form (x_i,y_i), where y_i is the predicted value when the input vector is x_i. X_l denotes the lth element of the vector x.

Several radial basis function algorithms have been proposed recently for both classification and real-valued function approximation. Significant contributions include those in [1]-[4], [6], [18], [26], [27], [28], [30]-[32], [34], [45]-[48], and others. It has been shown that RBF nets have the universal approximation property [12], [29].

4.1   Basic Ideas and the Algorithm

In forecasting, regression, signal processing and control theory, a linear or nonlinear function $f(x)$ is usually constructed from the data to model a certain phenomenon. The unknown parameters of the function $f(x)$ are generally found by some error minimizing technique. The following LP model can also be used to construct certain best-fit functions for the data [7], [23]:

$$\text{Minimize} \qquad \sum_{i=1}^{n} (d_i^+ + d_i^-) \qquad\qquad (5)$$

$$\text{subject to} \qquad f(x_i) + d_i^+ - d_i^- = y_i, \, i = 1,...,n$$

$$d_i^+, d_i^- \geq 0$$

$$a, b \text{ unrestricted in sign in } f(x),$$

where $f(x) = \sum_{p=1}^{m} a_p g_p(x) + b;$

$g_p(x)$ is a known real function of x; m is the total number of such functions; $a = (a_1, a_2,...,a_m)$ is the vector of coefficients of $g(x) = (g_1(x),...,g_m(x))$; y_i is the desired output for the ith input vector x_i; d_i^+ and d_i^- are the positive and negative deviation variables respectively for the ith input, and b is a constant. The function $f(x)$ in the LP can take a rich variety of forms. The following are some examples:

$$f(x) = \sum_{i=1}^{N} a_i X_i + \sum_{i=1}^{N} b_i X_i^2 + \sum_{i=1}^{N} \sum_{j=i+1}^{N} c_{ij} X_i X_j + d,$$

$$f(x) = \sum_{i=1}^{N} a_i |X_i| + \sum_{i=1}^{N} \sum_{j=i+1}^{N} c_{ij} Sin X_i X_j, \text{ and}$$

$$f(x) = \sum_{i=1}^{N} a_i e^{Xi} + \sum_{i=1}^{N} \sum_{j=i+1}^{N} c_{ij} X_i^2 |X_j|.$$

The LP solves for the unknown coefficients (a_i, b_i, c_{ij} and so on) of the function $f(x)$. Note that the LP minimizes the L_1 norm and not L_2, as is the usual practice.

In this algorithm, the idea of a compact and fixed model of the phenomenon, similar to one of the $f(x)$ functions above, is combined with the idea of using radial basis functions to handle any unknown nonlinearities in the phenomenon. From a purely RBF point of view, the addition of a fixed model $f(x)$ to the net can potentially assist the generalization process and reduce the need for a large number of RBF units. In computational experiments, a linear $f(x)$ function has been used in combination with Gaussian RBF units. Hence, the function $f(x)$ for the LP in (5) is more properly defined, for this algorithm, as

$$f_1(x) = \sum_{p=1}^{m} a_p g_p(x) + \sum_{q=1}^{\varrho} h_q G_q(x) + b, \tag{6}$$

which corresponds to the output of a "mixed" RBF net. When the effect of an RBF unit is small, it can be safely ignored. This idea of ignoring small RBF outputs leads to the definition of a truncated RBF unit as follows:

$$\overline{G}_q(x) = G_q(x) \quad \text{if } G_q(x) \geq \phi, \tag{7}$$

$$= 0 \qquad \text{otherwise,}$$

where $\overline{G}_q(x)$ is the truncated RBF function and ϕ a small constant. In computational experiments, ϕ was set to 10^{-4}. Thus, the function $f(x)$ for the LP in (5) is redefined in terms of $\overline{G}_q(x)$ as follows:

$$f_2(x) = \sum_{p=1}^{m} a_p g_p(x) + \sum_{q=1}^{\varrho} h_q \overline{G}_q(x) + b \tag{8}$$

where $f_2(x)$ now corresponds to the output of a "mixed" RBF net with truncated RBF units. Henceforth, solving the LP in (5) implies solving it using the function $f_2(x)$ instead of $f(x)$.

4.2   Generation of Gaussian Units for Function Approximation

The network constructed by this algorithm deviates from a typical RBF net. For example, there is truncation of RBF node outputs and, in addition, non-RBF units are used in the hidden layer. Besides that, in a clear departure from the kernel function idea, the basis functions are no longer viewed as purely local units, since it generally results in a very large net. Here, the basis functions are a combination of local and global feature detectors. For that purpose, a variety of overlapping Gaussians (different centers and widths) are created to provide for both global and local feature detection. Though both "fat" (i.e., ones with large widths) and "narrow" Gaussians can be provided, the "fat" ones, which detect global features, are created and explored first to see how well the broad territorial features work. The Gaussians, therefore, are generated incrementally, in stages, starting with the fat ones and they gradually become narrow local feature detectors in later stages. As new Gaussians are generated at each stage, the LP in (5) is solved using all of the Gaussians generated till that stage (the Gaussians are used in the function $f_2(x)$) and the resulting net evaluated for error. Whenever the incremental change in the error rates (both training and validation or test set errors) becomes small or overfitting occurs on the training set, the algorithm stops and either the current net (if the incremental change in the error rates is small) or the previous net (when overfitting occurs) is used as the final net. This incremental process of net generation, going from global to local Gaussian units, is consistent with the new learning theory requirement that an explicit attempt be made by the algorithm to obtain good generalization.

The Gaussians are generated incrementally, in stages, by random clustering and several Gaussians can be generated in a stage. Let k ($= 1,2,3...$) denote a stage of this process. A stage is characterized by a parameter δ that specifies the maximum radius for the hypersphere that includes the random cluster of points that is to define a Gaussian. The parameter δ essentially controls the nature of the Gaussian generated (fat or narrow). In random clustering, the starting point for a cluster is randomly selected and the cluster is grown around that starting point upto a radius δ. Therefore, each random cluster includes all points in the δ-neighborhood of the starting point. Let δ_k be the neighborhood radius at stage k.

The Gaussians at any stage k are randomly selected in the following way. Randomly select an input vector x_i from the training set and search for all other training vectors within the δ_k-neighborhood of x_i. The training vectors in the δ_k-neighborhood are used to define a Gaussian and then removed from the training set. To define the next Gaussian, another input vector x_i is randomly selected from the remaining training set and its δ_k-neighborhood similarly searched for other vectors. This process of randomly picking an input vector x_i from the remaining training set and searching for vectors in its δ_k-neighborhood to define the next Gaussian is then repeated until the remaining training set is empty.

Let V_j be the set of training vectors within the δ_k-neighborhood of starting vector x_i for the jth random cluster generated in stage k. The centroid of the set V_j becomes the center C_Q of the Qth Gaussian and the standard deviation of the distances of the points in V_j from C_Q becomes the width w_Q of the Gaussian, where the Gaussian being defined is the Qth overall Gaussian. That is, Q is the cumulative number of Gaussians generated over all of the past and current stages. When the number of vectors in V_j is less than a certain minimum, no Gaussian is created; the vectors in the set are however removed from the remaining training set. So a Gaussian is not necessarily produced from every random cluster.

Gaussians of various widths can be generated by repeating this process for various δ values. δ can be varied in many different ways. In the particular variation of the algorithm stated here, δ is initially set to the standard deviation of the distances of the training vectors from their centroid, and it is reduced at a fixed rate, $\delta_k = \alpha \delta_{k-1}$. In computational experiments, α values in the range 0.5 to 0.8 were tried and it was discovered that the method is fairly insensitive to the δ-reduction rate as far as the final error rate is concerned, although the size of the net may vary some.

4.3   The Sequential Approximation (SA) Algorithm for Function Approximation

The following notation is used to describe the algorithm. I denotes the initial training set and R denotes the training set remaining in a stage at any time after removal of random clusters. N_j denotes the number of vectors in the random cluster V_j, k is the stage counter and Q the counter for Gaussians generated. C_q and w_q are the center and width of the qth Gaussian unit. TRE_k is the training set error and TSE_k is the validation set error at the kth stage. γ is the minimum value for δ and β is the minimum number of points in a random cluster for a Gaussian to be defined. α is the δ-reduction rate and ρ is the standard deviation of the distances of the training points from their centroid. δ_k is the neighborhood radius at stage k. The Sequential Approximation (SA) algorithm is summarized below.

The Sequential Approximation (SA) Algorithm

1. Initialize counters and constants: $k=0$, $Q=0$, $\delta_1=\rho$, α =some fraction (say 0.8).
2. Increment stage counter: $k=k+1$.
   Reduce neighborhood radius: if $k > 1$, $\delta_k=\alpha\delta_{k-1}$. If $\delta_k < \gamma$, stop.
3. Select Gaussian units for the kth stage: $j=0$, $R=I$.
   a. Set $j=j+1$.
   b. Select an input vector x_i at random from R, the remaining training set.
   c. Search for all vectors in R within the δ_k-neighborhood of x_i. Let this set of vectors be V_j.
   d. Remove the set V_j from $R : R = R - V_j$.
      If $N_j < \beta$, go to (f).
   e. Increment Gaussian counter: $Q= Q + 1$. Compute the center C_Q and width w_Q of the Qth Gaussian unit:
      C_Q = centroid of the set V_j, and
      w_Q = standard deviation of the points in the random cluster V_j.
   f. If R is not empty, go to (a), else go to (4).
4. Solve LP (5) using function $f_2(x)$ with Q number of Gaussians.
5. Compute TSE_k and TRE_k.
   a. If $TSE_k < TSE_{k-1}$, go to (2);
   b. If $TSE_k > TSE_{k-1}$ and $TRE_k > TRE_{k-1}$, go to (2);

    c. Otherwise, stop. Overfitting has occurred. Use the net generated
    in the previous stage.

Other stopping criteria, like maximum number of Gaussians used or
incremental change in TSE, can also be used. Table 1 shows how
overfitting is detected during training. In problem 1, overfitting occurs
at stage 2, when the training set error TRE decreases, but the validation
set error TSE increases. So, the net generated in the first stage is used,
which has 15 Gaussian units. In problem 2, overfitting occurs in stage
4. So the net generated in the third stage is used, which has 43 Gaussian
units.

Table 1. Detection of overfitting by the SA algorithm.

stage or pass no. (k)	delta (δ_k)	Gaussians generated in this stage	cumulative no. of Gaussians (Q)	TRE_k (%)	TSE_k (%)
Problem 1 – A Neuro Controller					
1	1.2	15	15	3.11	3.53
2	0.96	26	41	2.07	5.14
Problem 2 – Another Neuro Controller					
1	2.1	10	10	19.86	13.65
2	1.68	13	23	12.637	11.478
3	1.34	20	43	6.694	6.31
4	1.07	26	69	4.0	19.14

5   Radial Basis Function (RBF) Nets for Classification

The algorithm for classification is slightly different. So it's discussed
here separately. Some additional notations first. Let T denote the total
number of classes and t a particular class. The method is for supervised
learning where the training set $x_1, x_2, ..., x_n$ is a set of n sample patterns
with known classification. In this method, a particular subset of the
hidden nodes, associated with class t, is connected to the tth output
node and those class t hidden nodes are not connected to the other
output nodes. Therefore, mathematically, the input $F_t(x)$ to the tth
output node (i.e., the class t output node) is given by

$$F_t(x) = \sum_{q=1}^{Q^t} h_q^t G_q^t(x), \tag{9}$$

$$G_q^t(x) = R(\|x - C_q^t\|/w_q^t) \tag{10}$$

Here Q^t is the number of hidden nodes associated with class t, q refers to the qth class t hidden node, $G_q^t(x)$ is the response function of the qth class t hidden node, R is a radially symmetric kernel function, $C_q^t = (C_{q1}^t,...,C_{qN}^t)$ and w_q^t are the center and width of the qth kernel function for class t, and h_q^t is the weight connecting the qth hidden node for class t to the tth output node. Generally, a Gaussian with unit normalization is chosen as the kernel function:

$$G_q^t(x) = \exp(-1/2 \sum_{l=1}^{N} (C_{ql}^t - X_l)^2/(w_q^t)^2), \tag{11}$$

The basic idea of the algorithm here is to cover a class region with a set of Gaussians of varying widths and centers. The output function $F_t(x)$, for class t, a linear combination of Gaussians, is said to cover the region of class t if it is slightly positive $(F_t(x) \geq \varepsilon)$ for patterns in that class and zero or negative for patterns outside that class. Suppose Q^t Gaussians are required to cover the region of class t in this fashion. The covering (masking) function $F_t(x)$ for class t is given by (9). An input pattern x, therefore, may be determined to be in class t if $F_t(x) \geq \varepsilon$ and and not in class t if $F_t(x) \leq 0$. This condition, however, is not sufficient, and stronger conditions are stated later.

As in function approximation, when the effect of a Gaussian is small, it can be safely ignored. Thus, as before, it leads to the notion of a truncated Gaussian unit as follows:

$$\bar{G}_q^t(x) = G_q^t(x) \quad \text{if } G_q^t(x) \geq \phi, \tag{12}$$
$$= 0 \qquad \text{otherwise,}$$

where $\bar{G}_q^t(x)$ is the truncated RBF function and ϕ a small constant.

Thus, the function $F_t(x)$ is redefined in terms of $\bar{G}_q^t(x)$ as follows:

$$F_t(x) = \sum_{q=1}^{Q^t} h_q^t \overline{G}_q^t(x),$$ (13)

where $F_t(x)$ now corresponds to the output of a RBF net with "truncated" RBF units.

So, in general, Q^t is the number of Gaussians required to cover class t, $t=1,...,T$, $F_t(x)$ is the covering function (mask) for class t, and $G^t_1(x),....,$ $G^t_{Qt}(x)$ are the corresponding Gaussians. Then an input pattern x' will belong to class t if and only if its mask $F_t(x)$ is at least slightly positive, and the masks for all other classes are zero or negative. This is the necessary and sufficient condition for x' to belong to class t. Here, each mask $F_t(x)$, $t=1,...,T$, will have its own threshold value ε_t as determined during its construction. Expressed in mathematical notation, an input pattern x' is in class t if and only if $F_t(x') \geq \varepsilon_t$, and $F_j(x') \leq 0$ for all $j \neq t$, $j=1,...,T$. If all masks have values equal to or below zero, the input cannot be classified. If masks from two or more classes have values above their ε-thresholds, then also the input cannot be classified, unless the maximum of the mask values is used to determine class ("ambiguity rejection").

Let TR_t be the set of pattern vectors of any class t for which masking is desired and TR'_t be the corresponding set of non-class t vectors, where $TR = TR_t \vee TR'_t$ is the total training set. As before, suppose Q^t Gaussians of varying widths and centers are available to cover class t. The following linear program is solved to determine the Q^t weights $h^t = (h^t_1,...., h^t_q)$ for the Q^t Gaussians that minimize the classification error:

Minimize $\alpha \sum_{x_i \in TR_t} d_i + \beta \sum_{x_i \in TR'_t} d_i$ (14)

subject to $F_t(x_i) + d_i \geq \varepsilon_t, \quad x_i \in TR_t$
                        $F_t(x_i) - d_i \leq 0, \quad x_i \in TR'_t$
                        $d_i \geq 0, \qquad\qquad x_i \in TR$
                     $\varepsilon_t \geq$ a small positive constant,
                     h^t in $F_t(x)$ unrestricted in sign,

where d_is are external deviation variables and α and β are the weights for the in-class and out-of-class deviations, respectively.

5.1   Generation of Gaussian Units for Classification

Again, as before, the network constructed by this algorithm deviates from a typical RBF net. In particular, there is truncation at the hidden nodes and the output nodes use a hard limiting nonlinearity [for the tth output node, the output is 1 if $F_t(x) \geq \varepsilon_t$, and 0 otherwise]. In addition, as before, the Gaussians here are not viewed as purely local units because it generally results in a very large net. An explicit attempt is made by the algorithm to obtain good generalization. For that purpose, a variety of overlapping Gaussians (different centers and widths) are created to act as both global and local feature detectors and to help map out the territory of each class with the least number of Gaussians. As usual, though both "fat" (i.e. the ones with large widths) and "narrow" Gaussians can be created, the "fat" ones, which detect global features, are created and explored first to see how well the broad territorial features work. The Gaussians, therefore, are generated incrementally and they become narrow local feature detectors in later stages. As new Gaussians are generated for a class at each stage, the LP model (14) is solved using all of the Gaussians generated till that stage and the resulting mask evaluated. Whenever the incremental change in the error rate (training and validation) becomes small or overfitting occurs on the training set, masking of the class is determined to be complete and the appropriate solution for the weights retrieved.

As in function approximation, the Gaussians for a class t are generated incrementally (in stages) and several Gaussians can be generated in a stage. As before, let k (=1,2,3....) denote a stage of this process. A stage for classification problems is characterized by its majority criterion, a parameter that controls the nature of the Gaussians generated (fat or narrow). A majority criterion of 60% for a stage implies that a randomly generated pattern cluster at that stage, which is to be used to define a Gaussian for class t, must have at least 60% of the patterns belong to class t. Let θ_k denote the majority criterion for any stage k. In the classification algorithm, θ_k starts at 50% (stage 1 majority criterion) and can increase upto 100% in, say, increments of 10%. Thus the method will have a maximum of six stages (θ_k = 50%, 60%, ..., 100%) when the increment is 10%. A 50% majority criterion allows for the creation of "fatter" Gaussians compared to, say, a 90% majority criterion and thus can detect global features in the pattern set that might not otherwise be detected by narrow Gaussians of a higher majority criterion.

The Gaussians for a given class t at any stage k are randomly selected in the following way. Randomly pick a pattern vector x_i of class t from the training set and search for all pattern vectors in an expanding δ-neighborhood of x_i. The δ-neighborhood of x_i is expanded as long as class t patterns in the expanded neighborhood retain the minimum majority of θ_k for stage k. The neighborhood expansion is stopped when class t losses its required majority or when a certain maximum neighborhood radius of δ_{max} is reached. When the expansion stops, the class t patterns in the last δ-neighborhood are used to define a Gaussian and are then removed from the training set. To define the next Gaussian, another class t pattern x_i is randomly selected from the remaining training set and its δ-neighborhood is similarly grown to its limits, as explained above. This process of randomly picking a pattern vector x_i of class t from the remaining training set and searching for pattern vectors in an expanding neighborhood of x_i to define the next Gaussian is then repeated until the remaining training set is empty of class t vectors.

The process of generating a Gaussian starts with an initial neighborhood radius δ_0 and then enlarges the neighborhood in fixed increments of $\Delta\delta$ ($\delta_r = \delta_{r-1} + \Delta\delta$). Here δ_r is the neighborhood radius at the rth growth step. Let V^r_j be the set of pattern vectors within the δ_r-neighborhood of starting vector x_i for the jth Gaussian being generated at stage k. A neighborhood size can be increased only if the current pattern set V^r_j from the δ_r-neighborhood satisfies the majority criterion and if $\delta_r < \delta_{max}$. Otherwise, further expansion is stopped. At any growth step r, if the current pattern set V^r_j fails the majority criterion, the previous set V^{r-1}_j (if there is one) is used to create the Gaussian. When a Gaussian is created from either V^r_j or V^{r-1}_j, the centroid of class t pattern vectors in the set becomes the center C^t_{Qt} and the standard deviation of their distances from C^t_{Qt} becomes w^t_{Qt}, assuming the Gaussian being defined is the Q^tth Gaussian for class t where Q^t is the cumulative total number of Gaussians generated over all of the past and current stages. When the number of patterns in a set V^r_j or V^{r-1}_j is less than a certain minimum, no Gaussian is created; however, the class t patterns in the set are removed from the remaining training set.

5.2   The Gaussian Masking (GM) Algorithm for Classification

The RBF classification algorithm is stated below. The following notation is used. I and R denote the initial and remaining training sets respectively. δ_{max} is the maximum neighborhood radius, δ_r is the neighborhood radius at the rth growth step, and $\Delta\delta$ is the δ_r increment at each growth step. V'_j is the set of pattern vectors within the δ_r-neighborhood of starting vector x_i for the jth Gaussian of any stage k. $PC'_j(t)$ denotes the percentage of class t members in V'_j. N'_j denotes the number of vectors in V'_j. k is the stage counter, θ_k is the minimum percentage of class t members in stage k, and $\Delta\theta$ is the increment for θ_k at each stage. S_t corresponds to the cumulative set of Gaussians created for class t. C'_{Qt} and w'_{Qt} are the center and width, respectively, of the Qth Gaussian for class t. TRE_k and TSE_k are the training and validation set errors, respectively, at the kth stage for the class being masked. γ is the minimum number of patterns required in V'_j to form a Gaussian and ρ is the maximum of the class standard deviations that are the standard deviations of the distances from the centroid of the patterns of each class. δ_{max} is set to some multiple of ρ. The fixed increment $\Delta\delta$ is set to some fraction of $\delta_{max} - \delta_0$, $\Delta\delta = (\delta_{max} - \delta_0)/s$, where s is the desired number of growth steps. s was set to 25 and δ_{max} was set to 10ρ for computational purposes.

The Gaussian Masking (GM) Algorithm

(0) Initialize constants: $\delta_{max} = 10\rho$, $\Delta\theta =$ some constant (e.g., 10%), $\delta_0 =$ some constant (e.g. 0 or 0.1ρ), $\Delta\delta = (\delta_{max} - \delta_0)/s$.

(1) Initialize class counter: $t = 0$.

(2) Increment class counter: $t = t + 1$. If $t > T$, stop. Else, initialize cumulative Gaussian counters: $S_t = 0$ (empty), $Q' = 0$.

(3) Initialize stage counter: $k = 0$.

(4) Increment stage counter: $k = k + 1$. Increase majority criterion: if $k>1$, $\theta_k = \theta_{k-1} + \Delta\theta$; otherwise $\theta_k = 50\%$. If $\theta_k > 100\%$, go to (2) to mask next class.

(5) Select Gaussian units for the kth stage: $j = 0$, $R = I$.
  (a) Set $j = j + 1$, $r = 1$, $\delta_r = \delta_0$.
  (b) Select an input pattern vector x_i of class t at random from R, the remaining training set.

(c) Search for all pattern vectors in R within a δ_r radius of x_i. Let this set of vectors be V^r_j.

    (i) if $PC^r_j(t) < \theta_k$ and $r > 1$, set $r = r - 1$, go to (e);

    (ii) if $PC^r_j(t) > \theta_k$ and $r > 1$, go to (d) to expand the neighborhood;

    (iii) if $PC^r_j(t) < \theta_k$ and $r = 1$, go to (h);

    (iv) if $PC^r_j(t) > \theta_k$ and $r = 1$, go to (d) to expand the neighborhood;

(d) Set $r = r + 1$, $\delta_r = \delta_{r-1} + \Delta\delta$. If $\delta_r > \delta_{max}$, set $r = r - 1$, go to (e). Else, go to (c).

(e) Remove class t patterns of the set V^r_j from R. If $N^r_j < \gamma$, go to (g).

(f) Set $Q^t = Q^t + 1$. Compute the center C^t_{Qt} and width w^t_{Qt} of the Q^tth Gaussian for class t. Add Q^tth Gaussian to the set S_t. $C^t_{Qt} =$ centroid of class t patterns in the set V^r_j, and $w^t_{Qt} =$ standard deviation of the distances from the centroid C^t_{Qt} of class t patterns in the set V^r_j.

(g) If R is not empty of class t patterns, go to (a), else go to (6).

(h) Remove class t patterns of the set V^r_j from R. If R is not empty of class t patterns, go to (a), else go to (6).

(6) From the set S_t, eliminate similar Gaussians (i.e., those with very close centers and widths). Let Q^t be the number of Gaussians after this elimination.

(7) Solve LP in (14) for class t mask using Q^t number of Gaussians.

(8) Compute TRE_k and TSE_k for class t. If $k = 1$, go to (4). Else:

    (a) If $TSE_k < TSE_{k-1}$, go to (4).

    (b) If $TSE_k > TSE_{k-1}$ and $TRE_k > TRE_{k-1}$, go to (4).

    (c) Otherwise, overfitting has occurred. Use the mask generated in the previous stage as class t mask. Go to (2) to mask next class.

Other stopping criteria, like maximum number of Gaussians used or incremental change in TSE, can also be used.

The GM algorithm needs a representative set of examples, other than the training set, to design and train an appropriate net. This set can be called the validation or control test set. This control test set can be created by setting aside some examples from the training set itself. The algorithm does not try to minimize the error on the control test set. Explicit error minimization is done only on the training set.

Proofs of polynomial-time complexity of these algorithms and computational results are in [37] and [38].

6   Conclusions

Through the new learning theory, this chapter has tried to define the "nature" of algorithms that should be developed in the neural network field. The theory defines very broadly how the neural network algorithms should be constructed and what they should accomplish. However, within this broad framework, many different algorithms can be developed. The algorithms discussed here demonstrate that this framework is workable and can indeed produce very robust and reliable algorithms. Increased competition within this framework can be very beneficial to the field and produce very powerful methods. The algorithms presented here are only a beginning in that direction.

Most of the issues addressed by this new learning theory have been long standing issues for the neural network field. They include issues like polynomial time complexity, network design, generalization, local minima and autonomous learning. The algorithms presented here demonstrate that all these problems can be dealt with using very simple ideas.

Acknowledgments

This research was supported, in part, by Arizona State University College of Business Summer Grants.

References

[1] Baldi, P. (1990), "Computing with arrays of bell-shaped and sigmoid functions," *Proceedings of IEEE Neural Information Processing Systems*, vol. 3, pp. 728-734.

[2] Botros, S.M. and Atkeson, C.G. (1991), "Generalization properties of radial basis functions," in Lippman, R.P., Moody, J.E., and Touretzky, D.S. (Eds.), *Advances in Neural Information Processing Systems 3*, San Mateo: Morgan Kaufmann, pp. 707-713.

[3] Broomhead, D. and Lowe, D. (1988), "Multivariable function interpolation and adaptive networks," *Complex Systems*, vol. 2, pp. 321-355.

[4] Chen, S., Cowan, C.F.N., and Grant, P.M. (1991), "Orthogonal least squares learning algorithm for radial basis function networks," *IEEE Transactions on Neural Networks*, vol. 2, pp. 302-309.

[5] Feldman, J.A. and Ballard, D.A. (1982), "Connectionists models and their properties," *Cognitive Science*, vol. 6, pp. 205-254.

[6] Girosi, F. and Poggio, T. (1990), "Networks and the best approximation property," *Biological Cybernetics*, vol. 63, pp. 169-176.

[7] Glover, F. (1990), "Improved linear programming models for discriminant analysis," *Decision Sciences*, vol. 21, no. 4, pp. 771-785.

[8] Freeman, W.J. (1995), *Societies of brains: a study in neuroscience of love and hate*, Hillsdale, NJ:Lawrence Erlbaum.

[9] Grossberg, S. (1982), *Studies of Mind and Brain: Neural Principles of Learning Perception, Development, Cognition, and Motor Control*, Boston: Reidell Press.

[10] Grossberg, S. (1987), "Competitive learning: from interactive activation to adaptive resonance," *Cognitive Science*, vol. 11, pp. 23-63.

[11] Grossberg, S. (1988), "Nonlinear neural networks: principles, mechanisms, and architectures," *Neural Networks*, vol. 1, pp. 17-61.

[12] Hartman, E.J., Keeler, J.D., and Kowalski, J.M. (1990), "Layered neural networks with Gaussian hidden units as universal approximations," *Neural Computation*, vol. 2, pp. 210-215.

[13] Hasselmo, M. (1995), "Neuromodulation and cortical function: modeling the physiological basis of behavior," *Behavioral and Brain Research*, vol. 67, no. 1, pp. 1-27.

[14] Hestenes, D.O. (1998), "Modulatory mechanisms in mental disorders," in Stein, D. (Ed.), *Neural Networks and Psychopathology*, Cambridge, U.K.: Cambridge University Press.

[15] Hinton, G.E. and Sejnowski, T.J. (1986), "Learning and relearning in Boltzmann machines," in Rumelhart, D.E., McClelland, J.L., and the PDP Research Group (Eds.), *Parallel Distributed Processing: Explorations in the Microstructure of Cognition*, vol. 1, pp. 282-317, Cambridge, MA: MIT Press.

[16] Houk, Davis, and Beiser (1995), *Models of Information Processing in the Basal Ganglia*, MIT.

[17] Kandel, E.R., Schwartz, J.H., and Jessel, T.M. (1993), *Principles of Neural Science* (3rd ed.), New York: Elsevier.

[18] Kardirkamanathan, V., Niranjan, M., and Fallside, F. (1991), "Sequential adaptation of radial basis function neural networks and its application to time-series prediction," in Lippmann, R.P., Moddy, J.E., and Touretzky, D.S. (Eds.), *Advances in Neural Information Processing Systems*, vol. 3, pp.721-727, San Mateo: Morgan Kaufmann.

[19] Kenny, A. (1971), "The homunculus fallacy," in Grene, M. (Ed.), *Interpretations of life and mind*, London.

[20] Kohonen, T. (1988), "An introduction to neural networks," *Neural Networks*, vol. 1, pp. 3-16.

[21] Kohonen, T. (1989). *Self-Organization and Associative Memory*, (3rd ed.), Berlin, Heidelberg: Springer-Verlag.

[22] Kohonen, T. (1993), "Physiological interpretation of the self-organizing map algorithm," *Neural Networks*, vol. 6, pp. 895-905.

[23] Mangasarian, O.L., Setiono, R., and Wolberg, W.H. (1990), "Pattern recognition via linear programming: theory and

application to medical diagnosis," in Coleman, T.F. and Li, Y. (Eds.), *Proceedings of the Workshop on Large-Scale Numerical Optimization*, Cornell University, Ithaca, New York, Oct. 19-20, 1989, pp. 22-31, Philadelphia, PA, SIAM.

[24] McClelland, J.L. (1985), "Putting knowledge in its place: a scheme for programming parallel processing structures on the fly," *Cognitive Science*, vol. 9, pp. 113-146.

[25] McGaugh, J., Weinberger, N., and Lynch, G. (1995). *Brain and Memory: Modulation and Mediation of Neuroplasticity*, Oxford University Press, New York.

[26] Moody, J. and Darken, C. (1989), "Fast learning in networks of locally-tuned processing units," *Neural Computation*, vol. 1, no.2, pp. 281-294.

[27] Moody, J. and Darken, C. (1988), "Learning with localized receptive fields," in Touretky, D., Hinton, G., and Sejnowski, T. (Eds.), *Proceedings of the 1988 Connectionist Models Summer School*, pp. 133-143, Morgan-Kaufmann, San Mateo.

[28] Musavi, M.T., Ahmed, W., Chan, K.H., Faris, K.B., and Hummels, D.M. (1992), "On the training of radial basis function classifiers," *Neural Networks*, vol. 5, no. 4, pp. 595-603.

[29] Park, J. and Sandberg, I.W. (1993), "Universal approximation using radial-basis- function networks," *Neural Computation*, vol. 5, pp. 305-316.

[30] Platt, J. (1991), "A resource-allocating network for function interpolation," *Neural Computation*, vol. 3, no. 2, pp. 213-225.

[31] Poggio, T. and Girosi, F. (1990), "Regularization algorithms for learning that are equivalent to multilayer networks," *Science*, vol. 247, pp. 978-982.

[32] Powell, M.J.D. (1987), "Radial basis functions for multivariable interpolation: a review," in Mason, J.C. and Cox, M.G. (Eds.), *Algorithms for Approximation*, pp. 143-167, Clarendon Press, Oxford, U.K.

[33] Reilly, D.L., Cooper, L.N., and Elbaum, C. (1982), "A neural model for category learning," *Biological Cybernetics*, vol. 45, pp. 35-41.

[34] Renals, S. and Rohwer, R. (1989), "Phoneme classification experiments using radial basis functions," *Proceedings of International Joint Conference on Neural Networks*, vol. I, pp. 461-467.

[35] Ricart, R. (1992), "Neuromodulatory mechanisms in neural networks and their influence on interstimulus interval effects in Pavlovian conditioning," in Levine, D.S. and Leven, S.J. (Eds.), *Motivation, Emotion, and Goal Direction in Neural Networks*. Hillsdale, NJ: Lawrence Erlbaum Associates.

[36] Roy, A., Kim, L.S., and Mukhopadhyay, S. (1993), "A polynomial time algorithm for the construction and training of a class of multilayer perceptrons," *Neural Networks*, vol. 6, no. 4, pp. 535-545.

[37] Roy, A., Govil, S., and Miranda, R. (1995), "An algorithm to generate radial basis function (RBF)-like nets for classification problems," *Neural Networks*, vol. 8, no. 2, pp. 179-202.

[38] Roy, A., Govil, S., and Miranda, R. (1997), "A neural network learning theory and a polynomial time RBF algorithm," *IEEE Transactions on Neural Networks*, vol. 8, no. 6, pp. 1301-1313.

[39] Roy, A. and Mukhopadhyay, S. (1997), "Iterative generation of higher-order nets in polynomial time using linear programming," *IEEE Transactions on Neural Networks*, vol. 8, no. 2, pp. 402-412.

[40] Rumelhart, D.E., and McClelland, J.L. (Eds.) (1986). *Parallel Distributed Processing: Explorations in Microstructure of Cognition, Vol. 1: Foundations*, MIT Press, Cambridge, MA., pp. 318-362.

[41] Rumelhart, D.E. (1989), "The architecture of mind: a connectionist approach," chapter 8 in Haugeland, J. (Ed.) (1997), *Mind Design II*, MIT Press, pp. 205-232.

[42] Scheler, G. (1998), "Dopaminergic regulation of neuronal circuits in prefrontal cortex," submitted to *Neural Networks*.

[43] Shanks, D. (1995). *The Psychology of Associative Learning*, Cambridge University Press, Cambridge, England.

[44] Shanks, D. (1996), "Learning and memory," chapter 10 in Green, D. (ed), *Cognitive Science, an Introduction*, 1996, Blackwell Publishers, Oxford, U.K.

[45] Vrckovnik, G., Carter, C.R., and Haykin, S. (1990), "Radial basis function classification of impulse radar waveforms," *Proceedings of the International Joint Conference on Neural Networks*, vol. I, pp. 45-50.

[46] Weymaere, N. and Martens, J. (1991), "A fast robust learning algorithm for feed-forward neural networks," *Neural Networks*, vol. 4, pp. 361-369.

[47] Xu, L., Klasa, S., and Yuille, A.L. (1992), "Recent advances on techniques of static feedforward networks with supervised learning," *International Journal of Neural Systems*, vol. 3, no. 3, pp. 253-290.

[48] Xu, L., Krzyzak, A., and Oja, E. (1993), "Rival penalized competitive learning for clustering analysis, RBF net and curve detection," *IEEE Transactions on Neural Networks*, vol. 4, pp. 636-649.

Chapter 11

Evolutionary Optimization of RBF Networks

E. Lacerda, A. de Carvalho, and T. Ludermir

The design of efficient Artificial Neural Networks (ANNs) is not an easy task. A number of parameters must be appropriately set before an adequate performance is achieved. There are no well-established set of rules to guide the definition of the parameter values. As a matter of fact, similar networks may have very different behaviors and very different networks may show similar performances. This chapter discusses how Radial Basis Function (RBF) networks can have their parameters defined by evolutionary algorithms. Initially, it presents an overall view of the problems involved and the different alternatives used to genetically optimize ANNs. Among the aspects to be considered, networks encoding, fitness evaluation and adapted genetic operators are mentioned. A few approaches proposed in the literature to optimize RBF networks using Genetic Algorithms (GAs) are discussed. Finally, a model proposed by the authors is described and experimental results using this model are presented.

1   Introduction

Although ANNs have usually achieved a very good performance when applied to a large number of application domains, their performance is directly influenced by the appropriate choice of architecture and learning parameters. As an example, the number and position of RBF networks [7] hidden nodes strongly influence their overall performance.

Several alternative approaches have been proposed to select the network parameters. These approaches may be grouped in five different categories:

- Trial and error;
- Heuristics;

- Pruning techniques;
- Constructive training algorithms;
- Evolutionary design.

When trial and error is employed, several different values for the network parameters must be selected, trained and compared before the choice of an ultimate network. This disadvantage becomes more apparent if, after the choice of the best values, the patterns set is changed, making necessary to re-start the design process. This search can be made more efficient if heuristics are used to guide it. The use of pruning techniques optimizes trained networks by removing neurons and connections that are irrelevant or redundant. In the constructive approach, a network starts its training with a minimal topology and, according to the problem complexity, new neurons and connection are inserted, aiming to improve the network performance. The evolutionary approach uses GAs to generate several networks variations and combine the features of those with the best performance, thus generating new networks with improved performances through a number of generations.

This chapter discusses how Radial Basis Function networks [6] can have their parameters defined by evolutionary algorithms. GAs [15] provide a very natural approach for the solution of this problem, especially because the human brain is also, somehow, a result of the biological evolution. According to Gerald Edelman [10], Nobel Prize winner in 1972, the human mind is a direct result of natural selection. He suggests that the organization of neurons and their connections were not pre-determined, but evolved to compete with the circumstances imposed by the environment.

The next section provides a brief review of RBF networks. Section 3 describes GAs, introducing the main concepts necessary to understand the RBF evolutionary design. The fourth section discusses how evolutionary design can be used to optimize ANNs. Networks representation, fitness evaluation and adapted genetic operators are mentioned. The fifth section analyses different approaches proposed in the literature that optimize RBF networks using GAs. Section 6 describes an evolutionary method to optimize RBF networks proposed by the authors and compares the performance achieved by this method with those achieved by other approaches in a classification task.

2   Radial Basis Function Networks

RBF Networks have their origin in the solution of the multivariate interpolation problem [31]. These networks have been used in a large number of applications, such as time series analysis [5], [26] and image processing [30]. RBF networks have traditionally only one hidden layer. Properly trained, they can approximate a function $f: \Re \rightarrow \Re^n$ by mapping:

$$f(\mathbf{x}) \approx w_0 + \sum_{i=1}^{m} w_i \phi\left(\|\mathbf{x} - \mu_i\|\right) \tag{1}$$

where $\phi(\cdot)$ denotes the activation function, also known as radial function; $\{w_i; \ i=1...m\}$ represents the output layer weights, $\|\cdot\|$ is the Euclidean norm, $\{\mu_i \in \Re^n; \ i=1...m\}$ are the center vectors and w_0 is a bias (which can be absorbed into summation if regarded as a weight from an extra basis function with $\phi(\mathbf{x})=1$ for all $\mathbf{x} \in \Re^n$). A common example of basis function is the Gaussian function:

$$\phi(v)=\exp(-v^2/2\sigma^2) \tag{2}$$

where σ represents the function width, which is a scaling factor for the radius $\|x-\mu\|$.

Usually, RBF networks employ a hybrid learning algorithm. The hybrid training combines unsupervised and supervised learning. In [26], the unsupervised learning stage uses the K-means clustering algorithm [2] to define the center vectors distribution over the input space.

The K-means algorithm initializes m centers fixing them on m input vectors randomly chosen from the training set. The p-m remainder input vectors are assigned to the nearest cluster S_i (i.e., the nearest center). Afterwards, it computes every center μ_i using Equation 3 (i.e., the mean point of the cluster S_i):

$$\mu_i = \frac{1}{|S_i|} \sum_{j \in S_i} \mathbf{x}_j \tag{3}$$

The following steps repetitively re-assign all input vectors to the nearest center and re-compute the centers until there is no further center position change. Commonly, the number of centers, m, is determined by trial and error and cross-validation. Other clustering algorithms can also be used to determine the center distribution, such as the self-organizing feature map [17].

The widths σ_i can be determined by a number of heuristics. A few of them use a single value σ for all basis functions. In [26], the use of $\sigma = \langle \|\mu_i - \mu^{nearest}\| \rangle$ is suggested, where $\mu^{nearest}$ is the nearest center from μ_i and $\langle \cdot \rangle$ indicates the average over all such pairs. Other methods use a different value σ_i for each basis function. As an example, consider Ψ as the set of the N nearest input vectors from μ_i. The local width σ_i is thus given by:

$$\sigma_i^2 = C \frac{1}{N} \sum_{j \in \Psi} \|\mu_i - x_j\| \qquad (4)$$

where C is an overlap factor.

In the supervised learning stage, the RBF network can be interpreted as a case of linear regression on the training set:

$$t = \Phi w + e \qquad (5)$$

where: $t = [t_1, t_2, ..., t_p]^T$, $w = [w_1, w_2, ..., w_m]^T$, $\Phi = [\phi_1, \phi_2, ..., \phi_m]^T$ and $\phi_i = [\phi_i(\|x_1 - \mu_i\|), \phi_i(\|x_2 - \mu_i\|), ..., \phi_i(\|x_m - \mu_i\|)]^T$. The weight vector w is determined minimizing the sum of squared errors . The solution to this least square problem can be obtained solving the linear system:

$$(\Phi^T \Phi) w = \Phi^T t \qquad (6)$$

In order to avoid possible numerical problems (ill conditioning) to solve (6), Singular Value Decomposition (SVD) has been employed [33]. SVD computes the pseudo-inverse matrix Φ^+. Thus, the weight w is given by:

$$w = \Phi^+ t \qquad (7)$$

where

$$\Phi^+ = (\Phi^T \Phi)^{-1} \Phi^T \qquad (8)$$

The next section gives a short introduction to Genetic Algorithms.

3   A Brief Look at Genetic Algorithms

Among the several AI methods available in the literature, Genetic Algorithms, in particular, have been highly successful in the solution of optimization and search problems. John Holland's group from the University of Michigan introduced GAs in the middle of 1976 [15]. However, its full use only started almost ten years later [11].

In contrast to conventional search methods, GAs use a population of individuals to solve a given problem. Each individual of the population, named chromosome, corresponds to a possible solution for the problem. A chromosome is composed by a set of genes, which are the features of the solution provided by the chromosome. A reproduction mechanism based on evolutionary processes is applied on the current population, generating a new population. The population usually evolves through several generations until a suitable solution is reached. This mechanism aims to explore the search space and to find better solutions for the problem.

GAs, which are a special case of evolutionary computation, operate on a population of candidates in parallel. Thus, they can simultaneously search different areas of the solutions space. Every search or optimization task has several components, such as the search space, where there is a large number of solution possibilities for the given problem, and the evaluation or cost function, which evaluates the possible solutions. According to [11], GAs differ from traditional methods of search and optimization, mainly, in four aspects:

- they work with a code of the group of parameters and not with the own parameters;
- they work with several possible solutions and not with a single solution point;
- they use cost information or reward functions and not derivative or other auxiliary knowledge;
- they use probabilistic rules of transition instead of deterministic rules.

GAs usually generate an initial population formed by a random group of individuals, which can be seen as first guesses to solve the problem.

During the evolutionary process, this population is evaluated and for each individual a score is given, reflecting the quality of the solution associated to it. A percentage of the most capable individuals is selected for an intermediate population, while the others are discarded.

The selected members can have a subset of their fundamental features, represented by their genes, modified through genetic operators, generating descending for the next generation. This process, named reproduction, is repeated until a group of satisfactory solutions is found. Figure 1 presents a general diagram of a GA life cycle.

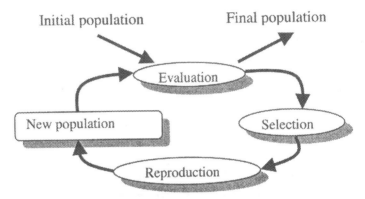

Figure 1. Genetic Algorithm cycles.

Different methods have been proposed to select individuals from a population. The most commonly used method is the roulette wheel sampling. In this method, each individual from the population occupies an area of the roulette wheel proportional to its fitness value. If N individuals are to be selected, the roulette wheel is spun N times. For each run, the individual pointed by the roulette wheel is selected. As a result, fittest individual has a higher chance of being selected and vice versa.

Although largely used, the roulette wheel method does not work with negative fitness values and suffer from premature convergence. This problem can be overcome by using tournament selection [25].

In the tournament selection method, N (usually, $N = 3$) chromosomes are randomly selected from the population, with the same probability. These chromosomes compete against each other and the chromosome with the highest fitness value is selected to an intermediate population. This process is repeated until the intermediate population is filled. Other selection methods have been proposed, like the Stochastic Universal Sampling (SUS) and the RANK selection [25].

Genetic operators are applied to the intermediate population individuals in order to produce new individuals. The main genetic operators employed are the crossover and the mutation operators.

The crossover operator is responsible for keeping the diversity of individuals in a population. It is the primary genetic operator. The crossover exchanges parts of a pair of individuals, creating new individuals. For ANNs optimization, it creates new networks by mixing parts of existing networks. Figure 2 illustrates a crossover operation.

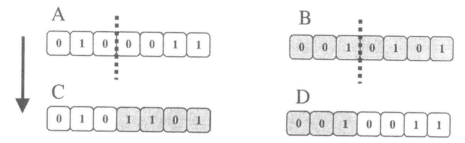

Figure 2. Crossover operation.

In this figure, a cut point is chosen and two chromosomes, A and B, contribute with a subset of their genes for the creation of the offsprings C and D.

The chromosome C inherits its first three genes from the chromosome A and its last four genes from the chromosome B. The chromosome D, on the other hand, receives its first three genes from the chromosome B and its last four genes from the chromosome A.

There are several variations of crossover operator, such as the two-cutpoints crossover and the uniform crossover. When the two-points crossover is used, the segments between the two cut points are exchanged between two parents [11], [25], as can be seen in Figure 3.

For the uniform crossover, a mask is used to define from which parent each offspring inherits each of its genes [11], [25].

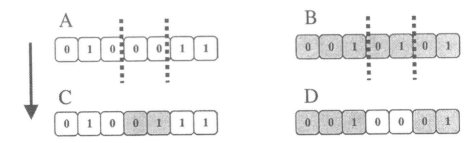

Figure 3. Two-point crossover operation.

The mutation operator guaranties that the probability of arriving in any point in the search space is larger than zero. This operator changes at random the value of a chromosome gene, also randomly chosen. Figure 4 shows a mutation operation.

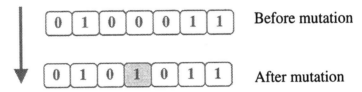

Figure 4. Mutation operation.

The mutation operation illustrated by Figure 4 changed the value of the fourth gene from 0 to 1.

4 Evolutionary Approaches for ANN Design

The evolutionary optimization of ANNs may occur in three different ways:

- **Optimization of topology and training parameters**. This may include the number of layers, the number of hidden units, the activation function, and the learning rate;
- **ANN training**. A GA may be used as a training algorithm to optimize the values of the network weights;
- **Learning rule optimization**. Given an ANN, this method looks for an efficient learning rule.

For ANNs evolutionary design, each individual can be seen as a state of the space of possible ANNs. Beginning the process with a population of genotypical representations of valid networks, usually randomly generated, a generator reconstructs each network (phenotype) from its representation (genotype), according to the encoding function used. Next, in order to evaluate their performances, all the networks are trained with the same training data set (and, ideally, a common validation data set).

Through a selection method, such as the roulette wheel [15], the networks are selected according to a relative probability associated to their fitness. The selection continues until the next population of candidates is completed. Later, the candidates go through a reproduction stage guided by mutation and crossover genetic operators. Through these operators, a new generation of neural architectures is constructed. In order to avoid the possible disappearance of the best networks from the population, an elitist policy can also be used, which automatically send these networks to the next generation.

This cycle is repeated and, with the passing of new generations, the population evolves gradually towards genotypes that correspond to phenotypes with higher performances. This cycle is carried out a certain number of times until the algorithm finds appropriate solutions to the problem, or, in extreme cases, until it comes to one best solution. During this process, the best networks, as well as some statistical data, can be collected and stored for a posterior analysis.

4.1   Representation Approaches

The question about how a neural architecture is genotypically represented is crucial in the design of an evolutionary approach. The representation used determines not only the classes of neural architectures that may evolve, but also the functioning of both the decoding process and the reproduction operators [3].

The representation of a Neural Network structure is usually a rather complex issue. Several factors must be considered:

- if the representation allows approximately optimum solutions to be represented;

- how invalid structures may be excluded;
- how the reproduction operators shall perform, so that each new generation has only valid ANNs;
- how the representation supports the creation of new neural architectures.

In the ideal representation, the genetically produced Neural Networks space excludes genotypes of invalid networks and allows the generation of all potentially useful ANNs [5].

Although different ANNs representations have been proposed [7], [13], [18], [22]-[24], [35]-[37], they can be roughly grouped into two main paradigms: the direct or low-level representation, and the indirect or high-level representation.

A direct representation specifies exactly each parameter of the network and requires little decoding effort, because the transformation from genotypes into phenotypes is straightforward.

A current method of direct representation, proposed by Miller [24], is the mapping of an ANN topology in a binary matrix. Each matrix element determines whether there is a connection between the two units represented by the row and column numbers. Figure 5 illustrates this representation.

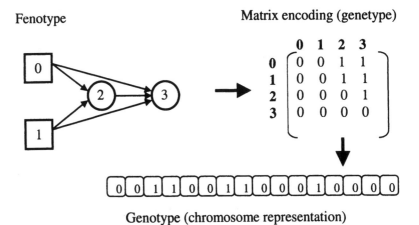

Figure 5. Miller's direct representation.

This method specifies in a direct and precise way the network connections, but all the other parameters must either be previously established or be defined by a training phase.

The main problem of this approach is that unfeasible structures can be produced, such as feedback connections for feedforward networks. Moreover, the network representation grows exponentially with the network size, bringing the need of very large codes for large networks. Thus, this method is useful only for relatively small network topologies. One advantage of this approach is that, by including the weights' values in the matrix, it can be easily modified to become a training algorithm or an initial weights selection algorithm.

Indirect representations, on the other hand, require a considerable effort for the decoding in the construction of the phenotypes. However, this kind of representation can employ abstract descriptions or grammatical encoding to characterize the networks. Besides, the networks can be pre-structured, using restrictions in order to exclude undesirable architectures, which makes the search space much smaller.

A few evolutionary methods work with indirect representations. Indirect encoding methods encode ANNs through set parameters. These parameters may be the number of layers, the size of the layers, the connections among them, etc.. It is also possible to include restrictions in the networks, thus either reducing or eliminating the chance of generating unfeasible ANNs. As a result, the number of structures to be trained and evaluated, as well as the number of evolutionary cycles necessary to produce good networks, is drastically reduced.

The network training algorithm determines the weight values, reducing the Genetic Algorithm search space.

Mendes Filho and Carvalho proposed a very simple indirect representation [23]. Their representation is a simplification of Mandisher representation [22], which is an improvement of the method proposed by Harp [13].

Mendes Filho and Carvalho representation describes the components in a parameter area and a layer area. The parameter area specifies the learning rate and the momentum term for the ANN. The layer area specifies the number of units in each hidden layer and, as a result, the number of layers (up to three layers can be used). All the ANNs are fully connected and strictly layered. Figure 6 illustrates this representation.

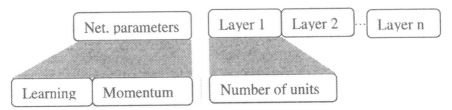

Figure 6. Mendes Filho and Carvalho indirect representation.

The Backpropagation training algorithm determines the weights of the connections. Pruning algorithms could be later used to eliminate redundant connections and units.

Due to its simplicity, this representation requires a smaller decoding effort than Mandisher's representation [22]. Different from the [22] and [13] representations, the decoding is direct and precise, in the sense that each representation generates just one architecture.

This representation only requires the specification of the number of input and output units, and the maximum number of units in hidden layers. Invalid structures could be generated in just one case: when there were not any units in the second intermediate layer although they could be found in the third hidden layer. However, this case is easily detectable and architectures with this characteristic are not generated for the initial population.

4.2   Evaluation

The current population of ANNs can only be evaluated after each ANN has been trained using the same data set. The training error rates can be used as fitness values to determinate the performance of these networks. Whenever possible, a validation data set should also be used to improve the networks' performances evaluation.

Different heuristics can be used for the definition of a fitness function, which is a function that associates a fitness value to each network. These heuristics may take several aspects into account, such as:

- error rates for the training and validation sets;
- training time;
- network size.

Such heuristics must weight these aspects according to the behavior desired for the application.

As the evaluation of neural architectures involves training, the computational cost is very high. However, due to the inherently parallel characteristics of the algorithms involved, its utilization in distributed environments or its parallel implementation can reduce these costs.

ANNs are selected by a selection method according to their fitness values. One of the simplest and most widely used selection methods for evolutionary design of Neural Networks is the roulette wheel method. The selected ANNs are put in a pool of candidates that can then be manipulated by the genetic operators.

4.3   Reproduction

The reproduction strategy must take into account the characteristics of the representation used, the necessities of the problem and the computational resources available. In the definition of the reproduction strategy, the elitist policy, the crossover and mutation operators, with their respective occurrence rates, must be specified.

The genetic operators are used to transform the population of ANNs through the generations, diversifying this population and keeping the desirable acquired characteristics.

The crossover genetic operator, the predominant operator, is responsible for the recombination of network characteristics during the reproduction, allowing the next generations to inherit characteristics of efficient ANNs. In the specification of the crossover operator there is a strong concern with the generation of feasible architectures. As an example, this operator should not produce architectures with connection to or from non-existent nodes. In order to reduce the chance of producing unfeasible ANNs, the cut points may be restricted to a limited number of positions.

The mutation genetic operator, a secondary operator, must cause only slight qualitative changes in the characteristics of the networks during the reproduction, allowing the next generations to diversify.

A subset of the networks' population is selected for mutation. A randomly chosen number specifies the genes that will have their current changed to a random value, restricted to maximum and minimum limits defined for each gene. In the specification of the mutation operator, care is also taken to avoid the production of unfeasible architectures.

5 Evolutionary Optimization of RBF Networks

Although most of the evolutionary approaches for Neural Networks design have been focused on MLP networks [13], [22], [23], [34], their long training time is a strong negative factor concerning the design efficiency. RBF networks are known for requiring a much shorter training period. To take advantage of this feature, a few methods have also been proposed to optimize the parameters of RBF networks.

RBF networks training optimization has been pursued by through other approaches like OLS (Orthogonal Least Square) [8] and RAN (Resource Allocating Network) [29]. Despite being very fast, these methods do local search; thus they can easily fall in local minima and produce sub-optimal solutions. GAs, on the other hand, are global search methods. They can provide an efficient alternative for the optimization of RBF networks.

When RBF networks are genetically optimized, several parameters may be considered, such as:

- Number of hidden units;
- Radial function used by each unit;
- Function center;
- Function width;
- Weight connections between hidden units and output units.

The current evolutionary optimization approaches usually optimize a subset of these parameters. The network weights, for example, are most of the time optimized by other techniques (like pseudo-inverse [33] and LMS [38] methods).

Next, a few methods that have been proposed in the literature to optimize RBF networks using GAs are discussed.

5.1   Billings and Zheng Model

One of the first attempts to genetically optimize RBF networks was due to Billings and Zheng [4]. The authors used GAs to select a subset of the input vectors to be used as the centers for the radial basis functions.

In their representation, each chromosome is list radial basis functions' centers. These centers are selected from the input training patterns. As an example, a RBF network whose centers are defined as the 1st, 3rd, 7th, 14th and 20th input patterns is represented by the vector shown on Figure 7.

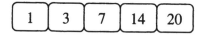

Figure 7. Chromosome representing the centers of a RBF network.

The authors used a Thin-Plate-Spline activation function for the hidden nodes and employed the crossover and mutation genetic operators proposed by Lucasius and Kateman [19]. These operators are suited to problems involving selection of a subset.

The crossover operation used considers only those genes whose value is exclusively present in the chromosome related to one of the parents. A few pairs of these genes are selected. Each pair is composed by one gene from each parent and the genes in a pair have different values. The genes from each pair are exchanged between the parents. Figure 8 illustrates this crossover operation.

The mutation operator changes the values of a chromosome to values randomly selected from the training set. It takes care to avoid genes with the same value in the same chromosome.

Addition and delete operators are also used. According to the authors, they help to keep the population diversity. The addition operator concatenates a random number of genes to the end of a chromosome.

The delete operator deletes a random number of genes from a chromosome, starting from a randomly defined chromosome position.

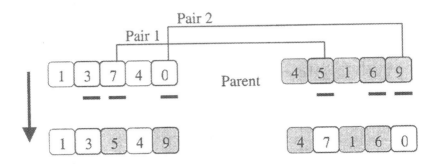

Figure 8. Crossover operator.

The networks were evaluated using a data set from a liquid level system. The authors used 500 training patterns, 500 validation patterns, a population of 60 individuals and each algorithm run comprised 400 generations.

In order to evaluate the network fitness, the authors used as objective function the Akaike Information Criterion (AIC) [1] over the training set. They also used the Pareto optimal set [11] for a multi-objective optimization.

5.2   Maillard and Gueriot Model

Maillard and Gueriot, in [21], modified the model proposed by Billings and Zheng by allowing the centers to be fixed anywhere, and not only on the training input vectors. In their model, the authors also investigated the use of different radial basis functions for the same network.

In the representation employed by Maillard and Gueriot, five genes represent each hidden unit. The first gene indicates the radial function used. The encoded position of the center is situated in the baricenter of two input vectors. The second and third genes give the identity of these vectors. The baricenter weight is given by the forth gene. Finally, the fifth gene indicates the radial function width. Figure 9 illustrates the chromosome representation proposed by Maillard and Gueriot.

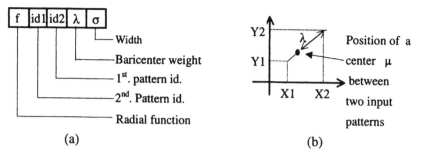

Figure 9. Crossover operator.

The following radial basis functions were used:
- Gaussian;
- Linear;
- Cubic;
- Thin-plate-spline;
- Quadratic;
- Multiquadratic inverse.

In order to evaluate the performance of their approach, the authors calculated the individuals' fitness using the AIC [1] over the training set. They used the chaotic time series Mackey-Glass [20] in their experiments. Two types of RBF networks were genetically designed:

- RBF networks using only Gaussian radial basis functions;
- RBF networks using several radial basis functions.

According to the authors, the networks with different radial basis functions presented a smaller number of hidden nodes and achieved lower error rates than those with only the Gaussian function. A population of 100 individuals was used in their experiments.

5.3   Carse and Fogart Model

Carse and Forgart [7] propose a method to genetically optimize the centers and widths of each hidden node in a RBF network. They used a Gaussian basis function for each hidden unit. In their representation, real value pairs (center, width) compose the chromosome. Equation 9 illustrates a chromosome representing a RBF network with n hidden nodes.

$$C_i = (\mu_{i1}, \sigma_{i1}, \mu_{i2}, \sigma_{i2},..., \mu_{in}, \sigma_{in}) \tag{9}$$

The authors employed a modified version of the two points crossover. In their version, the two cut positions belong to the vectors $\mathbf{a} = \{a_1, a_2, ..., a_n\}$ and $\mathbf{b} = \{b_1, b_2, ..., b_n\}$. The elements of these vectors are defined by:

$$a_j = MIN_j + (MAX_j - MIN_j)(Rd_1) \tag{10}$$

$$b_j = a_j + (MAX_j - MIN_j)(Rd_2)^{1/n} \tag{11}$$

where Rd_1 and Rd_2 are randomly selected from the interval $[0.0, 1.0]$ and $[MIN_j, MAX_j]$ is the allowed interval for the element x_j from the input vector $\mathbf{x}$. After the crossover, the first offspring inherits the genes from the first parent satisfying:

$$\forall j \; ((\mu_{ij} > a_j) \text{ AND } (\mu_{ij} < b_j)) \text{ OR } ((\mu_{ij} + MAX_j - MIN_j) < b_j) \tag{12}$$

Genes from the second parent not satisfying this condition are also added to the first offspring. The second offspring receives those genes from the first and second parents that were not inherited by the first offspring. Thus, this operator exchanges those hidden units whose centers are located inside the hypercube defined by the vectors $\mathbf{a}$ and $\mathbf{b}$. Rather than the genes position in the chromosome, this crossover operator considers the centers position in the input space. This reduces the occurrence of a problem known as the competing convention problem [28].

The authors also used the traditional mutation operators. The creep operator is applied to the center and width of the radial basis function. This creep operator either adds or subtracts a small value from a gene value. Besides these operators, operators to add and remove hidden units were also used.

Two sets of experiments were used to evaluate this model. The first set was composed by patterns generated from the function $y = sin(20x^2)$. For such, a population of 50 individuals and 50 generations were used. The second set of experiments was carried out with data from the chaotic time series Mackey-Glass [20]. This second set of experiments used 200 generations.

5.4 Neruda Model

Neruda's [28] model tackles the structural-functional problem, where networks with different structures may be functionally equivalent. For RBF networks, this problem happens for two networks whose hidden nodes are the same, but located at different positions. This problem substantially increases the search space by generating, without need, different chromosomes for networks with the same functionality. Figure 10 illustrates this situation.

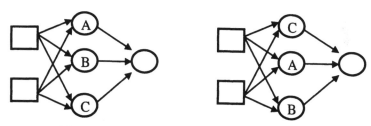

Figure 10. Functionally equivalent RBF networks.

In order to deal with this problem, Neruda created a unique representation for functionally equivalent RBF networks, named canonical parameterization. In this representation, the author associated a sequence of genes to each hidden node. Each sequence had a hidden node center, its width and weights from this node to the output nodes. The sequences were ordered in the chromosomes according to a relation defined by the author.

Neruda also proposed genetic operators specially suited to work with this representation. They preserve the sequences order in the chromosome. The mutation operator randomly changes the values inside a sequence, with the restriction that the new values cannot change the relative positions in the sequence The crossover operator chooses a cut position between sequences, assuming that the offsprings produced have their sequences in the correct order.

By eliminating structurally different chromosomes representing networks with the same functionality, this model clearly reduces the search space. It would be interesting to see its performance. However, in the article consulted, the author did not present any experimental results for his model.

5.5   Other Models

Additional models have been suggested for the evolutionary design of RBF networks. Whitehead and Choate, in [35], proposed a genetic representation that evolves space-filling curves to define the radial functions' centers. The basic idea behind their representation is the mapping of the centers m-dimensional space, situated along the space filling curves, to a unidimensional space in which the chromosome is encoded. A description of the algorithm used in this mapping can be found in [36]. Their model was evaluated with the Mackey-Glass chaotic time series data set [20] and the performance achieved was better than that obtained by the K-means algorithm [14].

In another model proposed by Whitehead and Choate [36], the centers and widths of the radial basis functions evolve through an elegant cooperative-competitive Genetic Algorithm. In this model, each individual encodes only one radial function (for one of the network's hidden layers). The whole population represents just one RBF network. The population individuals compete and cooperate among themselves at the same time, aiming to improve the overall performance of the network represented by the population. This model was applied to the Iris dataset [27] and the Mackey-Glass chaotic time series [20]. In both cases, the experimental results were better than those achieved using the K-means algorithm [14].

In [9], RBF networks are trained using the OLS algorithm with regularization. GAs are employed to evolve the widths and the regularization parameter λ, after the OLS algorithm defines automatically the number and position of the RBF centers.

The next section presents an evolutionary approach for RBF networks design proposed by the authors.

6   The Proposed Model

Lacerda and Carvalho [18] have proposed an alternative genetic approach to optimize RBF networks. Their method codifies each hidden unit into a gene G_j, which is given by:

$$G_j = (k, \mu_j, \sigma_j)$$ (13)

where k is the node index, σ_j is the width and $\mu_j = [\mu_{j1}, \mu_{j2}, \ldots \mu_{jn}]^T$ is the center vector. The index k represents a hypercube on the input space with the center μ_j inside. Each hypercube contains a cluster of patterns. The K-means algorithm determines the set of hypercubes and the authors restrict the search space to centers inside clusters of patterns, as shown in Figure 11. The chromosome representation is a variable length list of genes.

The use of the traditional crossover operator might produce duplicated genes in the same chromosome, as shown by Figure 12.

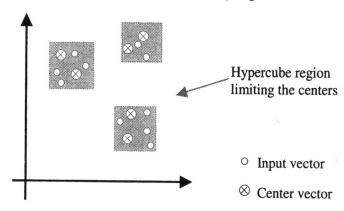

Figure 11. Search space restriction.

		Cut position	
Parent 1	(1; 0.3; 0.1) (2; 0.4; 0.2)	(3; 0.9; 0.1)	
Parent 2	(1; 0.2; 0.4) (3; 0.5; 0.7)	(2; 0.4; 0.2)	(1; 0.5; 0.2)
Offspring	(1; 0.3; 0.1) (2; 0.4; 0.2)	(2; 0.4; 0.2)	(1; 0.5; 0.2)
Offspring	(1; 0.2; 0.4) (3; 0.5; 0.7)	(3; 0.9; 0.1)	

Figure 12. Offspring produced using traditional crossover.

In order to avoid this problem, the authors proposed a new crossover, which is illustrated by Figure 13. This crossover avoids the previous problem by exchanging regions among the parents, rather than exchanging arbitrary genes. Figure 14 shows an algorithm for the proposed crossover operator.

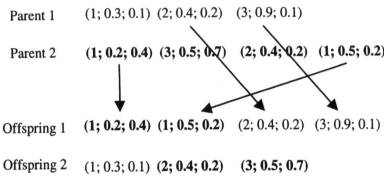

Figure 13. Offspring produced using the new crossover.

Create a template string $(b_1, b_2,...,b_n)$ randomly, where $b_i \in [1,0]$ and n is the number of hypercubes

   for $k=1$ **to** n **then**

      if $b_k = 1$ **then** copy all genes $G_j = (k, \sigma_j, \mu_j)$ from the first parent to the current offspring

      else copy all genes $G_j = (k, \sigma_j, \mu_j)$ from the second parent to the current offspring

Figure 14. Algorithm for the new crossover.

This crossover operator is similar to a uniform crossover and eliminates duplicated genes because it changes hypercubes (i.e., regions of the input space), rather than structural chunks of chromosomes. Four mutation operators were used: random mutation, creep mutation, addition of hidden units (genes) randomly generated and random deletion of hidden units. The fitness function was based on the Generalized Cross Validation (GCV) [12] on both the training and validation subsets. To deal with the training-validation trade-off, the concept of Pareto optimal [11] was used.

The next section compares the results achieved by using this approach with those obtained by different techniques used to set up RBF networks parameters. For such, a heart diagnosis disease dataset, obtained from the Proben1 repository [32], is used.

6.1   Experiments

The heart diagnosis disease dataset used in these experiments has 920 patterns with thirteen input attributes and one output attribute. The output may assume five different values. From the 920 patterns, only 299 have values defined for all attributes. According to [32], the attributes without value are represented by the addition of an attribute with a value equal to 1, if that attribute value is missing and 0, otherwise. In the experiments carried out, the GAs are run varying the number of regions n_R and the maximum number of centers allowed. Table 1 shows the parameters employed and their respective values.

Table 1.   AG parameters for the *heart disease dataset*.

Population	100
Number of generations	200
Number of regions	3
Crossover rate	0,8
Mutation rate	0,01
Creep rate	0,05
Creep operator range	[-0.01,+0.01]
Inclusion rate	0,05
Removal rate	0,05
Maximum number of centers allowed	7
Activation function	Gaussian

The experiments were performed following the methodology proposed in Proben1 [32]. In order to improve the statistical plausibility of the results achieved, three different partitions of the data set were used for the experiments. For each partition, the data set was divided into three subsets: training subset, validate subset and test subset. A random generator was used to define, for each partition, which data would be present in each subset. The results presented for the experiments represent the average of the results achieved by the three partitions run eight times each. The error function employed in the experiments is defined as follows:

$$E = \frac{o_{max} - o_{min}}{pc} \sum_{i=1}^{p} \left\| \mathbf{t}^{(i)} - \mathbf{y}^{(i)} \right\|^2 \qquad (14)$$

where c is the number of output nodes, p is the number of patterns, t is the desired output, y is the output produced by the network and o_{max} and o_{min} are the maximum and minimum desired output values, respectively.

The results achieved by the evolutionary RBF network were compared to those achieved by a MLP network trained with the backpropagation algorithm [32] and RBF networks trained with the M-RAN, RAN-EKF and RAN algorithms [39]. Table 2 illustrates these results.

The results obtained show the superiority of the evolutionary approach over the other approaches investigated both in terms of lower error rates and, for the RBF networks, smaller number of hidden nodes.

Table 2. Error rates and number of basis functions achieved.

Method	Average number of basis functions	Error rates for the test subset (%)
Evolutionary	5.5	3.77
M-RAN	8	4.14
RAN-EKF	13	4.21
RAN	13	5.20
MLP	-	4.55

It may be pointed out that the longest training time was achieved by the genetic approach. For a large number of applications, where recognition performance is more important than the training time, the results obtained suggest that the genetic approach is a strong option.

Experiments were also carried out by the authors using data from the chaotic time series Mackey-Glass [20], credit assessment data from the UCI Machine Learning repository [27], and data to model the Hermite polynomial. The performance achieved for these datasets was shown to be superior to those achieved by RBF networks using the RFS (which is the OLS algorithm [8] with regularization) and RAN-EKF [16] algorithms and MLP networks trained by the backpropagation algorithm [34].

7   Conclusions

The performance achieved by ANNs depends on an adequate setting of their parameters. This chapter discussed how RBF networks could have their parameters optimized by GAs. After a brief introduction to GAs, the main aspects involved in the evolutionary design of ANNs, in particular RBF networks, were discussed and different models proposed in the literature were described.

The authors presented an alternative approach for evolutionary design of RBF networks. In this approach, the authors introduced a new crossover operator. This new crossover operator disallows the incidence of duplicated genes in a chromosome, because it changes regions of the input space, instead of structural chunks of chromosomes.

The performance of this alternative approach was evaluated using a heart disease dataset and compared against those obtained by three different approaches for RBF training and by a MLP network trained with the backpropagation algorithm. The results achieved indicated the superiority of the proposed genetic approach. The genetically designed RBF networks presented the lowest classification error and the smallest number of radial functions.

It must be pointed out that the use of GAs leads to a longer processing time. However, the time required to design ANNs can be divided in conception time and processing time. By automatically defining the main network parameters, the evolutionary design largely reduces the conception time.

Further improvement can be pursued by: looking for alternatives to reduce the optimization time, using other approached for the evolutionary optimization, like hybrid GAs, and by including other parameters in the chromosomes, like different RBF functions.

Acknowledgements

The authors would like to thank CNPq, FAPESP and FINEP for the support received during this work.

References

[1] Akaike, H. (1974), "A new look at the statistical model identification," *IEEE Transactions on Automatic Control*, vol. 19, pp. 716-723.

[2] Anderberg, M.R. (1973), *Cluster Analisys for Applications*, New York, Academic Press.

[3] Balakrishnan, K. and Honavar, V. (1995), "Evolutionary design of neural architectures – a preliminary taxonomy and guide to literature," A.I. Research Group, Iowa State University, Technical Report CS TR #95-01.

[4] Billings, S.A. and Zheng, G.L. (1995), "Radial basis function network configuration using genetic algorithms," *Neural Networks*, vol. 8, no. 6, pp. 877-890.

[5] Branke, J. (1995) "Evolutionary algorithms for network design an training," Institute AIFB, University of Karlsruhe, Technical Report N. 322.

[6] Broomhead, D.S. and Lowe D. (1988), "Multivariable functional interpolation and adaptive networks," *Complex Systems*, vol. 2, pp. 321-355.

[7] Carse, B. and Fogarty, T.C. (1996), "Fast evolutionary learning of minimal radial basis function neural networks using a genetic algorithm," in Fogarty, T.C. (Ed.), *AISB Workshop on Evolutionary Computing*, Lectures Notes in Computer Science No. 1143, Springer-Verlag, pp. 1-22.

[8] Chen, S., Cowan C.F., and Grant, P. (1991), "Orthogonal least squares learning algorithm for radial basis function networks," *IEEE Transactions on Neural Networks*, vol. 2, pp. 302-309.

[9] Chen, S., Wu, Y., and Alkadhimi, K. (1995), "A two-layer learning method for radial basis function networks using combined genetic and regularised OLS algorithms," *Proceedings of the 1st*

IEE/IEEE International Conference on Genetic Algorithms in Engineering Systems: Innovations and Applications, pp. 245-249.

[10] Edelman, G. (1988), *Neural Darwinism*, New York Basic Books, New York.

[11] Goldberg, D. (1989*)*, *Genetic Algorithms in Search, Optimization, and Machine Learning*, Addison-Wesley.

[12] Golub, G.H., Heath, M., and Wahba, G. (1979) "Generalised cross validation as a method for choosing a good ridge parameter," *Technometrics*, vol. 21, no. 2, pp. 215-223.

[13] Harp, S.A., Samad, T., and Guha, A. (1991), "Towards the genetic synthesis of neural networks," *Proceedings of the 4th International Conference on Genetic Algorithms*, Morgan Kaufmann, pp. 360-369.

[14] Hartigan, J.A. and Wong, M.A. (1979), "A K-means clustering algorithm," *Applied Statistics*, vol. 28, pp.100-108.

[15] Holland, J.H. (1975), *Adaptation in Natural and Artificial Systems*, University of Michigan Press, Ann Arbor.

[16] Kadirkamanathan, V., and Niranjan, M. (1993), "A function estimation approach to sequential learning with neural networks," *Neural Computation*, vol. 5, no. 6, pp. 954-975.

[17] Kohonen, T. (1982), "Self-organized formation of topologically correct feacture maps," *Biological Cybernetics*, vol. 43, pp. 59-69.

[18] Lacerda E. and Carvalho, A. (1999), "Credit analysis using radial basis function networks," *Proceedings of the 3rd International Conference on Computational Intelligence and Multimedia Applications, ICCIMA'99*, New Deli, India, IEEE Computer Press, pp. 138-142.

[19] Lucasius, C.B. and Kateman, G. (1992), "Towards solving subset selection problems with the aid of the genetic algorithm," *Parallel Problem Solving from Nature*, vol. 2, Elsevier Science Publishers.

[20] Mackey, M.C. and Glass L. (1977), "Oscillations and chaos in physiological control systems," *Science,* pp. 197-287.

[21] Maillard, E.P. and Gueriot, D. (1997), RBF neural network, basis functions and genetic algorithm. *Proceedings of International Conference on Neural Networks*, vol. 4, pp. 2187-2192.

[22] Mandisher, M. (1993), "Representation and evolution of neural networks," University of Dortmund, Germany, Technical Report.

[23] Mendes Filho, E. and Carvalho, A. (1997) "Evolutionary design of MLP neural network architectures," *Proceedings of the IV Brazilian Symposium on Neural Networks, IV SBRN*, IEEE Computer Press, pp 58-65.

[24] Miller, G., Todd, P., and Hedge, S. (1989), "Designing neural networks using genetic algorithms," *Proceedings of the 3rd International Conference on Genetic Algorithms*, Morgan Kaufmann, pp. 379-384.

[25] Mitchell, M. (1996), *An Introduction to Genetic Algorithms*, MIT Press.

[26] Moody, J. and Darken, C.J. (1989), "Fast learning in networks of locally-tuned processing units," *Neural Computation*, vol. 1, no. 2, pp. 281-294.

[27] Murphy, C.A.M. and Aha, D.W., (1994), *UCI Repository of Machine Learning Databases*, Irvine, CA, University of California.

[28] Neruda, R. (1995), "Functional equivalence and genetic learning of RBF networks," in Pearson, D.W., Steele, N.C., and Albrecht, R.F. (Eds.), *Artificial Neural Nets and Genetic Algorithms*, Springer-Verlag, pp. 53-56.

[29] Platt, J.A. (1991), "Resource-allocating network for function interpolation," *Neural Computation*, vol.3, no.2, pp. 213-225.

[30] Poggio, T. and Girosi, F. (1990), "Networks for approximation and learning," *Proceedings of the IEEE*, vol. 78, no. 9, pp. 1481-1497.

[31] Powell, M. (1992), "The theory of radial basis function approximation in 1990," in Light, W. (Ed.), *Advances in Numerical Analysis*, Oxford, Clarendon, vol .3, pp. 105-210.

[32] Prechelt, L. (1994), "Proben1 – a set of neural networks benchmark problems and benchmarking rules," Fakultät füt Informatik. Universität Karlsruhe, Technical Report 21/94.

[33] Press, W.H., Flannery, B.P., Teukolsky, S.A., and Vetterling, W.T. (1988), *Numerical Recipes in C*, Cambridge University Press.

[34] Rumelhart, D.E., Hinton, G.E., and Williams, R.J. (1986), "Learning internal representation by error propagation," *Parallel Distributed Processing*, Cambridge, MIT Press, pp. 318-362.

[35] Whitehead, B.A. and Choate, T.D. (1994), "Evolving space-filling curves to distribute radial basis functions over an input space," *IEEE Transactions on Neural Networks*, vol. 5, pp.15-23.

[36] Whitehead, B.A. and Choate, T.D. (1996), "Cooperative-competitive genetic evolution of radial basis function centers and widths for time series prediction," *IEEE Transactions on Neural Networks*, vol.7, pp.869-880.

[37] Whitley, D. "The genitor algorithm and selection pressure: why rank-based allocation of reproductive trials is best," *Proceedings of the 3rd International Conference on Genetic Algorithms*, Morgan Kauffman, pp. 116-121.

[38] Widrow, B. and Hoff, M.E. (1960), "Adaptive switching circuits," *IRE-WESCON Convention Record*, New York, vol. 4, pp. 96-104.

[39] Yingwei, L., Sundararajan, N., and Saratchandran, P. (1997), "A sequential learning scheme for function approximation using minimal radial basis function neural networks," *Neural Computation*, vol. 9, pp. 461-478.

Index

List of Contributors

P. András
Department of Computer Science
University of Maastricht
the Netherlands

New address:
Department of Psychology
University of Newcastle upon Tyne
United Kingdom
andrasp@ieee.org

N.A. Borghese
Laboratory of Human Motion Study and Virtual Reality
Istituto Neuroscienze e Bioimmagini – CNR
c/o LITA
Via f.lli Cervi, 93
20090 Segrate (Milano)
Italy
borghese@inb.mi.cnr.it
http://www.inb.mi.cnr.it/Borghese/Borghese_page

A.G. Borş
Department of Computer Science
University of York
York YO10 5DD
United Kingdom
Adrian.Bors@cs.york.ac.uk

C. Campbell
Department of Engineering Mathematics
Bristol University
Bristol BS8 1TR
United Kingdom

D. Charles
Applied Computational Intelligence Research Unit
The University of Paisley
Scotland, United Kingdom

I.B. Ciocoiu
Faculty of Electronics and Telecommunications
Technical University of Iasi
Romania

A. de Carvalho
Department of Computing and Information Science
University of Guelph
Guelph, Canada, N1G 2W1
http://hebb.cis.uoguelph.ca/~andre/

C. Fyfe
Applied Computational Intelligence Research Unit
The University of Paisley
Scotland, United Kingdom

F.H. Hamker
Fachgebiet Informatik
J.W. Goethe Universität Frankfurt
Germany

New address:
California Institute of Technology
Division of Biology 139-74
Pasadena, CA 91125
U.S.A.
fred@klab.caltech.edu

M. Kubat
Center for Advanced Computer Studies
University of Louisiana at Lafayette
Lafayette, LA 70504-4330
U.S.A.

E. Lacerda
Department of Informatics
Pernambuco Federal University
Brazil

P.L. Lai
Applied Computational Intelligence Research Unit
The University of Paisley
Scotland, United Kingdom

E.L. Leiss
Department of Computer Science
University of Houston
Houston, TX 77204-3475
U.S.A.
coscel@cs.uh.edu

S.-T. Li
Department of Information Management
National Kaohsiung First University of Science and Technology
1 University Road
Yenchao, Kaohsiung 824
Taiwan, R.O.C.
stli@ccms.nkfust.edu.tw

T. Ludermir
Department of Informatics
Pernambuco Federal University
Brazil

D. MacDonald
Applied Computational Intelligence Research Unit
The University of Paisley
Scotland, United Kingdom

I. Pitas
Department of Informatics
University of Thessaloniki
Thessaloniki 540 06
Greece
`pitas@zeus.csd.auth.gr`

R. Rosipal
Applied Computational Intelligence Research Unit
The University of Paisley
Scotland, United Kingdom

A. Roy
School of Information Management
Arizona State University
Tempe, AZ 85287-3606
U.S.A.